JOURNEYS

Reader's Notebook

Grade 4

Printed in the U.S.A.

ISBN 978-0-544-59265-0

17 2536 23 22 21 20 19

4500745869 D E F G

Contents

Unit 1 **Good Citizens**

Lesson 1: Because of Winn-Dixie 1
Lesson 2: My Brother Martin 13
Lesson 3: My Librarian Is a Camel 25
Lesson 4: The Power of W.O.W.! 37
Lesson 5: Stormalong 49

Unit 2 **Express Yourself**

Lesson 6: Invasion from Mars 61
Lesson 7: Coming Distractions: Questioning Movies 73
Lesson 8: Me and Uncle Romie 85
Lesson 9: Dear Mr. Winston 97
Lesson 10: José! Born to Dance 109

Unit 3 **Learning Lessons**

Lesson 11: Hurricanes: Earth's Mightiest Storms 133
Lesson 12: The Earth Dragon Awakes 145
Lesson 13: Antarctic Journal: Four Months at the Bottom of the World 157
Lesson 14: The Life and Times of the Ant 169
Lesson 15: Ecology for Kids 181

Unit 4

Lesson 16: Riding Freedom 193
Lesson 17: The Right Dog for the Job: Ira's Path from Service Dog to Guide Dog 205
Lesson 18: Hercules' Quest 217
Lesson 19: Harvesting Hope: The Story of Cesar Chavez 229
Lesson 20: Sacagawea 241

Unit 5

Lesson 21: The World According to Humphrey 277
Lesson 22: I Could Do That! Esther Morris Gets Women the Vote 289
Lesson 23: The Ever-Living Tree: The Life and Times of a Coast Redwood 301
Lesson 24: Owen and Mzee: The True Story of a Remarkable Friendship 313
Lesson 25: The Fun They Had 325

Unit 6

Lesson 26: The Girl Who Loved Spiders 337
Lesson 27: Amphibian Alert! 348
Lesson 28: Museums: Worlds of Wonder 359
Lesson 29: Save Timber Woods! 370
Lesson 30: Mystery at Reed's Pond 381

Reading and Writing Glossary G1

Name ______________________ Date ____________

Because of Winn-Dixie

What Did You See, Miss Franny?

Complete Miss Franny's interview with a reporter about the bear sighting she had in the library. Use words that sound like Miss Franny is speaking directly to the reporter. Begin reading at page 26. Use the structure of the story to locate the details.

Reporter: We are here today at the Herman W. Block Memorial Library in Naomi, Florida. We are talking to head librarian Miss Franny about her amazing discovery in the library. Hello, Miss Franny! What did you see yesterday?

Miss Franny: ______________________________

____

Reporter: Wow! What were you doing before the bear arrived?

Miss Franny: ______________________________

____

____

Reporter: What did you do when you saw the bear?

Miss Franny: ______________________________

____

Name ______________________ Date ____________

Because of Winn-Dixie
Independent Reading

Reporter: What were you thinking?

Miss Franny: ____

____

____

Reporter: How did the bear react?

Miss Franny: ____

____

____

Reporter: Well, there you have it.
One remarkable encounter
from one remarkable woman!

Name ______________________ Date ____________

Prefixes *re-*, *un-*, and *dis-*

disagree	return	reappear	unlikely
dislike	review	unfair	unable

Read each sentence. Complete the sentence with a word from above.

1. I need a receipt to __________ the shirt that doesn't fit.
2. It is __________ that I will know everyone at the party.
3. My brother and I usually __________ about whose turn it is to take out the garbage.
4. Our class had to __________ our notes from the chapter before we took the test.
5. My sister loves talking on the phone, but I __________ it.
6. I think it is __________ that I have to do chores on my birthday.
7. Sometimes cleaning your room can cause a missing toy to __________.
8. He was __________ to go to the party because he was sick.

Name ______________________ Date ____________

Short *a* and Long *a*

Basic 1–10. Read the paragraphs. Below, write the Basic Words that best complete the sentences.

I spent a week of my summer vacation at my grandmother's house. At first I was (1) _____ that I would be bored, but I had a lot of fun. Every morning I helped my grandmother in her studio, where she paints pictures that would (2) _____ you.

I helped her (3) _____ some of the paintings that will go on (4) _____ soon. I also made a sign to put outside when the paintings are ready to sell. I used poster board and a black (5) _____ to make the sign. The most fun I had was creating my own painting. I learned how to apply paint to a canvas with a knife (6) _____ . I wore a smock so I wouldn't get a (7) _____ on my clothes. Grandma says that my painting was much improved from ones I've done in the (8) _____ .

On my last night there, Grandma took me out for a (9) _____ dinner. I know for a (10) _____ that I will be back to visit my grandmother next summer!

1. ____________________ 6. ____________________
2. ____________________ 7. ____________________
3. ____________________ 8. ____________________
4. ____________________ 9. ____________________
5. ____________________ 10. ____________________

Challenge 11–14. Read the headline. On a separate sheet of paper, write an article for it, using four of the Challenge Words.

EASTSIDE SCHOOL TRACK TEAM SETS NEW RECORDS

Spelling Words

1. blade
2. gray
3. past
4. afraid
5. magic
6. delay
7. amaze
8. drain
9. maybe
10. break
11. sale
12. hang
13. stain
14. glass
15. raft
16. jail
17. crayon
18. fact
19. stale
20. steak

Challenge

fraction
trait
champion
activity
graceful

Name ______________________________ Date ______________

Spelling Word Sort

Write each Basic Word beside the correct heading.

/ă/ spelled *a* followed by a consonant	**Basic Words:** **Challenge Words:** **Possible Selection Words:**
/ā/ spelled *a*-consonant-*e*	**Basic Words:** **Challenge Words:**
/ā/ spelled *ai*	**Basic Words:** **Challenge Words:** **Possible Selection Words:**
/ā/ spelled *ay*	**Basic Words:** **Possible Selection Words:**
/ā/ spelled *ea*	**Basic Words:**

Challenge Add the Challenge Words to your Word Sort.

Connect to Reading Look through "Because of Winn-Dixie." Find words that have the /ă/ and /ā/ spelling patterns like the ones on this page. Add them to your Word Sort.

Spelling Words

1. blade
2. gray
3. past
4. afraid
5. magic
6. delay
7. amaze
8. drain
9. maybe
10. break
11. sale
12. hang
13. stain
14. glass
15. raft
16. jail
17. crayon
18. fact
19. stale
20. steak

Challenge

fraction
trait
champion
activity
graceful

Proofreading for Spelling

Find the misspelled words and circle them. Write them correctly on the lines below.

The Avid Reader Bookstore is a popular place in town. The owner, Mr. Orville, unpacks a box of new books. He says he is afriad the weather will deley delivery, and some of the books on salee are on back order. The good news is that the book that Jenny wants to read about the magik raeft that goes down the kitchen drane and ends up in the middle of the ocean is not one on back order. But maibe Amanda will have to wait another week for the book about the cowboy who lands in jale for being falsely accused of stealing a graye mustang.

By the end of the day, Mr. Orville is ready for a glas of lemonade and a cookie. He's careful carrying the pitcher so he doesn't drop and braik it. The cold lemonade is refreshing, but the staile cookie has to go!

1. ____________ 7. ____________
2. ____________ 8. ____________
3. ____________ 9. ____________
4. ____________ 10. ____________
5. ____________ 11. ____________
6. ____________ 12. ____________

Spelling Words

1. blade
2. gray
3. past
4. afraid
5. magic
6. delay
7. amaze
8. drain
9. maybe
10. break
11. sale
12. hang
13. stain
14. glass
15. raft
16. jail
17. crayon
18. fact
19. stale
20. steak

Challenge

fraction
trait
champion
activity
graceful

Name ____________________ Date ____________

Simple Subjects and Predicates

A **sentence** is a group of words that tells a complete thought. The subject tells whom or what the sentence is about. The predicate tells what the subject does or is. A **simple subject** is the main word that tells whom or what the sentence is about. A **simple predicate** is the verb that tells what the subject is or does.

simple subject **simple predicate**
The trip to the supermarket takes five minutes.

Thinking Questions
What is the main word that tells whom or what the sentence is about? What is the main word that tells what the subject is or does?

1–4. Write the simple subject on the line.

1. Mr. Mota left his dog outside the supermarket.
   ____
2. The glass doors opened. ____________________
3. Mr. Mota's list had many items on it. ____________________
4. The dog outside the door watched Mr. Mota through the window. ____________________

5–8. Underline the simple subject once and the simple predicate twice.

5. Soup cans fell to the ground.
6. Mr. Mota sampled some cheese at the deli.
7. He bought some doggie treats for Chase.
8. The friendly cashier smiled.

Complete Subjects and Predicates

The subject of a sentence tells whom or what the sentence is about. All the words that name the person or thing the sentence is about make up the **complete subject**. All the words that tell what the subject of the sentence is or does is the **complete predicate**.

complete subject **complete predicate**

The new pet shop had many kinds of animals.

A dog that was whining became quiet when I picked him up.

Thinking Questions
Which words tell whom or what the sentence is about? What are all the words that tell what the subject does or is?

In each sentence, underline the complete subject and circle the complete predicate.

1. All the pets on our block are well behaved.
2. It is always fun to watch them play.
3. One little dog likes to chase sticks.
4. He scampers across Mrs. Parker's broad lawn.
5. Dr. James Moore owns a large German shepherd.
6. Dr. Moore's two daughters walk the dog every day.
7. The park down the street is a popular place for pets.
8. We often see the same dogs and people there every day.
9. My dog once saw a squirrel and ran away from me.
10. A girl who was jogging caught my dog before he got far.
11. I always wave hello to her now.
12. We make friends when we walk our dogs.

Name ______________________ Date ____________

Compound Subjects and Predicates

When a sentence tells about two or more people or things, the sentence has a **compound subject**. When a sentence tells about two or more things that the subject does, the sentence has a **compound predicate**. The word and is used to join compound subjects. It is also used to join compound predicates.

compound subject

My friend **and** I took our dogs to an obedience class.

compound predicate

My dog will learn **and** obey when I give commands.

Thinking Questions
How many subjects or predicates are there? What word is used to join the compound subject or compound predicate?

Underline the compound subject in each sentence.

1. William and I took our dog to an obedience class.
2. Most people and dogs made a lot of noise at first.
3. My dog Stanley and my friend's dog Fritz were quiet.
4. My friend and I were whispering.
5. Then the instructor and a trained dog showed us some commands.

Circle the compound predicate in each sentence.

6. First, the instructor held up one finger and said, "Sit."
7. The dog listened and sat.
8. Then, the instructor said, "Stay," and walked away.
9. The dog listened and did not move.
10. Finally, the instructor patted her pupil and said, "Good dog."

Nouns

Nouns can appear in the complete subject or in the complete predicate. A **common noun** tells about a person, animal, place, or thing. A**proper noun** names a certain person, animal, place, or thing. A proper noun starts with a capital letter.

proper **common**
Yesterday Thomas adopted a dog.

common
Today the dog is wearing a new collar.

Thinking Question
Does the word name a person, place, or thing?

1–5. Circle all the common nouns in each sentence.

1. Dogs can be great pets and helpers.
2. In our community, some animals assist people with special needs.
3. Our neighbor Ramon needs assistance when he shops for groceries.
4. His Labrador retriever leads him across busy streets.
5. My grandma has a collie that barks when her phone or doorbell rings.

6–10. Underline the proper noun in each sentence.

6. We took our dog Andy with us to Miami to visit Uncle Tito.
7. We passed through Daytona Beach and Titusville.
8. Then we took a detour to Everglades National Park.
9. We asked Park Ranger Sanchez whether our dog could enter the park.
10. Andy and I had never traveled so far from Jacksonville before.

Sentence Fluency

Short, Choppy Sentences	Combined Sentence with a Compound Subject
Rudy wants a pet. Her brothers want a pet.	Rudy and her brothers want a pet.

1–6. Combine the sentences by joining the subjects with the word *and* to form a compound subject. Write the new sentence on the line.

1. Children enjoy pets. Adults enjoy pets.

____

2. Large dogs can be good pets. Small dogs can be good pets.

____

3. My parents told me about different types of dogs. The vet told me about different types of dogs.

____

4. Poodles often live for more than ten years. Beagles often live for more than ten years.

____

5. My brother liked the beagle best. I liked the beagle best.

____

6. Our new dog slept soundly on the porch. Our cat slept soundly on the porch.

____

Focus Trait: Elaboration

Using Concrete Words

A. Read each sentence. Fill in the blanks with concrete words and phrases to create vivid details and to make each sentence more interesting.

Sentence	Sentence with Vivid Details
1. Some kittens slept in a box.	The ______________ kittens slept ______________________ in a ______________ box.
2. After the kittens woke up, we watched them play.	After the kittens ______________ ______________, we watched them ______________________.

B. Read each sentence. Rewrite each sentence using vivid details.

Pair/Share **Work with a partner to brainstorm concrete words and phrases to create vivid details.**

Sentence	Sentence with Vivid Details
3. Winn-Dixie looked in the window.	
4. Miss Franny was scared.	
5. Winn-Dixie smiled at Miss Franny.	

Name ______________________ Date ______________

My Brother Martin

Mother Dear, Why?

Christine writes about growing up with her famous brother, Martin Luther King, Jr. During the time when she and her brother were growing up, certain historical events influenced their lives. Think about details in the text to help you understand the historical events.

Read page 55. M. L. and A. D. came alone that day. Think about why they came home alone.

What did their playmates tell them?

____

____

____

____

Think about the historical events during the time. What allowed their playmates to treat M. L. and A. D. this way?

____

____

____

____

Read pages 56–57. M. L. finally asks his mother, "Why do white people treat colored people so mean?" What do you think Mother Dear says? Write her answer in her words. Make sure to include details about the historical events that caused colored people to be treated so unfairly.

Name ______________________ Date ____________

Prefixes *in-*, *im-*, *il-*, and *ir-*

injustice irresponsible impolite insecure
illegal imperfect irreplaceable

Read each underlined word. Use the meaning of the prefix to help you understand the meaning of the word. Then complete the sentence in a way that makes sense.

1. I know I am irresponsible when I

____.

2. It is impolite to

____.

3. The law says it is illegal to

____.

4. I feel insecure when I

____.

5. The imperfect pair of pants had

____.

6. Losing something that is irreplaceable

____.

7. One example of an injustice is

____.

Name ______________________ Date ____________

Short *e* and Long *e*

Basic 1–11. Write the Basic Word that best fits each clue.

1. inexpensive ______________________
2. a desire for more than one needs ______________________
3. a large animal ______________________
4. direction where the Sun sets ______________________
5. shine brightly ______________________
6. a small spot ______________________
7. rising at a very sharp angle ______________________
8. leader ______________________
9. water in the form of a gas ______________________
10. to think ______________________
11. a place for books or other items ______________________

Challenge 12–14. Write a paragraph about a place where you like to go to eat. Tell what you like about it. Use three Challenge Words. Write on a separate sheet of paper.

Spelling Words

1. west
2. steep
3. member
4. gleam
5. fresh
6. freedom
7. speed
8. steam
9. beast
10. believe
11. speck
12. kept
13. cheap
14. pretend
15. greed
16. shelf
17. least
18. eager
19. reason
20. chief

Challenge

echo
menu
creature
reveal
restaurant

Name ______________________ Date ____________

Spelling Word Sort

Write each Basic Word beside the correct heading.

/ĕ/ spelled *e* followed by a consonant	**Basic Words:** **Challenge Words:** **Possible Selection Words:**
/ē / spelled *ea*	**Basic Words:** **Challenge Words:** **Possible Selection Words:**
/ē / spelled *ee*	**Basic Words:** **Possible Selection Words:**
Other spellings for /ē /	**Basic Words:**

Spelling Words

1. west
2. steep
3. member
4. gleam
5. fresh
6. freedom
7. speed
8. steam
9. beast
10. believe
11. speck
12. kept
13. cheap
14. pretend
15. greed
16. shelf
17. least
18. eager
19. reason
20. chief

Challenge

echo
menu
creature
reveal
restaurant

Challenge Add the Challenge Words to your Word Sort.

Connect to Reading Look through "My Brother Martin." Find words that have the /ĕ/ or /ē / sounds. Add them to your Word Sort.

Name ______________________ Date ____________

Proofreading for Spelling

Find the misspelled words and circle them. Write them correctly on the lines below.

Many years ago, Africans were forced to come to the United States as slaves. They lived without fredom. Many people were against slavery. They, at leest, were eagre to spead change and worked hard to free slaves.

Slavery was abolished, but change was slow. When Dr. Martin Luther King, Jr. was a boy, his mother explained that she could no longer preten to beleeve that as a menber of the Atlanta community, she could eat at any restaurant in the city or stroll in the park and enjoy the freshh air. The reasen she gave was that some states still had unfair laws that kepp black people and white people separate.

Though Dr. King paid a steap price for working for equality, his contributions would offer a gleem of hope that change would come.

1. ______________ 7. ______________
2. ______________ 8. ______________
3. ______________ 9. ______________
4. ______________ 10. ______________
5. ______________ 11. ______________
6. ______________ 12. ______________

Spelling Words

1. west
2. steep
3. member
4. gleam
5. fresh
6. freedom
7. speed
8. steam
9. beast
10. believe
11. speck
12. kept
13. cheap
14. pretend
15. greed
16. shelf
17. least
18. eager
19. reason
20. chief

Challenge

echo
menu
creature
reveal
restaurant

Name ______________________ Date __________

Declarative and Interrogative Sentences

A sentence that makes a statement is a **declarative sentence**. It ends with a period. A sentence that asks a question is an **interrogative sentence**. It ends with a question mark. Every sentence begins with a capital letter.

declarative sentence	**interrogative sentence**
Martin Luther King Jr. gave many speeches.	What did you learn about Dr. King?

Thinking Questions
Does the sentence make a statement? Does the sentence ask a question?

Add the correct end punctuation. Write whether each sentence is *declarative* or *interrogative*.

1. Dr. King gave a famous speech in 1963 ____________

2. Were the words "I have a dream" in the speech ____________

3. Have you ever read the speech ____________

4. The occasion was a march in Washington ____________

5. At least 200,000 people were there ____________

6. What was the speech about ____________

7. How did listeners respond to the speech ____________

8. Dr. King spoke of his dreams of freedom ____________

9. Do you think a speech can change history ____________

10. Many said it was the best speech of 20th century America ____________

Name ______________________ Date ____________

Imperative and Exclamatory Sentences

A sentence that gives a command is an **imperative sentence**. It ends with a period or an exclamation point. A sentence that shows strong feeling is an **exclamatory sentence**. It ends with an exclamation point.

imperative sentence	**exclamatory sentence**
Discuss the fight for civil rights.	What a hard struggle it was!

Thinking Questions
Does the sentence give a command? Does the sentence show strong feeling?

1–10. Add the correct end punctuation. Write *imperative* or *exclamatory*.

1. Read about special laws for African Americans ______________
2. How unfair those laws were ______________
3. Find out why the laws changed ______________
4. Learn about freedom marches ______________
5. How inspiring the marches were ______________
6. Some people were so courageous ______________
7. Dr. King was an awesome speaker ______________
8. Imagine having thousands of people hear your words ______________
9. Think about how much our country has changed ______________
10. What an important part of our history ______________

Four Kinds of Sentences

A **declarative sentence** makes a statement and ends with a period. An **interrogative sentence** asks a question and ends with a question mark. An **imperative sentence** gives a command and ends with a period or exclamation point. An **exclamatory sentence** shows strong feeling and ends with an exclamation point.

Washington has many memorials.
Have you seen the Lincoln Memorial?
Decide what you want to see.
It will be a great trip!

Thinking Questions
What is the purpose of the sentence? What punctuation should be used?

Add the correct end punctuation. Write whether each sentence is *declarative*, *interrogative*, *imperative*, or *exclamatory*.

1. Look at this picture ________________
2. This is a national memorial in our nation's capital ________________
3. What is the memorial's purpose ________________
4. Martin Luther King Jr., is honored ________________
5. Some quotes by Dr. King are on a wall ________________
6. Isn't there a statue of Dr. King ________________
7. Try to go see the memorial ________________
8. I can't wait to see it ________________
9. Should we plan to visit Dr. King's memorial together ________________
10. There are many memorials in our nation's capital ________________

Name ______________________ Date ____________

Contractions

A **contraction** is a short way to write two words. An **apostrophe** takes the place of a letter or letters in a contraction.

contractions

She will — she'll

has not — hasn't

I have — I've

1–4. Write the contraction of the underlined words on the line.

1. They will share their stories. ____________
2. Caitlin should have written a report. ____________
3. I am going to write about kindness. ____________
4. I will write a report about Dr. Martin Luther King Jr. ____________

5–8. Write the words that make up the underlined contraction on the line.

5. People said that they'd march in the streets. ____________
6. Rosa Parks wouldn't give up her seat on the bus. ____________
7. Dr. King thought that people shouldn't ride the bus for a while. ____________
8. Every adult in America should've voted. ____________

Sentence Fluency

Statements	Varying Sentence Types
There were many civil rights leaders. They had many challenges. They fought for equality. You can find out what they did.	There were many civil rights leaders. They had so many challenges! How did they fight for equality? Find out what they did.

Change each underlined statement to a question, a command, or an exclamation. The word in parentheses ( ) tells you which kind of sentence to write. Write the sentences on the lines below.

Civil rights leaders brought about change. (question) They used different methods. Lawyer Thurgood Marshall worked for civil rights. You can study Marshall's accomplishments. (imperative) They were amazing. (exclamatory)

There are ways to challenge unfair laws. (question) Thurgood Marshall challenged them in court. He had a case against a Kansas public school system. He won. (exclamatory) As a result, African-American students could attend schools with white students. President Johnson appointed Marshall to the Supreme Court in 1964. He was the first African-American Supreme Court Justice. You can remember Thurgood Marshall as a great civil rights leader. (imperative)

1. ____________________
2. ____________________
3. ____________________
4. ____________________
5. ____________________
6. ____________________

Name ______________________________ Date ____________

Focus Trait: Purpose

Words That Describe

A. Read each sentence about the story. Look at the underlined words used to express feelings. Then rewrite the sentence using vivid words and details that describe.

Poor Word Choice	Vivid Word Choice
1. M. L. and A. D. did not like learning to play the piano.	
2. Many people cared about equal rights.	

B. Read each sentence about the story. Rewrite it, using vivid words that describe the characters' feelings.

Pair/Share **Work with a partner to brainstorm vivid words for your sentences.**

3. M. L. wanted people to treat each other better.	
4. M. L. was a kind person.	
5. M. L. admired his father's actions.	

Name ______________________ Date __________

My Librarian Is a Camel

My Library Card

Answer the questions below by rereading pages 80–81 and by looking at the photographs of "My Librarian Is a Camel."

In the picture on the left, what are the children doing?

____

____

____

How are they dressed? How do they look? What does this tell you about how much they want to get their books?

____

____

____

If they can use a sled all the way to the post office, what does this tell you about the area they live in?

____

____

____

Name ______________________ Date ______________

My Librarian Is a Camel
Independent Reading

Read page 81. Think about how important the books are to the boys in Cambridge Bay, Canada. Design a library card that shows the goals of the Northwest Territories Borrower-by-Mail system. Include visuals and a slogan. A slogan is a catchy phrase that tells the goals of an organization.

Front

Back

Signature ______________________________

Name ______________________ Date ____________

Using Context

energetic	generous	relative	grateful
homesick	negative	thoughtful	

Complete each sentence with a word from above. Use context clues to help you.

1. Having his own books to read at camp kept Mark from getting __________.
2. Mr. Cook's donation of 100 books to the town library was very __________.
3. A library boat takes books to Uncle Niko, a __________ of mine in Finland.
4. A camel must be very __________ to carry 400 pounds of books.
5. This cheerful book will get rid of __________ thoughts.
6. The residents are __________ for the workers who bring them books.
7. It was __________ of the librarian to save that book for Soren.

Name ______________________ Date ____________

Short *i* and Long *i*

Basic 1–9. Read the paragraph. Write the Basic Word that best replaces the underlined word or words in the sentences.

As I walk through the zoo, I (1) repeat to myself to visit the new monkey house. It is made of glass and red (2) hard clay block. There was a damp (3) coolness in the old monkey house. Now the monkeys (4) reside in a comfortable environment. There is a (5) trench between the trees and the glass that separates visitors from the monkeys. As I stand outside the glass, I give a (6) loud breath when I don't see any monkeys. I am about to (7) conclude that the monkeys are not in their new home yet, when I look up in the trees. The monkeys look down at me, and I smile with (8) happiness. I can't wait to tell my family about my zoo visit when we have dinner (9) this evening.

1. ______________
2. ______________
3. ______________
4. ______________
5. ______________
6. ______________
7. ______________
8. ______________
9. ______________

Challenge 10–12. Write some rules that visitors to a zoo might need to follow. Use three of the Challenge Words. Write on a separate sheet of paper.

Spelling Words

1. skill
2. crime
3. grind
4. tonight
5. brick
6. flight
7. live
8. chill
9. delight
10. build
11. ditch
12. decide
13. witness
14. wind
15. district
16. inch
17. sigh
18. fright
19. remind
20. split

Challenge

ignorant
recognize
advice
twilight
rigid

Name ______________________ Date ____________

My Librarian Is a Camel
Spelling: Short *i* and Long *i*

Spelling Word Sort

Write each Basic Word beside the correct heading. You will use two Basic Words more than once.

/ ĭ / spelled *i* followed by a consonant	Basic Words: Challenge Words: Possible Selection Words:
/ ĭ / spelled *ui*	Basic Words:
/ ī / spelled *i*-consonant-*e*	Basic Words: Challenge Words: Possible Selection Words:
/ ī / spelled *igh*	Basic Words: Challenge Words: Possible Selection Words:
/ ī / spelled *i* followed by a consonant	Basic Words: Possible Selection Words:
can be pronounced / ĭ / or / ī /	Basic Words:

Spelling Words

1. skill
2. crime
3. grind
4. tonight
5. brick
6. flight
7. live
8. chill
9. delight
10. build
11. ditch
12. decide
13. witness
14. wind
15. district
16. inch
17. sigh
18. fright
19. remind
20. split

Challenge

ignorant
recognize
advice
twilight
rigid

Challenge Add the Challenge Words to your Word Sort.

Connect to Reading Look through *My Librarian Is a Camel.* Find words that have / ĭ / and / ī /. Add them to your Word Sort.

Name ________________________ Date __________

Proofreading for Spelling

My Librarian Is a Camel
Spelling:
Short *i* and Long *i*

Find the misspelled words and circle them. Write them correctly on the lines below.

For children who liv in very isolated areas, new books are a treat. They cannot visit a local library or witniss a new bookstore opening. Many communities have no resources to bild such places. So leaders must deside how to get books to the children. It would be a crimme for children to go without books.

At an airport in the Arctic, three friends wait for the mail flite to arrive. A strong wynd blows. A moment of frite passes like a cill. What if the books do not come tonite? One boy lets out a loud sie. Then the children giggle with delite as the package appears. The new books are here!

1. ____________ 7. ____________
2. ____________ 8. ____________
3. ____________ 9. ____________
4. ____________ 10. ____________
5. ____________ 11. ____________
6. ____________ 12. ____________

Spelling Words

1. skill
2. crime
3. grind
4. tonight
5. brick
6. flight
7. live
8. chill
9. delight
10. build
11. ditch
12. decide
13. witness
14. wind
15. district
16. inch
17. sigh
18. fright
19. remind
20. split

Challenge

ignorant
recognize
advice
twilight
rigid

Quotation Marks with Direct Speech

A **quotation** is made up of the exact words that someone has said. Use **quotation marks** (" ") before and after the quotation.

Always capitalize the first word of a quotation and use correct end punctuation. When the quotation begins a sentence, use a comma at the end of the statement unless it is a question or exclamation. If the speaker's name begins a sentence, use a comma after *said*.

quotation
"I wish we lived near a library," said Arun.

quotation
Cristo said, "I'd take home books every day if we did."

Thinking Questions
What words tell that someone is speaking? What are the exact words that person says?

Write each sentence correctly. Capitalize words that should be capitalized. Add quotation marks, commas, and end marks where they are needed.

1. The bookmobile is coming today said Katie

____

2. Sam said I've never seen a bookmobile

____

3. it's a big bus that takes library books to people said Katie

____

4. Sam said let's visit the bookmobile this afternoon

____

____

Name ______________________ Date ____________

Split Quotations

Sometimes the words that tell who is speaking come in the middle of a quotation.

If the first part of the quotation is a complete sentence, use a comma before and then a period after the words that tell who is speaking. Capitalize the first letter in the second sentence of the quotation.

Example: "I lived near the North Pole," said Dad. "There were no libraries nearby."

If the entire quotation is one sentence, use a comma after the words that tell who is speaking. Do not capitalize the first letter in the second part of the quotation.

Example: "I love to read," he said, "so I found ways to get books."

Thinking Questions
Is the quotation broken into parts? Where does the punctuation belong?

1–4. Write the quotations correctly.

1. I read all the time exclaimed Anna it's nice to have plenty of books

____

2. some people are not so lucky said Ms. Owens they live far from a library

____

3. how do they get books asked Anna everyone needs books to read

____

4. some people get books by plane said Ms. Owens and others get them by boat

____

Name ______________________ Date ____________

Quotations from Text

For a report, you might use a quotation from a text. Use the same punctuation and capitalization rules that you use for other quotations. The name of the book or author that the quotation comes from is called the source. Be sure to include the source. Be sure to use the source's exact words.

Original text: "Camels are known for their ability to survive long periods without drinking water."
Source: "The Encyclopedia of Mammals"

quotation from text:
According to "The Encyclopedia of Mammals," "Camels are known for their ability to survive long periods without drinking water."

Original text: "People use camels much as they use horses, for transportation and other hard work."
Source: author Jennet Blanes

quotation from text:
"People use camels much as they use horses, for transportation and other hard work," writes Jennet Blanes.

Thinking Questions
What are the author's exact words? Where does the punctuation belong?

1. Quotation: "Camels have been helping people for centuries."
   Source: "Animals and People, Working Together"

   ____

2. Quotation: "In Africa, camels are an important means of transportation."
   Source: author James Silter

   ____

Name ______________________ Date __________

My Librarian Is a Camel
Grammar: Spiral Review

Contractions

Two Words	Contraction
I am already homesick.	**I'm** already homesick.
We are going away for the entire summer.	**We're** going away for the entire summer.
You will have a great time.	**You'll** have a great time.

1–5. Write the contractions for the underlined words.

1. You are going to miss summer baseball. ______________
2. I have heard that summers are hot in the islands. ______________
3. My grandmother said it is hot and humid every day. ______________
4. Mom said we will be close to the beach. ______________
5. She is looking forward to being with my grandparents. ______________

6–10. This note has five mistakes in the use of contractions. Underline the mistakes and write the contractions correctly on the lines below.

Hi Cody,

Iv'e been on the island for a week, and I'm having a great time. My cousins are so cool. Theyr'e baseball nuts, like you and I are. W'eve bought tickets to a baseball game. I can e-mail you some pictures. Your'e going to laugh when you see me in the straw hat. Its going to be a great summer after all.

Bye for now,
David

6. ______________
7. ______________
8. ______________
9. ______________
10. ______________

Name ______________________ Date ____________

Sentence Fluency

As you edit your writing, check for proper capitalization and punctuation of quotations. Also, make your writing more lively and precise by using different words for *said* in the words that tell who is speaking, such as *Terry said.*

A Quotation with *said*	A More Precise Word for *said*
"Maybe Lassie could take our books home on her back," Terry said.	"Maybe Lassie could take our books home on her back," Terry joked.

Rewrite each sentence. Add capital letters and punctuation. Replace *said* with a more precise word. Write the new sentence on the line.

1. our new library is awesome Jake said

____

2. what is the history of libraries Maria said

____

3. there haven't been public libraries for that long Ms. Chance said

____

____

4. early American towns had libraries Ms. Chance said it cost money to borrow books, though

____

____

5. Lucy said I'm glad we can borrow books for free now

____

6. Public libraries are a great resource Ms. Chance said

____

Name ______________________ Date ____________

Lesson 3
READER'S NOTEBOOK

My Librarian Is a Camel
Writing:
Narrative Writing

Focus Trait: Conventions

Informal Speech

Weak Dialogue	Informal, Natural Speech
"I very much like that book."	"That book is great!"

1–2. Read each line of dialogue. Rewrite the underlined phrases to make them sound more natural and informal.

1. "You will enjoy this book because it has many interesting characters."	"____________ this book because it has __________ characters."
2. "We can consult the librarian about worthwhile reading material for our book club."	"__________ the librarian about ______________ for our book club."

3–5. Read each line of dialogue. Rewrite it to make it sound more natural.

Pair/Share **Work with a partner to brainstorm words for your dialogue.**

3. "A frightening mystery story is often a popular choice."	
4. "There should be no problem locating the titles of current books on the Internet."	
5. "We can select our books based on members' recommendations."	

Name ______________________ Date ____________

The Power of W.O.W.!

Actor Call!

Imagine you are the director of the play *The Power of W.O.W.!* You would like to help the actress who will play Ileana understand her character. Complete the activity to write a description that helps the actress understand her role.

Read page 113. What line of dialogue on the page tells that Ileana is committed to helping save the W.O.W. program?

____

____

____

What is the stage direction for Ileana on page 116? What does the stage direction tell you about how Ileana feels about asking Uncle Carlos for a favor?

____

____

____

What can you infer about Ileana's character from her words and stage direction? How does it help you understand the play's theme?

____

____

____

Name ______________________ Date ____________

You are the director of the play, and you are trying to help the actress playing Ileana. Write a description of the character you can give to the actress. Be sure you tell what Ileana contributes to the theme of the play.

Name ______________________ Date ____________

Prefixes *non-, mis-*

misplace	mistreat	nonfiction
misspelled	misjudged	nonsense
misunderstand	nonbeliever	nonstop

Complete each phrase to make a complete sentence. In items 1–7, use your own words to complete the sentences in a way that makes sense. In items 8–9, choose a word from the box to complete the sentences.

1. To make sure I don't turn in an assignment with misspelled words, I ______________________.
2. I am a nonbeliever in ______________________.
3. If I misunderstand what was said, I ______________________.
4. The most important thing I have ever misplaced was my ______________________.
5. When you mistreat your belongings, they ______________________.
6. My favorite nonfiction book is ______________________.
7. One time I misjudged ______________________.
8. My sister Tina talks ______________________ on her phone with friends from school.
9. My dad thinks that buying a new school bag every year is ______________________.

Name ______________________ Date ____________

Words with Short *o* and Long *o*

Basic 1–10. Write the Basic Word that completes each analogy.

1. *Soup* is to *lunch* as ____________ is to *breakfast*.
2. *Typed* is to *e-mail* as ____________ is to *letter*.
3. *Shout* is to *yell* as *brag* is to ____________.
4. *Near* is to *close* as *distant* is to ____________.
5. *Normal* is to *usual* as *strange* is to ____________.
6. *Lose* is to *lost* as ____________ is to *found*.
7. *Climb* is to *hill* as ____________ is to *problem*.
8. *Approve* is to *disapprove* as *praise* is to ____________.
9. *Teacher* is to *students* as ____________ is to *guests*.
10. *Surf* is to *wave* as *ski* is to ____________.

Challenge 11–14. Write a paragraph about taking an ocean voyage to another country. Tell about your trip on the ocean. Use four of the Challenge Words. Write on a separate sheet of paper.

Spelling Words

1. block
2. shown
3. oatmeal
4. wrote
5. fellow
6. scold
7. coast
8. odd
9. locate
10. slope
11. throat
12. host
13. online
14. shock
15. solve
16. known
17. remote
18. stock
19. boast
20. globe

Challenge

bonus
approach
motion
continent
accomplish

Name ____________________ Date __________

Spelling Word Sort

Write each Basic Word beside the correct heading.

/ŏ/ spelled *o* followed by a consonant	**Basic Words:** **Challenge Words:** **Possible Selection Words:**
/ō/ spelled *o*-consonant-*e*	**Basic Words:** **Possible Selection Words:**
/ō/ spelled *oa*	**Basic Words:** **Challenge Words:**
/ō/ spelled *ow*	**Basic Words:** **Possible Selection Words:**
/ō/ spelled *o* followed by a consonant	**Basic Words:** **Challenge Words:** **Possible Selection Words:**

Spelling Words

1. block
2. shown
3. oatmeal
4. wrote
5. fellow
6. scold
7. coast
8. odd
9. locate
10. slope
11. throat
12. host
13. online
14. shock
15. solve
16. known
17. remote
18. stock
19. boast
20. globe

Challenge

bonus
approach
motion
continent
accomplish

Challenge Add the Challenge Words to your Word Sort.

Connect to Reading Look through "The Power of W.O.W.!" Find words that have /ŏ/ and /ō/. Add them to your Word Sort.

Name ______________________ Date ____________

Proofreading for Spelling

The Power of W.O.W.!
Spelling:
Words with Short *o* and Long *o*

Find the misspelled words and circle them. Write them correctly on the lines below.

People were in shok when they heard the news that Tim was involved in the disappearance of the ancient weaving from the local museum. Tim seemed like a nice enough feloe who was knowne and recognized by several of the volunteers at the gift shop. He wroat a silly note to enclose with the toy blok kit he bought for his nephew. He also tried to loccate a gloab for his niece, but there were none in stoc.

Tim did boaste about planning a trip to the coest of South America but said he had to postpone it because of a sore throte. Then he asked about the weavers' video shon during the day. Needless to say, the museum staff was surprised when the security video showed Tim taking the ancient weaving and then covering up with it while he took a nap in the back!

1. ____________ 7. ____________
2. ____________ 8. ____________
3. ____________ 9. ____________
4. ____________ 10. ____________
5. ____________ 11. ____________
6. ____________ 12. ____________

Spelling Words

1. block
2. shown
3. oatmeal
4. wrote
5. fellow
6. scold
7. coast
8. odd
9. locate
10. slope
11. throat
12. host
13. online
14. shock
15. solve
16. known
17. remote
18. stock
19. boast
20. globe

Challenge

bonus
approach
motion
continent
accomplish

Name ____________________ Date __________

Sentence Fragments

The Power of W.O.W.!
Grammar: Fragments and Run-on Sentences

A sentence must have a subject and a predicate to tell a complete thought. A **sentence fragment** is missing a subject, a predicate, or sometimes both.

fragment
Helped raise money for the soccer team.

Thinking Questions
Does this group of words have a subject that tells whom or what this sentence is about? Does it have a predicate that tells what happens or says something about the subject?

1–4. Write *sentence* if the group of words is a sentence. Write *fragment* if the group of words is not a sentence.

1. We made money for our team. ____________

2. Held a fun fair for little kids. ____________

3. Everyone on the team participated. ____________

4. Activities all over the soccer field. ____________

5–8. Write *subject* if the fragment is missing the part of the sentence that tells *whom* or *what*. Write *predicate* if the fragment is missing the part of the sentence that tells *what happens* or *what is*.

5. Tossed beanbags into a cardboard clown's mouth

____

6. A team member with a polar bear outfit

____

7. Posed for pictures with the bear ____________

8. Kids with clown makeup ____________

Name ________________________ Date ____________

Run-on Sentences

A **run-on sentence** has two complete thoughts that run together. To correct a run-on sentence, write each complete thought as a separate sentence or form them into a compound sentence.

run-on sentence: They all worked together the project was a success.

separate sentences: They all worked together. The project was a success.

compound sentence: They all worked together, and the project was a success.

Thinking Questions
How many complete thoughts are in the sentence? Is there proper punctuation and capitalization or a conjunction?

Write *run-on* if the sentence is a run-on sentence. Write *correct* if the sentence is not a run-on sentence. For each run-on sentence, draw a line between the two complete thoughts.

1. We wanted to raise money, our class needed a new computer.

____

2. Some people suggested a bake sale some wanted an arts-and-crafts fair.

____

3. The class decided on an arts-and-crafts sale.

____

4. One group made picture frames, another made baskets.

____

5. Some parents helped also they made candleholders.

____

6. We sold our arts and crafts to parents and students in other grades.

____

Name ______________________ Date ____________

Writing Complete Sentences

To change a sentence fragment to a complete sentence, first identify what information is missing. Then write a new sentence.

fragment	Worked together on a project.
complete sentence	Our school worked together on a project.
run-on	We raised money everyone had fun.
complete sentences	We raised money. Everyone had fun.

Thinking Questions
What information is missing from a fragment? How can I fix a run-on?

1–3. Change each fragment to a complete sentence.

1. Made money for a new playground.

____

2. Supported the kids in their community.

____

3. Each class in school.

____

4–6. Rewrite each sentence correctly.

4. We had a fair we sold food from many countries.

____

5. One booth sold tacos, another sold pizza.

____

6. It was a success, we'll do it again next year.

____

Name ______________________ Date __________

Writing Titles

When you write a title, capitalize

- the first word in the title.
- all important words in the title.
- a person's title, such as *Ms.* or *Dr.*

Do not capitalize *a*, *an*, or *the* unless it is the first word in the title.

1–4. Write each title correctly in the space below.

1. "the power of a community"

____

2. the dallas morning news

____

3. guide to volunteering

____

4. "how p.o.w.w.o.w. saved a program"

____

5–6. Write each sentence correctly in the space below.

5. The library has a copy of my favorite magazine, community service.

____

6. Doug read a great article on fundraising called "the basics of building support."

____

Name ______________________ Date __________

Sentence Fluency

When you edit your writing, make sure to correct all sentence fragments and run-on sentences. Many experienced writers make their writing flow smoothly by varying the length of their sentences.

For variety, combine two short, related sentences by inserting a comma and a conjunction between them. The words *and*, *but*, and *so* are conjunctions.

Dora got on her bike. She rode down the street.

Dora got on her bike**, and** she rode down the street.

1–5. Combine each pair of sentences using a comma and a conjunction. Use *and*, *but*, or *so*.

1. We belong to the service club at school. We find ways to help people.

____

2. Olivia was sick today. We took the homework assignment to her after school.

____

3. Every year, our class does a project to help the community. This year will not be different.

____

____

4. Gary called his friends to help. They were at football practice.

____

5. Dad cooks dinner every night. Bridget watches her little sister.

____

Name ______________________ Date __________

Focus Trait: Organization

Why Events and Actions Happen

Good writers show or hint at why events happen and why characters act the way they do. The plot helps direct the actions of the characters. A plot has a beginning, middle, and end.

Plot Event or Action	Reason Why
The Words on Wheels program is in its last week.	The library has no more money to pay for gas or buy books.

Read each event or action from "The Power of W.O.W.!" Then give the reason why it happened.

Plot Event or Action	Reason Why
1. Ileana, Shane, and Jason decide to have a car wash.	
2. Ileana does not accept a donation from her uncle, Mr. Diaz.	
3. A television news van comes to the car wash.	
4. The car wash becomes busier, and the kids begin making more money.	

Name ________________________ Date ____________

Stormalong

Post Cards to Home

Stormalong writes post cards to a friend back home in Cape Cod about his adventures. Use details from the story to complete Stormalong's post cards home.

Read pages 144–145. Stormalong impresses the crew of the *Lady of the Sea* by fighting a giant octopus. In Stormalong's post card, include details from the story that reflect his point of view.

Hello!
I fought an octopus today.
____
____
____
____

Stormalong

Next, read page 147. Now Stormalong is writing about his move to Kansas. As Stormalong, write in first person to explain why you are moving.

Hello!
____
____
____
____
____
____
____

Stormalong

Name ______________________ Date ____________

Finally, read about Stormalong's trouble on the English Channel on pages 149–151. What happened? How does Stormalong feel about it? Write another post card.

Stormalong

Think about the end of the story. What can you infer about how Stormalong feels? Explain how he feels and tell why. Use your own words.

Reference Materials

dispose, *v.* to throw away
harbor, *n.* a sheltered body of water where ships can anchor safely
mineral, *n.* a natural substance, such as diamonds or coal, that is not plant or animal
mine, *v.* to dig a tunnel or hole in order to find minerals
valuable, *adj.* worth a lot of money

1–4. Choose a word from the sample dictionary entries above to complete each sentence.

1. When silver was discovered in Colorado, thousands of people went west to ____________ for it and get rich.
2. Like gold, silver is rare, so even a little bit is ____________ .
3. If the silver is buried deep, miners must move a lot of earth and ____________ of it safely.
4. Silver is just one important ____________ . Others include coal, iron, and copper.

5–7. Use the given word in a sentence. Use a dictionary to confirm word meanings.

5. errand

____

6. popular

____

7. trampled

____

Name ______________________ Date ______________

Homophones

Basic 1–10. Write the Basic Word that best completes each sentence.

1. I cannot ______________ for my grandmother's birthday party.
2. We are going to celebrate in two ______________ with a picnic.
3. I hope that my sprained ankle will ______________ by then.
4. Organizing the party has been a real ______________.
5. People have ______________ gifts from all over the country.
6. I ______________ that my uncle is buying a piñata.
7. I asked my grandmother not to ______________ at the presents in the closet.
8. I bought Grandmother a spinning weather ______________.
9. She can put it on the ______________ of the roof.
10. Most of the guests will be adults. I will be the only ______________.

Challenge 11–14. Write a short article for your school about holding a book sale to help get money for new school playground equipment. Use four Challenge Words. Write on a separate sheet of paper.

Spelling Words

1. wait
2. weight
3. heard
4. herd
5. days
6. daze
7. heel
8. heal
9. peak
10. peek
11. sent
12. cent
13. scent
14. feet
15. feat
16. vain
17. vane
18. vein
19. miner
20. minor

Challenge

raise
raze
rays
principal
principle

Name ______________________ Date ____________

Spelling Word Sort

Write each Basic Word beside the correct heading.

/ā/ sound	**Basic Words:** **Challenge Words:** **Possible Selection Words:**
/ĕ/ sound	**Basic Words:**
/ē/ sound	**Basic Words:** **Possible Selection Words:**
/ī/ sound	**Basic Words:**
Other homophones	**Basic Words:** **Challenge Words:** **Possible Selection Words:**

Spelling Words

1. wait
2. weight
3. heard
4. herd
5. days
6. daze
7. heel
8. heal
9. peak
10. peek
11. sent
12. cent
13. scent
14. feet
15. feat
16. vain
17. vane
18. vein
19. miner
20. minor

Challenge

raise
raze
rays
principal
principle

Challenge Add the Challenge Words to your Word Sort.

Connect to Reading Look through "Stormalong." Find words that sound alike but have different spellings and meanings. Add them to your Word Sort.

Name ______________________ Date ____________

Proofreading for Spelling

Find the misspelled words and circle them. Write them correctly on the lines below.

To swim with manatees, you need a guide and snorkeling gear, including fins for your feete that fit your hele comfortably. You might feel like a minar in all of the gear, but it is all necessary. Sometimes your search for manatees is in vian and all you experience is the secnt of the sea, but often you can get a piek at the giant mammals moving slowly through the water if you wate long enough. You'll find you can stop on a cint when you see a manatee, and you can be so excited you'll feel like a vien might pop. Swimming with a hurd of manatees can put you in a daiz. A manatee's wieght can reach 3,000 pounds, and it can grow to be 13 feet long. If you ever get to swim with these gentle giants, you will be very lucky!

1. ______________ 7. ______________
2. ______________ 8. ______________
3. ______________ 9. ______________
4. ______________ 10. ______________
5. ______________ 11. ______________
6. ______________ 12. ______________

Spelling Words

1. wait
2. weight
3. heard
4. herd
5. days
6. daze
7. heel
8. heal
9. peak
10. peek
11. sent
12. cent
13. scent
14. feet
15. feat
16. vain
17. vane
18. vein
19. miner
20. minor

Challenge

raise
raze
rays
principal
principle

Name ______________________ Date ____________

Capitalizing Historical Events and Documents

Proper nouns are always capitalized. Proper nouns are words that name a particular person, place, or thing. The names of important historical events and documents are also proper nouns and should be capitalized.

a war the American Revolutionary War
a document the Declaration of Independence

Remember, do not capitalize small words like *and*, *of*, and *the*.

Thinking Question
What words name a particular event or document?

Write these sentences correctly. Add capital letters when they are needed.

1. After the war of 1812, many pioneers went west.

   ____

   ____

2. Clipper ships were used in the california gold rush.

   ____

   ____

3. Clipper ships were not common after the civil war.

   ____

   ____

4. Lincoln signed the emancipation proclamation during the war.

   ____

   ____

Name ______________________ Date __________

Capitalizing Titles

The titles of books, stories, and essays are**proper nouns** and should always be capitalized. Do not capitalize small words, such as *and*, *of*, and *the*, unless they begin the title.

book *Treasure Island*
story "Old Stormalong and the Octopus"

Remember, put the titles of book chapters, stories, and essays inside quotation marks.

Thinking Question
Which words are part of a title?

Write these sentences correctly. Add capital letters where they are needed. Be sure to underline book titles.

1. Is there a story about Stormalong in the book american tall tales?

____

____

2. The story "five fathoms tall" is about Stormy.

____

____

3. I wrote an essay for class called "why we like tall tales."

____

____

4. I loved the story "paul bunyan, the giant lumberjack."

____

____

Name ______________________ Date ____________

Capitalizing Languages, People's Names, and Nationalities

The names of languages, people, and nationalities are **proper nouns.** They should always be capitalized.

languages	English, Spanish, Quechua, Arabic, Swahili
peoples' names	Alfred Bulltop Stormalong, Paul Bunyan
nationalities	Canadian, Spanish, Chilean, Saudi Arabian

Thinking Question
What words name a language, person, or nationality?

1–4. Write these sentences correctly. Add capital letters where they are needed.

1. Did sailors speak chinese when they sailed to Asia?

____

____

2. Do william and janet know why the Dover cliffs are white?

____

____

3. Stormy delivered cargo to italians and to indians.

____

____

4. The tall tale hero john henry is an american hero.

____

____

Name ______________________ Date ____________

Writing Quotations

Stormalong
Grammar: Spiral Review

Capitalize the first word of a quotation. If a quotation comes at the end of the sentence, place a comma and a space before the first quotation mark. Place end punctuation before the last quotation mark.

The narrator said, "As he grew older, Stormy was the main attraction of Cape Cod."

Stormy said, "The sea's my best friend."

1–6. Write these sentences correctly. Add commas, capital letters, end marks, and quotation marks where they are needed.

1. The captain shouted hoist the anchor!

____

2. Stormy said, A sailor's life is the only one for me.

____

3. The book says, "the author uses exaggeration"

____

4. A sailor asked "where will you settle down, Stormy"

____

5. The first mate cried "we have to turn back"

____

6. No one quite remembers how old Stormalong died the narrator said.

____

Name _______________ Date _______________

Word Choice

Less Exact Nouns	More Exact Nouns
The boys signed up for a tour of the river.	The campers signed up for a tour of Rainbow River.

1–8. Rewrite each sentence. Change the underlined words to exact nouns.

1. This summer, some children and I are going to sailing camp.

   ____

2. We are looking forward to many exciting things.

   ____

3. Sailing a boat through water is a real challenge.

   ____

4. The early morning air can be chilly, so everyone wears warm clothes.

   ____

5. From time to time, someone spots animals in the open water.

   ____

6. One morning, a boy sees a dolphin and her calf swimming nearby.

   ____

7. It takes a lot of work to sail a boat.

   ____

8. At noontime, we catch a strong wind and speed toward shore.

   ____

Name ______________________ Date ____________

Focus Trait: Conventions

Beginning a Story

A. Identify the character and setting in the story opening. Then make a prediction about what the story problem might be.

1. Sui Li crept down the stairs. She opened the cellar door and stepped in. She smelled dust and dampness. Her flashlight gave off light. The door shut behind her.

Character: ______________________

Setting: ______________________

Story Problem: ______________________

B. Read each story opening. Then write sentences to introduce a story problem.

2. The waves slapped against the side of the sailboat, harder and harder. Tom's father said, "Look at how dark the sky is getting!"

____

____

____

3. The cave seemed miles wide. Amber stared in amazement at the strange rock formations.

____

____

____

4. James looked up and down the empty street. He called out into the silence, "Is anybody there?"

____

____

____

Name ____________________ Date __________

Invasion from Mars

PLAYBILL

A playbill is a program for a play. One of the things a playbill lists is a plot summary to entice viewers. Answer the questions below to help you create a plot summary for the playbill of *Invasion from Mars.*

Where and when does the story take place?

____

By whom is the story told?

____

List three major plot events.

- ______________________________
- ______________________________
- ______________________________

When the aliens come out of the object, how does the crowd feel? Find the stage direction on page 183 that tells you this information.

____

____

How does the character Phillip's narration of the event help you understand the event?

____

____

Write a summary of the play for the playbill using the information you gathered on the previous page. Make sure to include the setting, main characters, and the main events, but don't give away the most exciting parts! You want the audience to watch the play to find out more.

INVASION FROM MARS
PLOT SUMMARY

____
____
____
____
____
____
____
____
____
____
____
____
____
____
____

PLAYBILL

INVASION FROM MARS

Name ______________________ Date ____________

Suffixes *-y*, *-ous*

adventurous	handy	rocky
glorious	cloudy	chilly
scary	wondrous	glamorous

Complete each sentence with a word from above.

1. A pencil is a ________________ thing to have when you are taking a test.

2. The ________________ princess wore an expensive gown and jewels to the ball.

3. The ________________ skier raced down a steep mountain.

4. The ________________ sky made the air seem ________________.

5. The climb up the ________________ cliff was difficult and tiring.

6. The ________________ monster frightened the villagers.

7. At the end of the day, we watched a ________________ sunset.

8. Their mouths dropped open at the ________________ sight.

Name ______________________ Date __________

Vowel Sounds /u/, /yoo/, and /oo/

Basic 1–11. Read the paragraph. Write the Basic Words that best complete the sentences.

The puppy running through the grocery store was the first (1) ______________ something was wrong. Diana stood next to the (2) ______________ and vegetable section. She looked at a (3) ______________ of bananas but chose an orange instead. Suddenly, the (4) ______________ dog jumped into Diana's cart! It tore open a loaf of bread, causing a (5) ______________ to fly into Diana's face. Startled, Diana squeezed the orange, and (6) ______________ exploded over Diana and a nearby man. He was (7) ______________ to Diana. He began to (8) ______________ with her. He said it was her fault that his business (9) ______________ was ruined! One worker had to (10) ______________ the dog. The cleaning (11) ______________ had to mop the floor.

Challenge 12–14. Write sentences that tell about jobs that people might have. Use three Challenge Words. Write on a separate sheet of paper.

Spelling Words

1. bunch
2. fruit
3. argue
4. crumb
5. crew
6. tune
7. juice
8. refuse
9. truth
10. young
11. clue
12. trunk
13. amuse
14. suit
15. rude
16. trust
17. dew
18. stuck
19. rescue
20. brush

Challenge

computer
mustard
tissue
customer
attitude

Name ______________________ Date __________

Spelling Word Sort

Invasion from Mars
Spelling: Vowel Sounds /ŭ/, /yōō/, and /ōō/

Write each Basic Word beside the correct heading.

/ŭ/ spelled *u* followed by a consonant	Basic Words: Challenge Words: Possible Selection Words:
Other spellings for /ŭ/	Basic Words:
/yōō/ and /ōō/ spelled *u*-consonant-*e*	Basic Words: Challenge Words: Possible Selection Words:
/yōō/ and /ōō/ spelled *ue*	Basic Words: Challenge Words:
/yōō/ and /ōō/ spelled *ui*	Basic Words:
/ōō/ spelled *ew*	Basic Words: Possible Selection Words:
Other spellings for /yōō/ and /ōō/	Basic Words: Challenge Words:

Challenge Add the Challenge Words to your Word Sort.

Connect to Reading Look through "Invasion from Mars." Find more words that have the /ŭ/, /yōō/, and /ōō/ spelling patterns on this page. Add them to your Word Sort.

Spelling Words

1. bunch
2. fruit
3. argue
4. crumb
5. crew
6. tune
7. juice
8. refuse
9. truth
10. young
11. clue
12. trunk
13. amuse
14. suit
15. rude
16. trust
17. dew
18. stuck
19. rescue
20. brush

Challenge

computer
mustard
tissue
customer
attitude

Name ______________________ Date ____________

Proofreading for Spelling

Invasion from Mars
Spelling: Vowel Sounds /ŭ/, /yoo/, and /oo/

Find the misspelled words and circle them. Write them correctly on the lines below.

Sometimes trooth and fantasy are easily confused. That is what happened when a radio play, meant to amuise, created a panic. At that time, people were very in toon with stories of aliens from space. So, when a radio crue described a strange extraterrestrial crash, few people would argew that they didn't believe it.

According to the newsman, a bunsh of people were gathered beside the crash when suddenly an alien emerged. Old and yung alike were stuk to their seats as the story unfolded.

It was hours before people had a clew that the broadcast was a hoax. Frantic citizens called on authorities to rescew them. Finally, people settled down, but they grew skeptical. From then on, many would refuise to trest everything they heard on television or radio.

1. ____________ 7. ____________
2. ____________ 8. ____________
3. ____________ 9. ____________
4. ____________ 10. ____________
5. ____________ 11. ____________
6. ____________ 12. ____________

Spelling Words

1. bunch
2. fruit
3. argue
4. crumb
5. crew
6. tune
7. juice
8. refuse
9. truth
10. young
11. clue
12. trunk
13. amuse
14. suit
15. rude
16. trust
17. dew
18. stuck
19. rescue
20. brush

Challenge

computer
mustard
tissue
customer
attitude

Name _______________ Date _______________

Action Verbs

An **action verb** tells what a person or thing does.

action verb
A strange object lands near the school.
It came from the sky.

Thinking Question
Which words tell what a person or thing does?

1–10. Write the action verb in each sentence.

1. The object glows like the moon. _______________
2. Students watch the object in shock. _______________
3. A strange creature peers out a window.
____
4. The event begins earlier in the day. _______________
5. Many people hear a loud buzzing sound.
____
6. A silver streak flashes overhead. _______________
7. The object rises with a roar. _______________
8. It disappears into the clouds. _______________
9. The students stare at one another in amazement.
____
10. Everyone returns to their work. _______________

Name ______________________________ Date ____________

Main Verbs and Helping Verbs

Some verbs are more than one word. The **main verb** is the most important verb. The **helping verb** comes before the main verb.

helping verb **main verb**
Ryan is writing a science fiction story.

Thinking Questions
Which is the most important verb? Which verb comes before it?

1–10. Write *HV* above each helping verb. Write *MV* above each main verb.

1. Ryan has read much science fiction.

2. He was thinking about his favorite stories.

3. They have described distant galaxies.

4. Ryan is imagining a strange planet.

5. Ryan will write about the planet's creatures.

6. His characters are traveling to Earth.

7. They are dressed as humans.

8. They will visit New York City.

9. The extraterrestrials are living among us.

10. The story will frighten his friends.

Linking Verbs

A **linking verb** tells what someone or something is, or what someone or something is like. Most linking verbs are forms of the verb *be*.

linking verb
That story is scary.

Thinking Questions
Which word tells what a person or thing is? Which word tells what a person or thing is like?

1–8. Underline the linking verb in each sentence.

1. Science fiction was always my favorite type of story.
2. The stories are very imaginative.
3. In one story, a creature from Mars becomes lost on Earth.
4. The creature appears human.
5. A boy is kind to the creature.
6. Soon, the creature is comfortable at the boy's home.
7. The Martian becomes homesick on Earth.
8. That story seemed realistic in some ways.

Name ______________________________ Date ____________

Complete Sentences

A complete sentence expresses a complete thought. It contains a subject and a predicate. To change a sentence fragment to a complete sentence, identify what is missing. Then write a new sentence.

The movie characters.	The movie characters see a spaceship.

To correct a run-on sentence, write each complete thought as a separate sentence.

The spaceship appears out of the blue it lands in a field.	The spaceship appears out of the blue. It lands in a field.

1–3. Change each fragment to a complete sentence.

1. Streaking across the sky.

____

2. The pattern of the lights.

____

2. Could be on a helicopter or an airplane.

____

4–6. Rewrite each run-on sentence correctly.

4. The lights at the top were red the lights around the bottom were yellow.

____

5. The lights hovered over the park people started backing away.

____

6. Then the strange lights disappeared the streetlights suddenly disappeared also.

____

____

Name ______________________ Date ____________

Word Choice

Weak Verb	Strong Verb
Scientists made a spaceship for a flight to Venus.	Scientists designed a spaceship for a flight to Venus.

1–6. Replace each underlined verb with a stronger verb. Write the new sentence on the line.

1. Many astronauts thought about a trip to Venus.

____

2. The rocket finally took off.

____

3. It went through space at thousands of miles per hour.

____

4. Its metal sides shone in the sunlight.

____

5. The spaceship moved past the moon within hours.

____

6. Soon the astronauts will walk on Venus.

____

Name ______________________ Date ____________

Focus Trait: Organization

News Report

Strong news reports include specific, relevant facts, quotations, and other details. The information should be organized in a logical manner to guide readers through the events.

Weak, General Ideas	Specific, Relevant Details
A comet came close to Earth recently. Some people feared it could hit Earth, but scientists said it came apart and won't be near Earth again for many years.	A comet passed within 22 million miles of Earth on October 16, 2011. "It broke apart," said Don Yeomans of NASA. The remains of the comet won't be near Earth again for 12,000 years.

Write a paragraph reporting on a fictional asteroid that approached Earth. Begin with the topic sentence shown below and include the most relevant and specific details from the list of ideas.

Topic Sentence: An asteroid came near Earth on Tuesday.

____

____

____

____

Ideas

1. People called the asteroid 2427.
2. People said the asteroid was not a danger.
3. The asteroid came within 500,000 miles of Earth.
4. Some people worried about the asteroid.
5. An asteroid might have hit Earth and killed the dinosaurs.
6. "We can protect Earth from all asteroids," said a popular astronaut.

Name ______________________ Date ____________

Coming Distractions: Questioning Movies

Thumbs Up or Thumbs Down

Reread pages 204–208 of "Coming Distractions: Questioning Movies." Then answer the questions below.

List three opinions that the author states about movies.

1. ____

2. ____

3. ____

List one fact that the author uses to support each opinion above.

1. ____

2. ____

3. ____

Name ______________________ Date ____________

Lesson 7
READER'S NOTEBOOK

Coming Distractions: Questioning Movies
Independent Reading

Imagine you read the author's article online and want to send an e-mail to the author telling him what you think of it. Choose one opinion from your list. Do you think the author did a good job of supporting his opinions with facts? Tell the author what you think of his opinion. Make sure to support your opinion with reasons.

New Message

To: **Frank W. Baker**

From:

Subject: **Your Article**

Name _______________________ Date ___________

Greek and Latin Word Parts *phon, photo, graph, auto, tele*

autograph	autobiography	automobile	symphony
photograph	telephone	photocopy	cinematographer

Read the words in the box above. Look for Greek and Latin word parts to help you understand the meaning of each word. Then use a word from the box to complete each sentence below.

1. The movie actress signed an _______________ for her fan.
2. I used the _______________ to call the theater for the movie schedule.
3. My mom drove the _______________ to the movie theater.
4. At the movie premiere, I used a camera to take a _______________ of the actors.
5. The movie director wrote an _______________ about his life.
6. The _______________ won an award for his filming technique.
7. The movie soundtrack features a _______________ by a famous composer.
8. I will _______________ this movie article from the library to share with the class tomorrow.

Name _______________ Date _______________

Coming Distractions: Questioning Movies
Spelling: Vowel Sounds /o͞o/ and /o͝o/

Vowel Sounds /o͞o/ and /o͝o/

Basic 1–10. Complete the puzzle by writing the Basic Word for each clue.

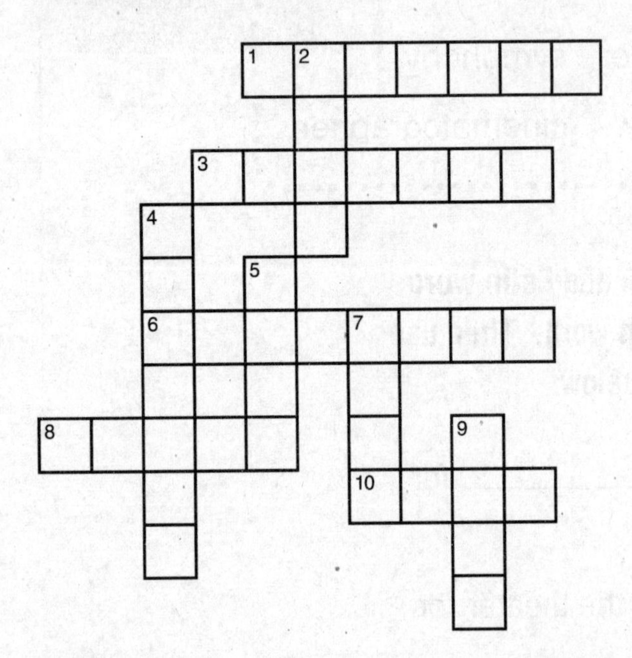

Across

1. bent or twisted
3. not sensible
6. a collection of recipes
8. a seat with legs but no arms
10. a bent object used to hold something

Down

2. the cover on a house
4. mammal with masklike face markings
5. thick hair from sheep
7. low, woody plant; a shrub
9. instrument used for work

Challenge 11–14. You've just finished your homework assignment. Before putting it in your backpack, you check it over for errors. Tell what you might find. Use four Challenge Words. Write on a separate sheet of paper.

Spelling Words

1. bloom
2. cookbook
3. tool
4. shampoo
5. put
6. wool
7. stool
8. proof
9. prove
10. group
11. brook
12. foolish
13. bush
14. crooked
15. booth
16. raccoon
17. hook
18. groom
19. roof
20. soup

Challenge

bulletin
cocoon
cushion
proofread
marooned

Spelling Word Sort

Write each Basic Word beside the correct heading.

/o͞o/ spelled *oo*	**Basic Words:** **Challenge Words:** **Possible Selection Words:**
Other spellings for /o͞o/	**Basic Words:**
/o͝o/ spelled *oo*	**Basic Words:** **Possible Selection Words:**
/o͝o/ spelled *u* followed by a consonant	**Basic Words:** **Challenge Words:**

Spelling Words

1. bloom
2. cookbook
3. tool
4. shampoo
5. put
6. wool
7. stool
8. proof
9. prove
10. group
11. brook
12. foolish
13. bush
14. crooked
15. booth
16. raccoon
17. hook
18. groom
19. roof
20. soup

Challenge

bulletin
cocoon
cushion
proofread
marooned

Challenge Add the Challenge Words to your Word Sort.

Connect to Reading Look through "Coming Distractions: Questioning Movies." Find words in the selection that have the /o͞o/ and /o͝o/ spelling patterns on this page. Add them to your Word Sort.

Name ______________________ Date ____________

Lesson 7
READER'S NOTEBOOK

Coming Distractions: Questioning Movies
Spelling: Vowel Sounds /o͞o/ and /o͝o/

Proofreading for Spelling

Find the misspelled words and circle them. Write them correctly on the lines below.

The next time you go to a movie, be sure to stay putt until the end to watch the credits. Some people think it's fullish, but the credits list the people involved in the movie. They are also prouf of the work the groop did.

I now invite you to take a moment to picture some of the following scenes that might be created on the set: flowers in blewm, a family in a restaurant buth enjoying bowls of hot sewp, a bottle of shampo on a rock by a brock, and a veterinarian showing a young girl how to properly groum her puppy. It takes many people to create these simple scenes.

I recently visited a movie studio and went behind the scenes. I met some of the people who make movie scenes scary, exciting, or magical. I can proov it, too. I took a zillion pictures!

1. ______________ 7. ______________
2. ______________ 8. ______________
3. ______________ 9. ______________
4. ______________ 10. ______________
5. ______________ 11. ______________
6. ______________

Spelling Words

1. bloom
2. cookbook
3. tool
4. shampoo
5. put
6. wool
7. stool
8. proof
9. prove
10. group
11. brook
12. foolish
13. bush
14. crooked
15. booth
16. raccoon
17. hook
18. groom
19. roof
20. soup

Challenge

bulletin
cocoon
cushion
proofread
marooned

Name _______________ Date _______________

Past, Present, and Future Tenses

The **present tense** shows action happening now.

The **past tense** shows that an action already happened. Form the past tense by adding *-ed* to the end of a regular verb. If the verb ends in *e*, drop the *e* before adding *-ed*.

The **future tense** shows action that has not happened yet. The future tense is formed by using the helping verb *will* plus a verb.

present tense
I watch a movie with my family.

past tense
I watched a movie with my family.

future tense
I will watch a movie with my family.

Thinking Question
When does the action take place?

1–3. Write the verb given in parentheses in the past tense.

1. (walk) I _______________ to the movie theater with my dad.
2. (amaze) The special effects in the movie _______________ us!
3. (impresses) The actress _______________ the critics with her moving performance.

4–5. Write the verb given in parentheses in the future tense.

4. (look) The new movie _______________ great!
5. (walk) I _______________ to the movie theater with my dad.

Name ______________________ Date ____________

Helping Verbs and Past Participles

A **helping verb** such as *have, has,* or *had* comes before the main regular verb and tells more about what happened in the past. Helping verbs must agree with the subject of the sentence. Use these helping verbs with past participles.

The **past participle** of a regular verb is the the past-tense form: add *-ed* to the end of the regular verb. If the verb ends in *e,* drop the *e* before adding *-ed.* Past participle forms use helping verbs show past action.

They have watched that movie three times.

She has liked the movie as well.

Thinking Questions
Does the main verb end with -ed? Is it used with a helping verb?

Write the past participle of the verb in parentheses. Underline the helping verb.

1. Jane's aunt has (perform) ______________ stunts for movies.
2. She has (work) ______________ on a movie about spies.
3. Many action movies have (include) ______________ amazing stunts.
4. Jane's aunt had (learn) ______________ how to do stunts safely.

Underline the past participle in each sentence. Write the appropriate helping verb.

5. I __________ enjoyed many comedy movies.
6. That director __________ filmed some of the funniest comedies.
7. We __________ waited to see that actor's latest movie.
8. He __________ appeared on the movie screen many times.

Name ______________________ Date ____________

Consistent Use of Tenses

Choose a verb tense to write in and continue to write in that tense. When you write about a particular time in a paragraph or sentence, all of the verbs should be in the same tense.

past tense: I watched a movie with a friend. After the movie, we discussed it.

present tense: We still remember and laugh at the funny parts.

future tense: Next time, we will watch a scary movie.

Thinking Question
Are the verbs telling about a particular time all in the same tense?

1–5. Choose the correct verb tense for the sentences. Write the correct verb on the line.

1. (go/will go) Tomorrow I will see a movie with my family. Then we ______________ out to dinner.
2. (will like/liked) The scenery amazed me! I especially ______________ the scene at the beach.
3. (admire, admired) We chose the movie because my mom has ______________ its star for a long time.
4. (will buy/buy) First, we will buy movie tickets, and then we ______________ some popcorn and drinks.
5. (liked/like) I love movies about cats! I also ______________ movies about dogs.

Name ________________________ Date ____________

Fragments and Run-On Sentences

A sentence **fragment** is missing a subject, a predicate, or sometimes both. To correct a fragment, identify what is missing. Then write a new sentence with the missing part.

fragment: Has produced some amazing movies.

complete sentence: That studio has produced some amazing movies.

A **run-on sentence** has two complete thoughts that run together. To correct a run-on sentence, write each complete thought as a separate sentence.

run-on sentence: I will see the movie soon animated movies are my favorites.

correct sentences: I will see the movie soon. Animated movies are my favorites.

Write *correct* if the group of words is a correctly written sentence. Write *fragment* if the group of words is a fragment. Write *run-on* if the group of words is a run-on sentence. Change each fragment to a complete sentence. Rewrite each run-on sentence correctly.

1. An animated movie about a baby penguin.

____

2. Everyone will enjoy that character he is cute and funny.

____

3. Many animated movies have featured animal characters.

____

Name ________________________ Date __________

Lesson 7
READER'S NOTEBOOK

Coming Distractions: Questioning Movies
Grammar: Connect to Writing

Sentence Fluency

When you write about a particular time in a sentence or paragraph, make sure the verbs are all in the same tense. Change the tense only to show a change in time.

Mixed Tenses	Same Tense
My cousin Susan takes acting lessons. She will want to be an actress.	My cousin Susan takes acting lessons. She wants to be an actress.

Rewrite each pair of sentences by changing the underlined verbs to the tense shown in parentheses.

1. Last year, Susan got a small role in a comedy. She will play a waitress. (past)

____

____

2. My entire family will go to opening night. We clapped loudly at the end! (past)

____

____

3. Now I own the DVD. I kept it on my bookshelf. (present)

____

4. Maybe someday I will act in the movies. Maybe I design costumes. (future)

____

____

Name ______________________ Date ____________

Coming Distractions: Questioning Movies
Writing: Informative Writing

Focus Trait: Evidence

Using Precise Language

Read each sentence. Then rewrite the sentence using more precise language and concrete details.

Poor Word Choice	Precise Word Choice
1. Everybody doesn't like movies where a lot of things happen fast.	
2. Most newspapers provide articles that tell whether a movie is good or bad.	
3. Different sounds in movies make them better.	
4. The clothes that actors wear are an important part of a movie.	
5. A good movie advertisement makes you want to see the movie.	

Name ______________________ Date __________

Me and Uncle Romie

Drawing the Bridge

When James arrives in New York, he feels very far from home. Answer the questions below to draw a picture of what James learns about people who live in different places.

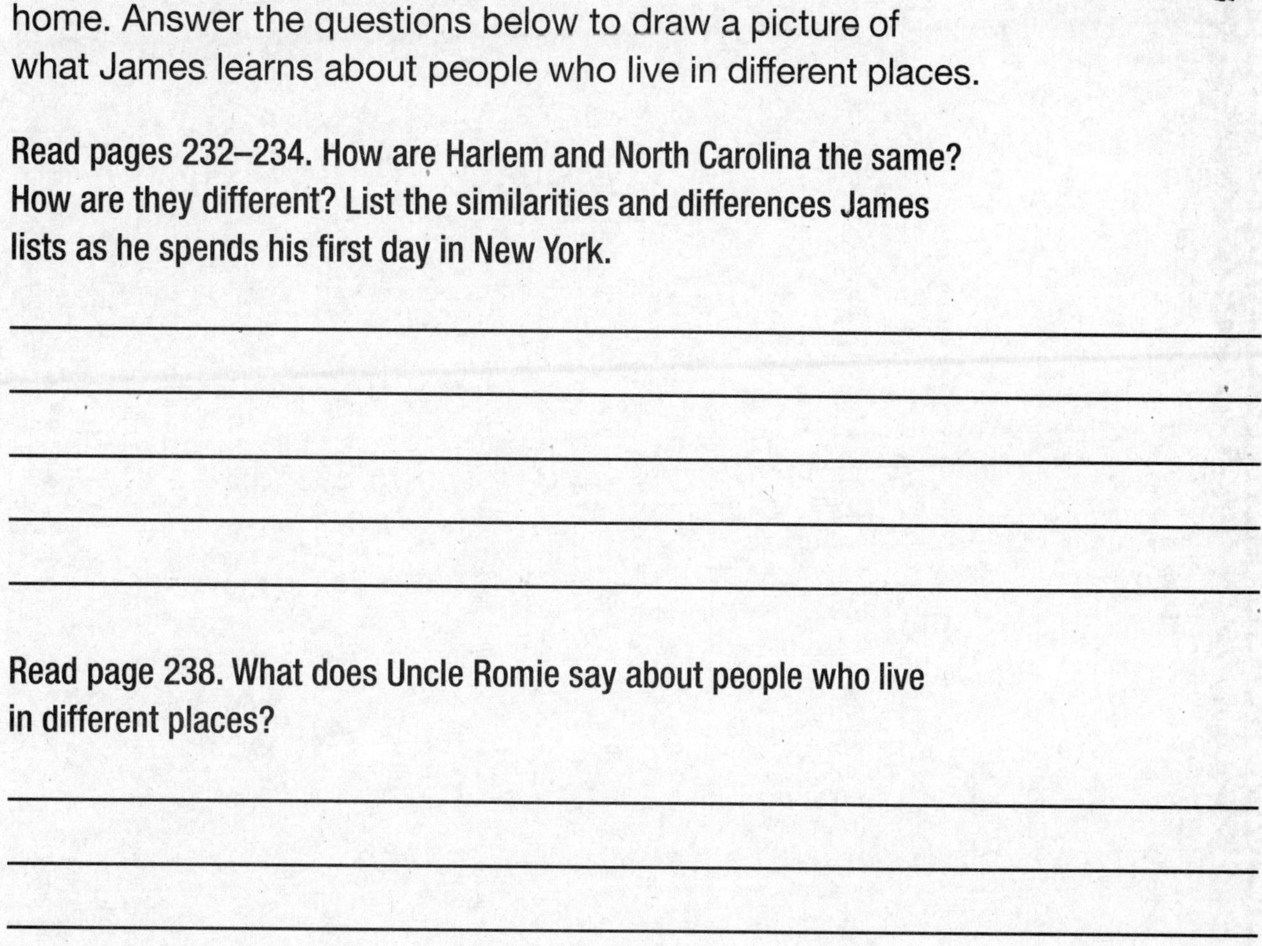

Read pages 232–234. How are Harlem and North Carolina the same? How are they different? List the similarities and differences James lists as he spends his first day in New York.

____

____

____

____

____

Read page 238. What does Uncle Romie say about people who live in different places?

____

____

____

Which details on page 239 help you confirm that this is true?

____

____

____

____

Name ______________________ Date ____________

Me and Uncle Romie
Independent Reading

What has James learned about people who live in places different from his home? Imagine that you are James writing in his journal about his experiences. Draw a picture and write what you have learned.

Name ______________________ Date __________

Figurative Language

chow down	head over heels	good as gold
heart of gold	feast or famine	safe and sound

Rewrite each sentence using one of the idioms above.

1. My mother helps others because she is so kind and loving.

   ____

2. The quiet children were very well behaved during the long car trip.

   ____

   ____

3. When I finally sat down for lunch, I ate quickly without talking.

   ____

   ____

4. My best friend really loves the movie we watched.

   ____

5. The mother couldn't rest until all her children were tucked in their beds at home.

   ____

   ____

6. When I go to the library, I either see many books I want to read or none at all. It's always too many or too few.

   ____

   ____

Name ______________________ Date ____________

Vowel Sounds /ou/, /ô/

Basic 1–10. Read the paragraph. Write the Basic Words that best complete the sentences.

I am a (1) __________ member of my school's bird-watching club. Every Saturday we leave at (2) __________ to go to the national park. Today, we looked for a (3) __________. It was sunny at first, but then it got (4) __________. Our adviser reminded us not to speak (5) __________ as we scanned the skies. Megan thought she saw something, but it was a (6) __________ alarm. Then we saw a bird fly from the (7) __________. We watched it (8) __________ a field mouse. The bird spread its wings wide, and it seemed to (9) __________ in the air. Suddenly, the bird dived and grabbed its meal with a sharp (10) __________!

Challenge 11–14. Write an e-mail message to your friend telling about a sporting event you have seen. Use four Challenge Words. Write on a separate sheet of paper.

Spelling Words

1. aloud
2. bald
3. hawk
4. south
5. faucet
6. proud
7. claw
8. tower
9. stalk
10. couple
11. howl
12. false
13. dawn
14. allow
15. drown
16. pause
17. fault
18. cause
19. amount
20. cloudier

Challenge

applaud
foul
browse
gnaw
doubt

Name ____________________ Date __________

Spelling Word Sort

Write each Basic Word beside the correct heading.

/ou/ spelled *ou*	Basic Words: Challenge Words: Possible Selection Words:
/ou/ spelled *ow*	Basic Words: Challenge Words: Possible Selection Words:
Other sounds for *ou*	Basic Words:
/ô/ spelled *aw*	Basic Words: Challenge Words:
/ô/ spelled *au*	Basic Words: Challenge Words: Possible Selection Words:
/ô/ spelled *a* before *l*	Basic Words: Possible Selection Words:

Spelling Words

1. aloud
2. bald
3. hawk
4. south
5. faucet
6. proud
7. claw
8. tower
9. stalk
10. couple
11. howl
12. false
13. dawn
14. allow
15. drown
16. pause
17. fault
18. cause
19. amount
20. cloudier

Challenge

applaud
foul
browse
gnaw
doubt

Challenge Add the Challenge Words to your Word Sort.

Connect to Reading Look through "Me and Uncle Romie." Find more words that have the /ou/ and /ô/ spelling patterns on this page. Add them to your Word Sort.

Name ______________________ Date ____________

Proofreading for Spelling

Find the misspelled words and circle them. Write them correctly on the lines below.

Mr. Rico's students are planning to paint a mural on the wall outside their classroom. Mr. Rico turns on the fawcet and rinses the brushes off. He checks the amont of paint available for the project while the students think alowd.

Everyone has a different idea. Rosa wants to paint a cuple of bawld eagles sitting high up on a towor. Jason thinks the mural should show a coyote letting out a houl at the silvery moon. Aidan says he wants to paint a box of matches with the words "Do Not Play With Matches." Matches are the cauze of many fires due to human falt. And Victoria wants to know if Mr. Rico will alow her to paint a race car. Mr. Rico likes everyone's ideas.

Before the students get started, Mr. Rico says, "Don't droun your brush with too much paint."

1. ____________ 7. ____________
2. ____________ 8. ____________
3. ____________ 9. ____________
4. ____________ 10. ____________
5. ____________ 11. ____________
6. ____________

Spelling Words

1. aloud
2. bald
3. hawk
4. south
5. faucet
6. proud
7. claw
8. tower
9. stalk
10. couple
11. howl
12. false
13. dawn
14. allow
15. drown
16. pause
17. fault
18. cause
19. amount
20. cloudier

Challenge

applaud
foul
browse
gnaw
doubt

Name ______________________ Date ____________

Present Progressive Tense

Progressive forms of verbs show action that continues over time. To make the progressive form of a verb, add *-ing* to the main verb. Use a form of *be* as a helping verb.

The **present progressive tense** describes something that is continuing to happen now. It uses the verb *is*, *am*, or *are* as a helping verb.

He is playing.

Thinking Questions
Is the action taking place over a period of time? Is it happening in the present?

1–7. Write the words that form the present progressive tense in each sentence.

1. The kids are kicking a ball in the street.

   ____

2. I am enjoying my game with the neighbors.

   ____

3. The boys and girls are forming two teams.

   ____

4. The ball is bouncing over the curb.

   ____

5. The city street is getting noisier and livelier.

   ____

6. I am remembering the quiet streets in my hometown.

   ____

7. The sky is becoming darker by the minute.

   ____

Name ______________________ Date __________

Past Progressive Tense

The **past progressive verb tense** describes something that continued in the past. It uses the verb *was* or *were* as a helping verb.

He was working.

Thinking Questions
Is the action taking place over a period of time? Is it happening in the past?

1–12. Underline the words that form the past progressive verb in each sentence.

1. The artist was making amazing pictures in his studio.
2. An art gallery was showing them last month.
3. Everyone was admiring his art.
4. We were working together on some collages.
5. The pictures were hanging on the walls of the studio.
6. They were creating collages last year at school.
7. I was using photographs for my collages last year.
8. My friends were collecting photos of animals for me.
9. Also, I was cutting out comic strips for another collage.
10. I was showing that collage at my school's art show last winter.
11. I was telling my friends about my plans for the next collage.
12. They said they were wondering what I would do next.

Name ______________________ Date ____________

Me and Uncle Romie
Grammar: Progressive Verb Tenses

Present, Past, and Future Progressive

Use progressive forms of verbs to show action that continues over time.

To make the progressive form of a verb, add *-ing* to the present-tense form of the main verb. Use a form of *be* as a helping verb.

For future progressive, use *will be* as the helping verb.

present progressive	I am learning about the city.
past progressive	I was missing my family.
future progressive	I will be remembering my visit.

Thinking Questions
Is the action taking place over a period of time? Is it happening in the present, past, or future?

1–4. Write the sentences. Change each underlined verb into a progressive form. Use the progressive form identified in parentheses.

1. I visit my cousins in Chicago. (present progressive)

____

2. The streets overflow with traffic and people. (present progressive)

____

3. The crowds will stay until late in the evening. (future progressive)

____

4. I planned to go home on Sunday, but now I want to stay longer! (past progressive)

____

Name ______________________ Date ____________

Kinds of Sentences

Kind of Sentence	End Mark	Example
Statement	period (.)	Tomoko is waiting at the bus stop.
Question	question mark (?)	Does this bus go by the aquarium?
Command	period (.)	Get in line to buy a ticket.
Exclamation	exclamation mark (!)	That line is so long!

1–6. Write the correct end mark for each sentence. Then label each sentence *statement, question, command,* or *exclamation.*

1. The city streets are very busy ____________
2. That bus is going so fast ____________
3. Can you give me directions ____________
4. Look both ways ____________
5. I've never seen such a big crowd

   ____
6. I am headed uptown ____________

7–12. Correct six errors in this ad. There are two missing capital letters and four incorrect or missing end marks.

Are you visiting our beautiful city soon! do you wonder how you'll ever find your way around town? Jonny's Guided Walking Tour is here to help. let one of our cheerful tour guides show you around, or use one of our easy-to-read maps? Either way, you'll learn about our city's rich history and see all of its important landmarks Everyone agrees. Jonny's Guided Walking Tours are totally cool

Name ______________________ Date ____________

Ideas

Help readers follow your ideas and the events you write about by using verb forms and verb tenses correctly.

Use progressive verb forms for actions that happen over a period of time.

Use the same verb tense for actions that happen at the same time.

Read each pair of sentences. Choose the correct verb tense or form for the second sentence. Write the correct verb form on the line.

1. I plan to visit my cousin's house this summer. Now I ______________ what I will want to do there. (listed/am listing)
2. My cousin lives on a farm out west. I ______________ in a big city in the east. (live, lived)
3. I was nervous about going. I ______________ scared about being so far from home. (was getting, will get)
4. Then I talked to my cousin and his parents. I ______________ how much fun we had when he came to visit me. (will be remembering, remembered)
5. Last time I visited him, we were three years old. We ______________ everywhere with the adults. (will go, went)
6. This time, we will be doing things by ourselves. I hope we ______________ in his pond most of the time. (will be swimming, swam)

Name ______________________ Date ____________

Focus Trait: Purpose

Book Report

A. Read the book report sentences. Write the letters of the sentences in the correct order.

(A) I like this book because it compares two settings. (B) However, my favorite setting is the farm in North Carolina. (C) The book also has realistic characters. (D) The first setting is New York City. (E) My favorite character is the boy's uncle. (F) New York is crowded and exciting.

____

B. Read the topic sentence below. Organize a complete paragraph that supports the topic with details.

Topic Sentence: The book I have read that has the most interesting setting is ________________ .

____

____

____

____

____

____

Name ______________________ Date ____________

Dear Mr. Winston

Mixed Messages

Reread page 262. Use details from Cara's letter to summarize what Cara writes to the librarian.

____

____

____

Based on the letter, write in the thought ballon what Cara wants to tell her dad.

What text evidence from the letter did you use to infer Cara's thoughts on page 262?

____

____

____

Name ______________________________ Date ______________

Now turn to page 266 and respond to the items below.

Reread paragraphs 3, 4, and 5 of the letter on page 266. Use details from Cara's letter to summarize what happened to the box.

____

____

____

Based on the letter, write in the thought bubble what Cara wants to tell her dad.

What text evidence from the letter helped you make inferences about Cara's thoughts on page 266?

____

____

____

Antonyms

honest	thoughtful	borrow	healthy
genuine	ashamed	guilty	nearby

Read each sentence. Rewrite each using one of the antonyms above.

1. My wallet is made from fake leather.

   ____

2. I was proud when I threw the baseball through my neighbor's window.

   ____

   ____

3. We went shopping at a distant mall.

   ____

4. Monica asked if I could lend her my book.

   ____

5. My sister was sick.

   ____

6. I was lying when I said I liked to eat liver and onions.

   ____

7. She is a very thoughtless person.

   ____

8. My brother thinks that I am innocent of taking his baseball glove.

   ____

   ____

Name ______________________ Date __________

Vowel + /r/ Sounds

Basic 1–10. Complete the puzzle by writing the Basic Word for each clue.

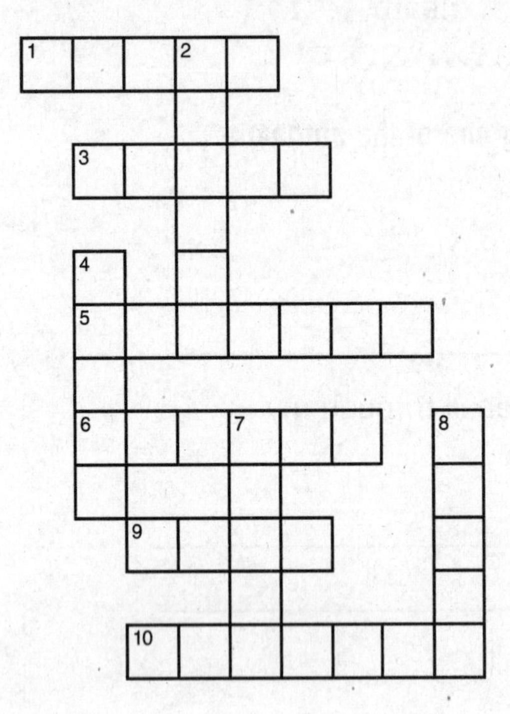

Across

1. unkind
3. a piece of cloth worn around neck or head
5. to make something ready
6. to mend
9. back
10. to discover differences and similarities

Down

2. not enough
4. a flash of light
7. a warning signal
8. to frighten

Spelling Words

1. spark
2. prepare
3. cheer
4. tear
5. scarf
6. scare
7. repair
8. earring
9. scarce
10. weird
11. sharp
12. rear
13. spare
14. gear
15. hairy
16. compare
17. alarm
18. harsh
19. upstairs
20. square

Challenge

weary
startle
appear
barnacle
awareness

Challenge 11–14. You have watched a movie about taking a submarine trip deep in the ocean. Write a story about it. Use four Challenge Words. Write on a separate sheet of paper.

Name ______________________ Date ____________

Dear Mr. Winston
Spelling:
Vowel + /r/ Sounds

Spelling Word Sort

Write each Basic Word beside the correct heading.

/îr/ spelled *ear*	Basic Words: Challenge Words:
/îr/ spelled *eer*	Basic Words:
Other spellings for /îr/	Basic Words:
/är/ spelled *ar*	Basic Words: Challenge Words: Possible Selection Words:
/âr/ spelled *are*	Basic Words: Challenge Words:
/âr/ spelled *air*	Basic Words:
Other spellings for /âr/	Basic Words: Possible Selection Words:

Spelling Words

1. spark
2. prepare
3. cheer
4. tear
5. scarf
6. scare
7. repair
8. earring
9. scarce
10. weird
11. sharp
12. rear
13. spare
14. gear
15. hairy
16. compare
17. alarm
18. harsh
19. upstairs
20. square

Challenge

weary
startle
appear
barnacle
awareness

Challenge Add the Challenge Words to your Word Sort.

Connect to Reading Look through "Dear Mr. Winston." Find words that have the vowel + /r/ spelling patterns in the chart. Add them to your Word Sort.

Name ______________________________ Date ____________

Proofreading for Spelling

Dear Mr. Winston
Spelling:
Vowel + /r/ Sounds

Find the misspelled words and circle them. Write them correctly on the lines below.

I'm so jazzed! On our way to visit my grandparents, we saw a Grizzly Giant. You're probably thinking we saw a huge black, heiry bear with sharpp teeth, or that maybe we saw a very tall, weard person wearing a teer-shaped diamond earing. Nope. The Grizzly Giant is at least 200 feet tall and 30 feet around. It's a Sequoia tree!

Dad shifted into first geer, pulled over, and stopped the car. We went for a walk to look at these giant trees and discovered that you can even walk through some of them!

We heard clapping and a loud cher coming from the visitors center. Since we were on vacation and had lots of spar time, we decided to explore. Inside, the park ranger told us the upsteirs theater had a short movie about the park. She looked at her squar-shaped watch and said the next show started in five minutes.

1. ____________ 6. ____________
2. ____________ 7. ____________
3. ____________ 8. ____________
4. ____________ 9. ____________
5. ____________ 10. ____________

Spelling Words

1. spark
2. prepare
3. cheer
4. tear
5. scarf
6. scare
7. repair
8. earring
9. scarce
10. weird
11. sharp
12. rear
13. spare
14. gear
15. hairy
16. compare
17. alarm
18. harsh
19. upstairs
20. square

Challenge

weary
startle
appear
barnacle
awareness

Name ______________________ Date ____________

Compound Sentences

A **compound sentence** has two simple sentences joined together. The separate sentences are joined by a comma (,) and a coordinating conjunction such as *and*, *or*, *but*, or *so*.

complete sentence **complete sentence**
Some people read books, and others talked quietly.
comma **coordinating conjunction**

Thinking Questions
Is the sentence made up of two simple sentences? Is one word a coordinating conjunction with a comma before it?

1–8. Underline the simple sentences in each compound sentence. Circle the coordinating conjunction.

1. The girls went to the library, and they worked on their project.
2. They could do a report, or they could write a skit.
3. The library was quiet, but the girls were getting noisy.
4. Sophie made a joke, so everyone laughed.
5. Ms. Walker came over, and she put her finger to her lips.
6. The library is for everyone, but people should be considerate of others.
7. People must work quietly, or they will disturb others.
8. The girls could be quieter, or they could work at Sophie's house.

Name ______________________ Date ____________

Complex Sentences

A **complex sentence** is made up of a simple sentence and a dependent clause, or a group of words that has a subject and a predicate. The two parts are joined by a subordinating conjunction such as *after, although, because, before, until, if, since,* and *while.*

The snake slithered under a rock	**simple sentence**
before the sun became too hot.	**dependent clause**

Thinking Question
Is the sentence made up of a simple sentence and a dependent clause with a subordinating conjunction?

1–4. Read each complex sentence. Underline the simple sentence once. Underline the dependent clause twice. Circle the subordinating conjunction that joins the two.

1. Although Rodney loved most animals, he didn't like snakes.
2. Snakes startled him because they moved so quickly.
3. He ran away from a snake in the grass though he knew it wasn't poisonous.
4. He learned more about the snake after he saw it.

5–8. Write a complete sentence by adding a simple sentence to the dependent clause. Put a comma between the two parts of the complex sentence.

5. Because that snake is poisonous

____

6. Although this snake is large

____

7. While you are at the zoo

____

8. After you look at the snake exhibit

____

Name ______________________ Date ____________

Commas in Compound Sentences

A **compound sentence** has two or more complete thoughts joined together. Use a comma after each complete thought. Always put the comma before the coordinating conjunction.

Jane has a mouse, Mike has a snake, and I have a dog.

Thinking Question
Where is the coordinating conjunction?

1–6. Write each sentence. Put in commas where necessary.

1. I'm sorry my dog, Chipper, went into your yard and he will not do it again.

____

____

2. Chipper likes flowers so he wanted to smell your roses.

____

____

3. He crushed some plants but he didn't do it on purpose.

____

____

4. He jumped over the violets but he stepped on the daisies.

____

____

5. I looked over the fence I saw Chipper and I called him.

____

____

6. I could plant some more flowers or I could weed your garden for you.

____

____

Name ____________________ Date ____________

Kinds of Nouns

Dear Mr. Winston
Grammar: Spiral Review

Common Nouns	Proper Nouns	Singular Nouns	Plural Nouns
girl	Ann	apple	apples
city	Orlando	day	days
day	Thanksgiving	class	classes
month	June	fox	foxes

1–3. Write each noun and tell whether it is *common* or *proper*.

1. Joe and Sal each sneaked a box into their classroom.

____

____

2. Several holes had been poked into each lid with a pencil.

____

____

3. That morning, Ms. Li heard a strange noise under her desk.

____

____

4–6. Write the plural form of the noun in parentheses.

4. (sandwich) The children were eating their ____________.

5. (box) Then, the lids popped off the two ____________.

6. (frog) Suddenly, ____________ were jumping all over the room.

Conventions

A **compound sentence** has two or more complete thoughts joined together. The separate ideas can be joined with a comma (,) and a conjunction such as *and*, *or*, *but*, or *so*.

Use a comma after each complete thought. Always put the comma before the conjunction.

Minnie is Alicia's dog. Alicia takes her everywhere.
Minnie is Alicia's dog, and Alicia takes her everywhere.

1–6. Combine the simple sentences into one compound sentence. Use a conjunction to join the two sentences. Use commas correctly.

1. The ice cream shop was empty. Alicia went in.

   ____

2. She put her bag on the counter. She looked at the menu.

   ____

3. The bag moved. A tiny dog peeked out.

   ____

4. The lady behind the counter smiled. She spoke seriously.

   ____

5. You can't bring pets here. You can bring service animals.

   ____

6. You can leave the dog outside. You can come back later.

   ____

Name ______________________ Date ____________

Focus Trait: Evidence

Opinions, Reasons, and Details

Good writers support their ideas with details and reasons. When you explain your thoughts in an essay, group your evidence and related ideas together so they make sense to readers. Include only those ideas that are relevant to your topic.

The organization of your essay will depend on your topic. For example, if you are explaining a process, describe the process in the proper order.

Main Idea	Cara in "Dear Mr. Winston" is a likeable character.
Unrelated Detail	Mr. Winston knew Cara for several years.
Relevant Detail	She makes an honest mistake when she accidentally tells him who sold her the snake.

Read each idea about "Dear Mr. Winston." Write two related, relevant details to support each idea.

1. **Idea:** Cara truly wants to know more about her snake.

   Detail ______________________________

   ____

   Detail ______________________________

   ____

2. **Idea:** Cara's father is more upset than her mother is.

   Detail ______________________________

   ____

   Detail ______________________________

   ____

Name ______________________ Date ____________

José! Born to Dance

José's Performance Was Like…

A simile is a type of figurative language that compares two things using *like* or *as*. Read page 296. List three similes the author uses to describe José's dancing.

Imagine you are reporter and have attended one of José Limón's performances. Using the similes you found on page 296, write a review of José's performance. A review tells what is good and bad about something. What might the reporter say about José's career?

José Limón's Debut

José Limón performed at the theater on Saturday night. His performance was …

Name ______________________ Date ____________

Shades of Meaning

Synonyms are words that have similar meanings. They do not mean exactly the same thing. Synonyms may give us different feelings about the subject. For example, if you call someone's actions **bold,** you are praising him or her. If you call the actions **reckless,** you are criticizing.

Circle the synonym that best fits the context for each sentence. On the line, write why you chose this word.

1. Janelle sang all the time, and her teacher praised her (good, lovely) voice.

   ____

2. She was so (determined, stubborn) to succeed that she practiced every day.

   ____

3. She moved to the big city and rented a (cramped, little) room.

   ____

4. The busy city streets were (exciting, terrifying).

   ____

5. She worked at a restaurant to support herself, but she knew her real (job, profession) would be in music.

   ____

6. Janelle was (happy, thrilled) when she got her first paid singing job.

   ____

Name ____________________ Date ____________

More Vowel + /r/ Sounds

Basic 1–10. Write the Basic Word that best replaces the underlined word or words in each sentence.

1. My older sister Pam gets up at the beginning of the day to run cross-country. ____________
2. Running is her favorite competition. ____________
3. There are a little more than a dozen students on her team. ____________
4. Their updated uniforms are red and gold. ____________
5. The race path goes through the woods near the creek. ____________
6. Pam's teammates fight hunger and dryness as they train. ____________
7. They often get grubby as they run through mud and under tree branches. ____________
8. Their shoes get old and used up very quickly. ____________
9. Muscles get painful and ache from all the activity. ____________
10. The good feeling running gives Pam is well deserving of the effort. ____________

Spelling Words

1. learn
2. dirty
3. worn
4. sore
5. thirst
6. burn
7. record
8. cure
9. board
10. course
11. worth
12. early
13. return
14. pure
15. world
16. search
17. worse
18. thirteen
19. sport
20. current

Challenge

curious
thorough
earnest
portion
foreign

Challenge 11–14. A friend of yours is planning a trip to another country. Write a letter wishing your friend a good trip. Use four Challenge Words. Write on a separate sheet of paper.

Name ______________________ Date ____________

José! Born to Dance
Spelling:
More Vowel + /r/ Sounds

Spelling Word Sort

Write each Basic Word beside the correct heading.

/ôr/ spelled *or*	Basic Words: Challenge Words: Possible Selection Words:
/ôr/ spelled *ore*	Basic Words: Possible Selection Words:
Other spellings for /ôr/	Basic Words: Possible Selection Words:
/ûr/ spelled *ir* or *ur*	Basic Words: Possible Selection Words:
/ûr/ spelled *ear* or *or*	Basic Words: Challenge Words:
/yŏŏr/ spelled *ure*	Basic Words:
Other spellings for /yŏŏr/	Challenge Words:

Spelling Words

1. learn
2. dirty
3. worn
4. sore
5. thirst
6. burn
7. record
8. cure
9. board
10. course
11. worth
12. early
13. return
14. pure
15. world
16. search
17. worse
18. thirteen
19. sport
20. current

Challenge

curious
thorough
earnest
portion
foreign

Challenge Add the Challenge Words to your Word Sort.

Connect to Reading Look through "José! Born to Dance." Find more words that have the vowel + /r/ spelling patterns on this page. Add them to your Word Sort.

Name ______________________ Date __________

Proofreading for Spelling

Find the misspelled words and circle them. Write them correctly on the lines below.

Doris Humphrey was born in 1895 in Oak Park, Illinois. It was pur joy for her as a young child to lirn new dance routines. At first, she was stiff like a bord. Doris soon opened her own dance studio. In 1928, Doris and Charles Weidman left to form their own group in New York. They would go on to rekord their choreographic works and produce some of the outstanding performers in the wurld.

Her career ended due to arthritis, for which there was no kure. Not being able to dance hurt Doris werse than her ailment itself. Dance would always bern in her like a fire. However, she did not retern to California in serch of other work. Instead, she became José's mentor and the artistic director of his dance company. Doris was one of the founders of American modern dance.

1. ______________ **6.** ______________

2. ______________ **7.** ______________

3. ______________ **8.** ______________

4. ______________ **9.** ______________

5. ______________ **10.** ______________

Spelling Words

1. learn
2. dirty
3. worn
4. sore
5. thirst
6. burn
7. record
8. cure
9. board
10. course
11. worth
12. early
13. return
14. pure
15. world
16. search
17. worse
18. thirteen
19. sport
20. current

Challenge

curious
thorough
earnest
portion
foreign

Name ______________________ Date ___________

Subject and Object Pronouns

A **subject pronoun** is a pronoun that tells who or what does the action of a sentence. An **object pronoun** is a pronoun that tells who or what receives the action of the verb.

subject pronoun
He studied dance for many years.
object pronoun
Grandmother made breakfast for him every morning.

Thinking Questions
What pronoun tells who or what does the action of the sentence? What pronoun tells who or what receives the action of the verb?

1–4. Underline the subject pronoun in each sentence.

1. We watched José dance in the show.
2. I couldn't wait to see the performance.
3. Have you ever seen a dance recital?
4. He should dance in all of the shows.

5–8. Write the pronoun in parentheses that can take the place of the underlined word or words.

5. (him, you) The birds sang to José during breakfast. ______
6. (them, us) Mama drank hot chocolate with José and Grandmother. ______
7. (him, me) José said to Grandmother, "Please give José more!" ______
8. (you, us) "Can you save some for Mama and me?" Grandmother asked, with a smile. ______

Name ______________________ Date __________

Reflexive and Demonstrative Pronouns

Reflexive pronouns show that a subject is performing an action on itself. They may also call attention to an action.
Demonstrative pronouns point out specific people, places, things, or ideas.

Reflexive pronouns	Demonstrative pronouns
myself, yourself, himself, herself, itself, ourselves, yourselves, themselves	this, that, these, those
In dance class I can watch **myself** in the mirror. Jeff and Maria moved the mats **themselves**.	**This** is a new dance to learn. **These** are your fellow students. **That** is where we practice. **These** are the lockers we use.

1–4. Write the correct reflexive pronoun on the line in the sentences below.

1. (herself, himself) Henry injured __________ while practicing a dance routine.
2. (myself, ourselves) I made the dance costumes __________!
3. (yourself, itself) Help __________ to some juice after you've mastered the dance steps.
4. (ourselves, yourselves) We dressed __________ before the dance recital.

5–8. Write the correct demonstrative pronoun on the line in the sentences below.

5. It's Saturday! __________ is the day of our recital!
6. Find the gray chairs in the closet. __________ are the chairs to set up in rows.
7. See the circle on the stage floor? __________ is where you stand at first.
8. Take this box. __________ are the programs to hand out to the audience.

Name ______________________________ Date ____________

Pronoun-Antecedent Agreement

An **antecedent** is a word or phrase that a following word refers back to. Pronouns often have antecedents.

antecedent **pronoun**
Musicals are popular, and (they) feature singing and dancing.

In the above sentence, musicals is the antecedent. The word they is the pronoun that is used instead of repeating the word musicals. The pronoun agrees with its antecedent in number.

1–4. Write the correct pronoun to complete each sentence.

1. (she, he) Fred Astaire was a famous actor, and ________ was well-known for his dancing.
2. (They, You) Ginger Rogers danced with Fred Astaire. _______ moved gracefully together.
3. (They, He) Gene Kelly danced in many movies. ________ are worth watching!
4. (They, It) Gene Kelly and Leslie Caron danced in *An American in Paris*. ______ was a great movie.

5–8. Circle the pronoun in each sentence. Underline the antecedent.

5. Shirley Temple was a child star, and she could tap dance, too.
6. Musicals are fun, but they can be long.
7. Dancers need to be careful when they perform.
8. When my sister and I took tap dance lessons, we wore special shoes.

Name ______________________ Date __________

Plural Nouns

Singular	Plural
one **valley**	several **valleys**
a **bunny**	some **bunnies**
this **tooth**	these **teeth**
one **moose**	both **moose**

1–6. Write the plural form of the noun in parentheses to complete each sentence.

1. (hobby) Ballroom dancing is one of my aunt's __________.

2. (country) This type of dance is performed in many __________.

3. (man) Women and __________ wear fancy costumes.

4. (foot) Dancers kick their __________ and glide across the floor.

5. (city) Some __________ host ballroom dancing contests.

6. (key) One of the __________ to winning is practice, practice, practice!

7–12. Correct six errors in this paragraph. There are six plural nouns written incorrectly. Use proofreading marks.

My brother takes dance lessons on Fridayes. There are girls and boyes in his class. Last week, my parents and I watched his dance recital with many other families. I sat in the front row with several childs I knew. Some dancers wore tap shoes on their foots. Other dancers acted out stories. In one dance, the performers were dressed as sheeps! After the show, we went to two partys for the dancers.

Name ______________________ Date __________

Sentence Fluency

You can combine sentences with pronouns and subordinating conjunctions.

Choppy Sentences	Combined Sentences
José and his family stayed in Nogales. José and his family waited for permission to enter the United States.	José and his family stayed in Nogales while they waited for permission to enter the United States.

1–4. Combine each pair of sentences. Replace the underlined subject with a pronoun. Use the subordinating conjunction in parentheses. Write the new sentence on the line.

1. Papa decided to leave Mexico. Papa was worried about the war. (because)

   ____

   ____

2. José drew such beautiful pictures of trains. Everyone thought José would become an artist. (since)

   ____

   ____

3. José studied for three years. José learned English. (before)

   ____

   ____

4. José felt lonely. José walked around on a cold day. (when)

   ____

   ____

Name ____________________ Date __________

Focus Trait: Elaboration

Using Precise Words

To elaborate your topic, use words that are specific to the topic. These key words give readers a precise idea of what you are explaining.

Topic: Pet food	
Too General	**Precise**
dog food, water, scraps	nutrients, water, proteins, carbohydrates, fats, vitamins, minerals, kibble

Rewrite each sentence. Replace the underlined general words with more precise words. Choose words that are specific to the topic shown in parentheses.

1. (cooking) I cooked some bread yesterday.

   ____

2. (science) We did an activity in the room after school.

   ____

3. (math) Cut the paper in two pieces, and then fold each piece into a different shape.

   ____

4. (sports) Janet made a point when she kicked the ball into the net.

   ____

5. (computers) Use the thing that rolls around to move the pointer on your monitor screen.

   ____

Name ______________________ Date ____________

Discovering Mars

Mars Trading Card

Design a trading card about Mars to include in a deck of cards for the solar system. Using information on pages 7–9, draw a picture of Mars and fill in the blanks.

Solar System Trading Cards

MARS

Another name for Mars:

____

Where the name came from:

____

____

____

Name ______________________ Date ____________

Now answer some Frequently Asked Questions (FAQs) about Mars for the back of your trading card. What are some fun facts about Mars? Reread pages 9–11 and answer the questions to complete your card.

Solar System Trading Cards

DID YOU KNOW?

- Why does Mars look different over time?

____

____

- What are the large white areas at the poles?

____

____

- Why did people think Martians existed?

____

____

____

____

____

Name ______________________ Date ____________

Discovering Mars

Mars Makes News

Mars made news in 1938 when a radio program caused panic among listeners in New Jersey. Use the information from pages 12–14 to write a news article that tells what caused the panic and how people reacted.

• NEWS TODAY •

1938

PANIC IN NEW JERSEY!

New Jersey ______________________________

____

____

____

____

____

____

____

____

____

____

____

Name ______________________ Date ____________

The planet Mars has made news many times since its discovery. Write a news article telling about the discovery of its two moons in 1877. Read page 15 to find the important facts to include in your article. Then, use pages 16–17 to help you complete a diagram to accompany your article.

NEWS OF THE DAY

1877

MOONS DISCOVERED NEAR MARS!

Washington D.C. ______________________________

____

____

____

____

____

Name: ______________ ______________

Diameter: ______________ ______________

Distance from Mars: ______________ ______________

Label the moons. Then write a caption for the diagram that compares the moons.

____

____

____

____

____

____

Discovering Mars

Mission: A Space Rover to Mars

Imagine you are an engineer at NASA sending a space rover to explore the surface of Mars. Use the information on pages 19–25 to fill in the web below with details about the surface of Mars.

How big is Mount Olympus?

____

____

____

What is the weather like on Mars?

____

____

____

How long is Valles Marineris?

____

____

____

Surface of Mars

What is the Northern Hemisphere of Mars like?

____

____

____

What is the Southern Hemisphere of Mars like?

____

____

____

Write a memo to your fellow colleagues at NASA explaining what kinds of things they should think about when planning the space rover mission to Mars. What special conditions should the engineers consider? What will the space rover need to be able to do? In your memo, give your solutions to the challenges the space rover mission may have.

MEMO

TO: NASA Engineers

FROM: ______________________________

SUBJECT: Planning the Rover Mission to Mars

In planning the space rover mission, we will need to consider ______________________

____

____

____

____

____

____

____

____

____

____

____

Name ______________________ Date ____________

Discovering Mars

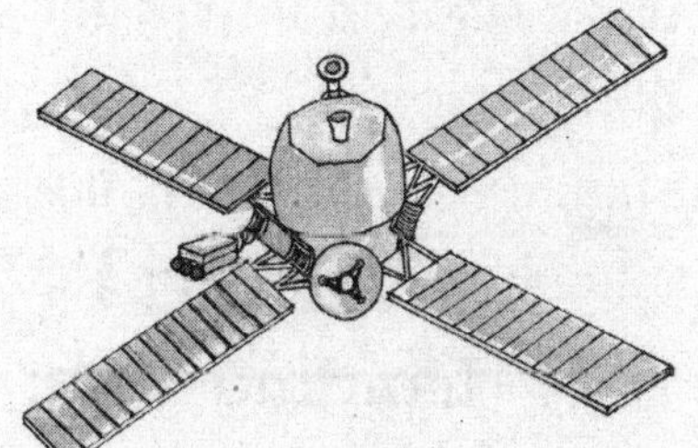

NASA Discovery Mission Series

Help create a timeline of NASA's discovery missions to Mars. Reread pages 28–29 about NASA's Mariner missions. For each mission, write a caption that tells how close the Mariner got to Mars and why the mission was a success. Fill in the year of the mission on the lines. Then write a caption that summarizes the progress of the missions.

Mariner 4
Year: ____________

Mariner 6 & 7
Year: ____________

Mariner 9
Year: ____________

Name ______________________ Date __________

Reread pages 34–37 about NASA's Viking missions. Draw a picture to show the two tasks the missions had. Then write a caption for your illustrations.

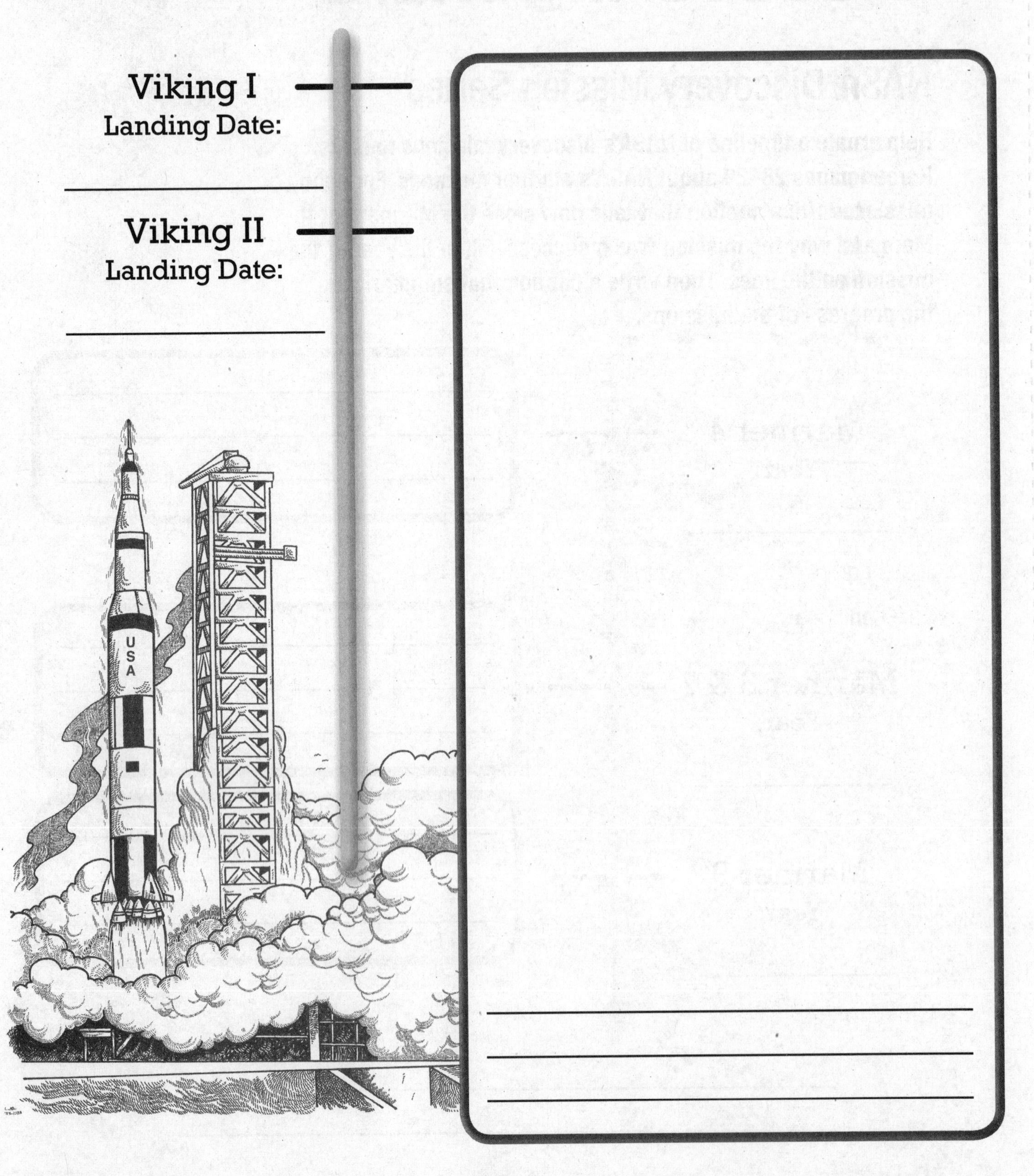

Discovering Mars

Volunteer: Mission to Mars

Astronauts need to be able to do many things to handle a mission in space. NASA interviews people who are interested in becoming astronauts to find the best people for the job. What kinds of questions should NASA officials ask to find good astronauts for the job?

Reread page 42.
Write a question based on what the astronauts on the cargo ship do.

Question: ____

____

____

Write a question based on what the mission to Mars is about.

Question: ____

____

____

Reread pages 44–45.
Write a question based on what is required for the astronauts physically.

Question: ____

____

____

Name ______________________ Date __________

Now imagine you are applying for the astronaut job. Answer the questions that you wrote on the previous page. Give answers that show why you would be a good astronaut for this mission.

Answer 1: ______________________

Answer 2: ______________________

Answer 3: ______________________

Name ______________________ Date ____________

Discovering Mars

Illustrated Guide to Terraforming Mars

Imagine you are on a committee that has come up with a plan to terraform Mars. Reread the ideas presented on pages 50–53.

First, summarize your plan for readers. How is Mars different from Earth? Tell what your plan will do to make Mars more like Earth.

____

____

____

____

____

Now draw a three-step illustrated guide to your plan to terraform Mars. Include a caption for each step.

STEP 1:

____

Name ______________________ Date __________

STEP 2:

____

STEP 3:

____

Name ______________________ Date __________

Hurricanes: Earth's Mightiest Storms

Caption the Diagram

Read the first two paragraphs on page 324 of "Hurricanes: Earth's Mightiest Storms." Why does drawing air into the low-pressure area cause it to spiral?

____

____

____

Take a close look at the diagram. In which hemisphere is the storm in the diagram located? How do you know? Write a caption to explain the diagram to readers.

____

____

____

How does the diagram help you understand what the winds in a hurricane are like? Write a caption that describes them.

____

____

____

____

Hurricanes: Earth's Mightiest Storms

Independent Reading

Read page 325. What is the eye of the storm like?

____

____

Why would people caught in the eye of a storm think that the storm has ended?

____

____

____

Write a caption that explains what is happening in the eye of the storm and why it happens.

____

____

____

Explain how the diagram helps you to understand what the eye of the storm is like.

____

____

____

Suffixes -*ful*, -*less*, -*ness*, -*ment*

cheer	use	assign	still
success	dark	entertain	

To complete each sentence below, select a word from the box and add the suffix *-ful, -less, -ness,* or *-ment.* Read the completed sentence to be sure it makes sense.

1. I have trouble being ______________ when I hear a hurricane is coming.
2. The sudden ______________ of the air told us the storm was approaching.
3. As the storm hit, doors and windows seemed ______________ against a raging wind.
4. The storm knocked out our electricity, so we used candles and flashlights in the ______________.
5. After the storm, my ______________ was to take care of my little brother while the adults checked the storm damage.
6. I was ______________ at keeping him busy for a while, but then he got bored.
7. It's difficult to find ______________ for a five-year-old when you can't go outside and you don't have electricity!

Name ______________________ Date ____________

Compound Words

Basic 1–10. Write the Basic Word that best replaces the underlined word or words.

My parents asked me to (1) look after my little sister. We waved (2) see you later as they drove down the (3) lane from our garage. Then we headed for town to get Amelia a (4) short trim. She was tired of always pushing her hair off her (5) part of the face above her eyes. Suddenly, it was like (6) a person we did not know had turned the sky green. People were yelling to get inside because a tornado was (7) in the area. We took shelter in a store's basement with (8) more than twenty other people. Fortunately, the storeowner kept a (9) small, battery-powered lamp in the basement, so we weren't stranded in the dark. In the end, the tornado missed our town, and we were (10) fine. Amelia and I had quite an adventure!

1. ____________ 6. ____________
2. ____________ 7. ____________
3. ____________ 8. ____________
4. ____________ 9. ____________
5. ____________ 10. ____________

Challenge 11–14. Write a journal entry about taking a school trip with your class. Use four Challenge Words. Write on a separate sheet of paper.

Spelling Words

1. somebody
2. fireplace
3. nearby
4. toothbrush
5. homesick
6. make-believe
7. anything
8. all right
9. goodbye
10. forehead
11. classmate
12. flashlight
13. haircut
14. twenty-two
15. driveway
16. alarm clock
17. baby-sit
18. airport
19. forever
20. mailbox

Challenge

field trip
absent-minded
life jacket
skyscraper
nevertheless

Name ______________________ Date ____________

Spelling Word Sort

Write each Basic Word beside the correct heading.

One word	**Basic Words:** **Challenge Words:** **Possible Selection Words:**
With a hyphen	**Basic Words:** **Challenge Words:** **Possible Selection Words:**
Two separate words	**Basic Words:** **Challenge Words:** **Possible Selection Words:**

Spelling Words

1. somebody
2. fireplace
3. nearby
4. toothbrush
5. homesick
6. make-believe
7. anything
8. all right
9. goodbye
10. forehead
11. classmate
12. flashlight
13. haircut
14. twenty-two
15. driveway
16. alarm clock
17. baby-sit
18. airport
19. forever
20. mailbox

Challenge

field trip
absent-minded
life jacket
skyscraper
nevertheless

Challenge Add the Challenge Words to your Word Sort.

Connect to Reading Look through "Hurricanes: Earth's Mightiest Storms." Find compound words. Add them to your Word Sort.

Name ______________________ Date ____________

Hurricanes: Earth's Mightiest Storms
Spelling: Compound Words

Proofreading for Spelling

Find the misspelled words and circle them. Write them correctly on the lines below.

Becky and her family heard that a hurricane was neerby. The local air porte was already closed to prepare for the high winds. That night, Becky found her flashlite and set her allarm clock so she would wake up early. In the morning, she called her friends to make sure they didn't need annything.

The hurricane's power seemed make beleive. Their brick fireplayce shook. The family took shelter in the basement. After the hurricane passed, they checked the damage and found trees in the driv-way. The mail box was sticking out of Becky's bedroom window. Becky realized how lucky she was to be all rite. She waved good-by to her broken window and wiped her fourhead in relief.

1. ____________ 7. ____________
2. ____________ 8. ____________
3. ____________ 9. ____________
4. ____________ 10. ____________
5. ____________ 11. ____________
6. ____________ 12. ____________

Spelling Words

1. somebody
2. fireplace
3. nearby
4. toothbrush
5. homesick
6. make-believe
7. anything
8. all right
9. goodbye
10. forehead
11. classmate
12. flashlight
13. haircut
14. twenty-two
15. driveway
16. alarm clock
17. baby-sit
18. airport
19. forever
20. mailbox

Challenge

field trip
absent-minded
life jacket
skyscraper
nevertheless

Name ______________________ Date ____________

To, Too, and *Two*

Do not confuse the words *to, too,* and *two*. They sound the same, but they have different spellings and meanings.

Thinking Question
Which word makes sense in the sentence?

to means "in the direction of"	I ran **to** the porch when the rain started.
too means "also" or "in addition"	I brought my bike up on the porch **too.**
two is a number	My **two** brothers came out to watch the rain.

Complete each sentence with *to, too,* or *two,* as appropriate. Write the correct sentence on the line.

1. The forecast says we will get (to, too, two) inches of rain.

____

2. Lightning strikes are amazing, but they can be scary, (to, too, two).

____

3. A storm with lightning has thunder (to, too, two).

____

4. Between the (to, too, two), I prefer thunder with its deep rumbling sounds.

____

5. I had planned on going (to, too, two) my friend's house until the storm was over.

____

Name ______________________ Date __________

There, They're, and *Their*

Do not confuse the words *there, they're,* and *their.* They sound the same, but they have different spellings and meanings.

Thinking Question
Which word makes sense in the sentence?

There means "in that place."	We go **there** to watch storms roll in.
They're is a contraction of *they are.*	**They're** my cousins.
Their means "belonging to them."	I love to spend time at **their** house.

Complete each sentence with *there, they're,* or *their.* Write the correct sentence on the line.

1. My friends Joe and Julie told me (there, they're, their) neighborhood was hit by the tornado.

 ____

2. I went over (there, they're, their) to help clean up the damage.

 ____

3. (There, They're, Their) house is still standing, but the roof is gone.

 ____

4. It looks like (there, they're, their) in better shape than others in the neighborhood.

 ____

5. "Pile the fallen tree limbs over (there, they're, their)," said my friends' father.

 ____

Name ______________________ Date __________

Its and *It's*

Do not confuse the words *its* and *it's.* They sound the same, but they have different spellings and meanings.

Thinking Question
Which word makes sense in the sentence?

Its means "belonging to it."	The dog hides in **its** bed during a storm.
It's is a contraction of *it is* or *it has.*	The storm was fierce, but now **it's** over.

Complete each sentence with *its* or *it's.* Write the correct sentence on the line.

1. The storm did lots of damage on (its, it's) way through town.

   ____

2. The news said that (its, it's) been twenty years since we've had such a terrible storm.

   ____

3. The town garage had (its, it's) roof collapse.

   ____

4. The school district says all of (its, it's) school buses are stuck in the parking lot.

   ____

5. At my house, the snow is so deep that (its, it's) drifted up to our windows.

   ____

Name ______________________ Date __________

Kinds of Verbs

Action Verb	Helping Verb and Main Verb
I enjoy thunderstorms.	The cats are running in from the storm.

1–4. Underline the action verb in each sentence.

1. Little balls of ice battered everything in yesterday's hailstorm.
2. The hail broke several windows around town.
3. Cars suffer more damage than other things in a hailstorm.
4. Now, little round dents cover the top of our car.

5–8. Underline the helping verb once and the main verb twice.

5. Jamie is reading an article about extreme weather.
6. He has collected many books about storms.
7. For school, he will be writing a paper on lightning storms.
8. His science teacher had approved his topic last fall.

9–10. Combine each pair of sentences to make one sentence with a compound predicate. Write the sentence on the line.

9. The rain pours down. It soaks everyone.

   ____

10. People in the desert suffer heat during the day. They enjoy cooler temperatures at night.

   ____

Name ____________________ Date ____________

Conventions

Use the correct words to make your writing clear. Avoid being confused by words that sound the same but have different spellings and meanings.	
to, too, two	I am going **to** Jenna's house before the storm. Shani will come **too.** The weather report says we have about **two** hours before the storm hits.
there, they're, their	**There** are the umbrellas. **They're** going to come in handy today! Jenna and Shani are wearing **their** rain boots.
its, it's	Check the car to make sure **its** windows are closed. It's going to be a very rainy day!

1–10. Circle the correct word in parentheses.

1. "Did you see the lightning over (there, they're)?" Shani asked.
2. "Yes, and I heard the thunder, (two, too)," I replied.
3. Shani thinks (its, it's) exciting to watch thunderstorms.
4. Jenna likes storms (too, two).
5. Jenna and Shani have agreed that (their, they're) going to stay on the porch and watch the storm come in.
6. The porch has glass windows, and (it's, its) roof will protect them from rain.
7. I really would rather go (too, to) the movies and avoid the storm!
8. However, those (two, to) are my friends, so I will watch the storm with them.
9. Maybe I will begin to agree with (there, their) opinion of storms.
10. (Its, It's) been a long time since I watched a storm.

Name ______________________ Date __________

Focus Trait: Purpose

Vivid Details

Use strong reasons and vivid details to support your opinion and make your writing more persuasive.

Reason	Vivid Detail
Hurricanes bring winds and rain that cause terrible damage.	The wind howls like an angry monster and tosses things around. Metal scrapes along the roads like nails on a chalkboard. Rain lashes everything and turns streets into rivers.

A. Fill in the blank with the title of your favorite book. Then write two vivid supporting details that would help persuade others that the book is good.

My favorite book is ______________________

I like this book because ______________________

Vivid supporting detail: ______________________

____

Vivid supporting detail: ______________________

____

B. Work with a partner. Choose the kind of storm you think is the most dangerous. Work together to write a paragraph to persuade others to agree. Start an opinion statement about the type of storm. Add your main reason for your opinion. Then include at least two vivid details that support your reason.

____

____

____

____

____

____

Name ______________________ Date ____________

The Earth Dragon Awakes

Ah Sing's Journal

Chin's father, Ah Sing, wrote in his journal describing the events of April 18, 1906. Use details from the story to infer what Chin's father may have been thinking as the earthquake unfolded.

Reread pages 350–351. Then use the sentence starters to complete this journal entry.

Wednesday, April 19, 1906

I was washing up yesterday with my son when ...

____

____

____

Reread pages 354–355. Then continue the journal entry.

The worst had happened.

____

____

____

Name ______________________ Date ____________

Reread pages 356–357. Then continue the journal entry.

Chin started to panic...

____

____

____

____

____

If Ah Sing could speak to the Earth Dragon, what do you think he would say to it? Support your idea with what you know about Ah Sing's character.

____

____

____

____

____

Name ______________________ Date ____________

Synonyms

damaged	dangerous	flee	protective
daring	wobbles	frightened	

Read each sentence. Rewrite each sentence by using one of the synonyms above in place of the underlined word or words.

1. The <u>brave</u> warrior led his troops in battle.
____

2. We practiced how to <u>escape</u> if there was a fire in the school.
____

3. Some parts of the world experience <u>harmful</u> earthquakes.
____

4. The vase was <u>broken</u> during the move.
____

5. My older brother is very <u>caring</u> for me.
____

6. During a storm, my dog is <u>scared</u> by the thunder.
____

7. During an earthquake, the ground <u>shakes</u>.
____

Name ______________________ Date ____________

Words with *-ed* or *-ing*

Basic 1–10. Complete the puzzle by writing the Basic Word for each clue.

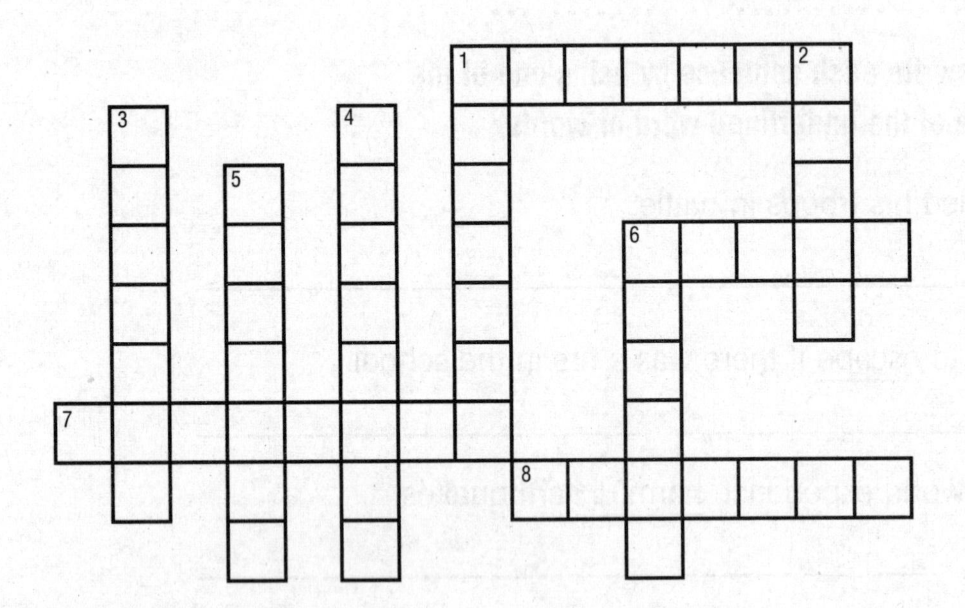

Across

1. fell in drops
6. rushed at top speed
7. shutting with a click
8. gaining a victory

Down

1. moving to music
2. challenged
3. punching or slapping
4. boasting
5. a lined pattern
6. going up

Spelling Words

1. rising
2. traced
3. stripped
4. slammed
5. dancing
6. striped
7. winning
8. snapping
9. bragging
10. handled
11. dripped
12. begged
13. dared
14. skipped
15. hitting
16. spotted
17. raced
18. dimmed
19. spinning
20. escaped

Challenge

urged
striving
whipped
breathing
quizzed

Challenge 11–14. Your class had a spelling bee yesterday. Write a short paragraph about it for your school paper. Use four of the Challenge Words. Write on a separate sheet of paper.

Name ____________________ Date ____________

The Earth Dragon Awakes
Spelling: Words with *-ed* or *-ing*

Spelling Word Sort

Write each Basic Word beside the correct heading.

Adding *-ed*: final *e* dropped	**Basic Words:** **Challenge Words:**
Adding *-ing*: final *e* dropped	**Basic Words:** **Challenge Words:** **Possible Selection Words:**
Adding *-ed*: final consonant doubled	**Basic Words:** **Challenge Words:** **Possible Selection Words:**
Adding *-ing*: final consonant doubled	**Basic Words:** **Possible Selection Words:**

Spelling Words

1. rising
2. traced
3. stripped
4. slammed
5. dancing
6. striped
7. winning
8. snapping
9. bragging
10. handled
11. dripped
12. begged
13. dared
14. skipped
15. hitting
16. spotted
17. raced
18. dimmed
19. spinning
20. escaped

Challenge

urged
striving
whipped
breathing
quizzed

Challenge Add the Challenge Words to your Word Sort.

Connect to Reading Look through "The Earth Dragon Awakes." Find words that have *-ed* or *-ing*. Add them to your Word Sort.

Name ______________________ Date ____________

Proofreading for Spelling

Find the misspelled words and circle them. Write them correctly on the lines below.

My grandfather beged his parents to let him leave home to see the world. When they finally agreed, my grandfather began danceing and spining across the spoted rug in the living room. He escapt disaster as he nearly slamed into the wall. But with excitement in the air, he skiped dinner and racd upstairs to get his suitcase. He packed some pants and his favorite stiped shirts.

He was a young man when he left his home in Peru, South America. My grandfather handld all his own travel arrangements, and before he left, he tracid a map for his parents, showing the route the steamship would be traveling. For twenty-one days he did not see land. When the lights on the steamship dimed, my grandfather sat and thought about his future. The steamship arrived in San Francisco on the day of the big earthquake.

1. ____________ 7. ____________
2. ____________ 8. ____________
3. ____________ 9. ____________
4. ____________ 10. ____________
5. ____________ 11. ____________
6. ____________ 12. ____________

Spelling Words

1. rising
2. traced
3. stripped
4. slammed
5. dancing
6. striped
7. winning
8. snapping
9. bragging
10. handled
11. dripped
12. begged
13. dared
14. skipped
15. hitting
16. spotted
17. raced
18. dimmed
19. spinning
20. escaped

Challenge

urged
striving
whipped
breathing
quizzed

Name ______________________ Date __________

Singular Possessive Nouns

A **singular possessive noun** shows ownership by one person or thing. Add *-'s* to a singular noun to make it possessive.

singular possessive noun
the Earth Dragon's anger

Thinking Question
What word shows ownership by one person or thing?

1–8. Write each phrase another way. Use the possessive form of the underlined noun.

1. the father of Chin ______________ father
2. the son of Ah Sing ______________ son
3. the rumble of an earthquake an ______________ rumble
4. the shout of a person a ______________ shout
5. the courage of a father a ______________ courage
6. the fear of the boy the ______________ fear
7. the help of a friend a ______________ help
8. the smile of the rescuer the ______________ smile

Name ______________________ Date ____________

Plural Possessive Nouns

A **plural possessive noun** shows ownership by more than one person or thing. When a plural noun ends with *-s*, add only an apostrophe to make it possessive. When a plural noun does not end in *-s*, add an apostrophe and *-s* to make it possessive.

plural possessive noun

the dragons' caves the men's stories

Thinking Question
What word shows ownership by more than one person or thing?

1–6. Write each phrase another way. Use the possessive form of the underlined noun.

1. legends of different countries

   different ______________________ legends

2. the long necks of the sea serpents

   the ______________________ long necks

3. the footprints of the children

   the ______________________ footprints

4. the huge wings of the dragons

   the ______________________ huge wings

5. the brave actions of the young women

   the ______________________ brave actions

6. the towers of the castles

   the ______________________ towers

Name ______________________ Date ____________

Apostrophes in Possessive Nouns

Some plural nouns do not end in *-s*. To make these plural nouns possessive, add *-'s*.

plural possessive nouns
her feet's soles his teeth's braces

1–8. Write each phrase another way. Use the possessive form of the underlined noun.

1. the choice of the people ______________________
2. the soft wool belonging to the sheep ______________________
3. the nests belonging to the mice ______________________
4. the tracks of the deer ______________________
5. the annoying honks of the geese ______________________
6. the stubbornness of the oxen ______________________
7. the colored fins belonging to fish ______________________
8. the safety of the children ______________________

Name _______________ Date __________

Progressive Verb Tenses

Present Progressive Tense	is quaking
Past Progressive Tense	was quaking
Future Progressive Tense	will be quaking

1–5. Underline the progressive verb in each sentence. Write *present progressive, past progressive,* or *future progressive* for each verb.

1. Scientists are studying the San Andreas Fault. _______________
2. In science class, I am learning that this fault causes many earthquakes.
   ____
3. This week alone several small earthquakes will be occurring there.
   ____
4. A few years ago, Southern California was experiencing a very strong earthquake.
   ____
5. People in the area were moving to safe places.
   ____

6–9. Correct this paragraph. There are four mistakes in verb tense. Write the correct progressive verbs on the lines below.

In class yesterday, we are listening to an old eyewitness radio account of an earthquake. During the earthquake, the reporter said, "The ground will be shaking so violently that I can hardly stand up. Residents were fleeing the scene!" After the earthquake stopped, he said, "People were returning tomorrow to start rebuilding their homes."

6. _______________ 8. _______________

7. _______________ 9. _______________

Name ______________________ Date __________

Ideas

You can use possessive nouns to make details clearer by showing ownership.

Unclear Detail	Clear Detail
The siren was louder than the cries.	The siren was louder than my baby brother's cries.

1–6. Rewrite each sentence to show ownership of the underlined word or words by the noun in parentheses. Write the new sentence on the line.

1. The tornado siren frightened our visitors. (town)

 ____

2. The loud, shrill sound made the windows rattle. (house)

 ____

3. Jacob said we should hurry to the shelter. (neighbors)

 ____

4. The shelter is a basement room with emergency supplies. (people)

 ____

 ____

5. My uncle entertained us with songs while we waited for the all-clear signal. (artists)

 ____

 ____

6. The music helped everyone to relax, even the dog. (my brother)

 ____

Name ______________________ Date ____________

Focus Trait: Organization

Connecting Opinions and Reasons

When you write a problem-solution paragraph, follow these steps:

1. State the problem clearly.
2. Explain why you think it is a problem.
3. Give a possible solution.
4. Use facts and details to provide reasons for that solution.
5. Clearly link supporting facts and connecting words to your opinion with words and phrases.

Think of a problem that you can help to fix. Complete the outline for a problem-solution paragraph. Use linking words when possible.

1. Problem: ______________________

____

2. Reason: ______________________

____

3. Possible solution: ______________________

____

a. Fact/example: ______________________

____

b. Fact/example: ______________________

____

4. My solution: ______________________

____

Name ______________________ Date ____________

Antarctic Journal: Four Months at the Bottom of the World

Don't Try This at Home!

On December 24, the author of the *Antarctic Journal* found herself in a very dangerous situation. Find the journal entry and reread it. Then answer the questions below.

How is the text for this entry structured, or organized?

____

What is the author's problem in this section?

____

What can you infer happened to cause the author to fall? What details help you make this inference?

____

____

What does the author do to solve her problem? How does she make sure she gets out of the glacier safely?

____

____

What do you think a tour guide would tell the author she did wrong?

____

____

Name ______________________ Date ____________

Antarctic Journal: Four Months at the Bottom of the World
Independent Reading

Suppose that you are the author and are writing the introduction to *Antarctic Journal*. Write an introduction to the book in which you:

- use main ideas and details to give a brief overview of the contents of the book,
- tell how the book is structured and why you structured it that way, and
- explain the dangers of visiting Antarctica and warn readers to follow the rules if they visit.

Introduction

Name ____________________ Date __________

Greek and Latin Word Parts
spect, struct, tele, vis

Each word in the box comes from a Greek or Latin word. *Spect* means "look," *vis* means "see," *struct* means "build," and *tele* means "far away." Use the meanings of the Greek and Latin word parts to help you understand the meanings of the words.

respect	instruct	telescope	vision
inspected	visible	television	construction

Complete each sentence using one of the words from the box above. Write the correct word on the line.

1. We used a __________ to see the planet Jupiter.
2. The class watched an interesting program on __________ .
3. The teacher will __________ us on what to do in a fire drill.
4. Be polite and show __________ to all people.
5. Germs are small and only __________ with a microscope.
6. I need glasses to correct my __________ .
7. Get your car __________ to make sure it is safe.
8. Wear a hard hat at the building __________ site.

Name ____________________ Date __________

More Words with *-ed* or *-ing*

Basic 1–11. Write the Basic Word that best replaces the underlined word or words.

1. My family likes to go walking for exercise on summer vacation. ____________
2. We are placing together a plan for our next trip. ____________
3. We are looking for information about what to do. ____________
4. Last summer, we journeyed to a national park. ____________
5. My brother and I planned our route. ____________
6. Our mother volunteered to help us. ____________
7. My brother had a habit of rambling off on his own. ____________
8. Mom was starting to get worried, but he returned. ____________
9. We may try going to the lake! ____________
10. My dad is calling ahead for cabin reservations. ____________
11. I am inspecting our raft for leaks. ____________

Challenge 12–14. Write a short paragraph about having dinner and then playing a game with your family or friends. Use three of the Challenge Words. Write on a separate sheet of paper.

Spelling Words

1. wiped
2. covered
3. mapped
4. pleasing
5. slipped
6. putting
7. traveled
8. seeking
9. visiting
10. mixed
11. shipped
12. phoning
13. offered
14. smelling
15. hiking
16. checking
17. fainted
18. landed
19. becoming
20. wandering

Challenge

amusing
entertained
admitted
stunning
starving

Name ______________________ Date ____________

Spelling Word Sort

Antarctic Journal
Spelling: More Words with *-ed* or *-ing*

Write each Basic Word beside the correct heading.

***-ed*: no spelling change**	**Basic Words:** **Challenge Words:** **Possible Selection Words:**
***-ing*: no spelling change**	**Basic Words:**
***-ed*: final *e* dropped**	**Basic Words:** **Possible Selection Words:**
***-ing*: final *e* dropped**	**Basic Words:** **Challenge Words:** **Possible Selection Words:**
***-ed*: final consonant doubled**	**Basic Words:** **Challenge Words:** **Possible Selection Words:**
***-ing*: final consonant doubled**	**Basic Words:** **Challenge Words:** **Possible Selection Words:**

Spelling Words

1. wiped
2. covered
3. mapped
4. pleasing
5. slipped
6. putting
7. traveled
8. seeking
9. visiting
10. mixed
11. shipped
12. phoning
13. offered
14. smelling
15. hiking
16. checking
17. fainted
18. landed
19. becoming
20. wandering

Challenge

amusing
entertained
admitted
stunning
starving

Challenge Add the Challenge Words to your Word Sort.

Connect to Reading Look through "Antarctic Journal." Find words that have *-ed* or *-ing*. Add them to your Word Sort.

Name ______________________ Date ____________

Lesson 13
READER'S NOTEBOOK

Antarctic Journal
Spelling: More Words with *-ed* or *-ing*

Proofreading for Spelling

Find the misspelled words and circle them. Write them correctly on the lines below.

I liked smeling the fresh coffee while I miksed pancake batter and the blueberries that were shiped to Palmer Station. As I was mixing one day, I heard a loud rumbling noise. Before I could go outside to investigate, I had to put on my parka, a wool hat, and boots. I also coverd my face with sunscreen and grabbed my sunglasses because I didn't want to risk a bad sunburn or snow blindness. My sunglasses were dirty and needed to be wipet. They landded on the snow when I was out wandereng around and sliped on the ice last night. My friends thought I'd faintted, but that was not the case. I am new here and hikeing on open ground is a bit tricky.

When I got outside, I saw a big blue whale and a newborn calf exhaling a blast of hot wet air. It was such a pleaseing sight! I really enjoy visitting new places!

1.	______________	**7.**	______________
2.	______________	**8.**	______________
3.	______________	**9.**	______________
4.	______________	**10.**	______________
5.	______________	**11.**	______________
6.	______________	**12.**	______________

Spelling Words

1. wiped
2. covered
3. mapped
4. pleasing
5. slipped
6. putting
7. traveled
8. seeking
9. visiting
10. mixed
11. shipped
12. phoning
13. offered
14. smelling
15. hiking
16. checking
17. fainted
18. landed
19. becoming
20. wandering

Challenge

amusing
entertained
admitted
stunning
starving

May, *Might*, *Can*, and *Could*

Modal Auxiliary	What It Expresses	Examples
may	permission to do an action; possibility that an action will happen	My parents said my sister **may** go on the field trip. She **may** see penguins in the arctic exhibit.
might	possibility that an action will happen	The class **might** also see polar bears.
can	certain ability to do an action	We **can** go on Tuesday or Thursday.
could	possibility of having the ability to do an action	Perhaps we **could** also visit the desert exhibit.

Thinking Questions
Which word is a helping verb? Does it tell about the certainty of the action?

1–5. Complete each sentence by writing a modal auxiliary from the chart.

1. Whenever it snows, Chantal _______________ watch the snow fall from her window.
2. She wonders whether she _______________ visit the Arctic some day.
3. Her parents have said she _______________ go after she graduates from high school.
4. Chantal thinks she _______________ work hard and save enough money for a trip.
5. She _______________ imagine how exciting it would be to see a polar bear.

Would, Should, and *Must*

Antarctic Journal
Grammar: Modal Auxiliaries

Modal Auxiliary	What It Expresses	Examples
would	willingness to do an action	I would go to Antarctica if I had the chance.
should	the action probably ought to happen	People going to Antarctica should learn about the area before they go.
must	the action absolutely has to happen	Visitors to Antarctica must go with an experienced guide.

Thinking Questions
Which word is a helping verb? Does it express the writer's feelings or opinion?

1–6. Complete each sentence by writing a modal auxiliary from the chart.

1. You ______________ hear my uncle talk about his work in Antarctica.
2. If he ever goes back, I ______________ love to go with him.
3. Before he will let me go, he says, I ______________ take special training to know what to expect there.
4. Also, he thinks I ______________ work hard to be in good physical shape.
5. Of course, I ______________ get my parents' permission to go!
6. I ______________ really enjoy seeing all that ice and visiting penguins in their natural habitat!

Name ______________________ Date __________

Using Modal Auxiliaries

Antarctic Journal
Grammar: Modal Auxiliaries

Modal Auxiliary	What It Expresses
may	Someone has permission to do an action.
should	I think the action probably ought to happen.
must	I think the action absolutely needs to happen.
can	Someone has the ability to do an action.
will	This forms a future tense.

Thinking Question
Which modal auxiliary helps express my idea clearly?

1–4. Circle the modal auxiliary in parentheses that clearly expresses the idea in the sentence.

1. Today our teacher told us that we (may, must) write our term papers on Antarctica.
2. "You all (will, can) do research at the library or online, so use whichever you prefer," our teacher said.
3. "Everyone (should, will) choose a specific topic and begin researching by Tuesday," she advised.
4. According to the assignment sheet, we (can, may) write about the weather, the land, or the animals in Antarctica.

5–6. Write a modal auxiliary on the line that best expresses the idea.

5. To do my best on this report, I ______________ find a topic I want to learn about.
6. Tomorrow, I ______________ ask whether I may write about scientific expeditions to Antarctica.

Name ______________________ Date ____________

Compound and Complex Sentences

For compound sentences, use a comma and coordinating conjunction to join two simple sentences. Use *and* to join ideas together, *but* to show a contrast, and *or* to show a choice.	The man arrived at the cabin, **and** his dog came with him. They could walk, **or** they could swim before dark. Swimming would be fun, **but** the weather was too cold.
For complex sentences, use a subordinating conjunction to join a simple sentence and a clause.	The dog loves winter walks **because** he enjoys the snow. **Since** snow was about to fall, the man and his dog took a short walk.

1–3. For these compound sentences, write the conjunction that has the purpose shown in parentheses. Add a comma (,) before the conjunction.

1. (join together) Clouds are forming __________ snow will fall.
2. (show contrast) The temperature rises __________ the wind blows harder.
3. (show choice) Will Milo get home in time __________ will Ed fall asleep first?

4–6. For each complex sentence, underline the simple sentence once and the clause twice. Circle the subordinating conjunction.

4. When the blizzard hits, everyone stays snug indoors.
5. Although Milo loves snow, he sleeps by the fireplace during snowstorms.
6. The cabin doors and windows rattle because the wind is so strong.

Name ______________________ Date ____________

Conventions

Modal Auxiliary	What It Expresses	Examples
can	present ability	I can walk with snowshoes.
could	past ability present possibility	Years ago, people could only travel to Antarctica by ship. I could go there next year, if I wanted to.
will	willingness future tense	I will help you plan your trip. The expedition will leave in October.
would	usual activity willingness	Explorers would travel by sled over dangerous ice. Would you do that?

1–7. Complete each sentence by writing a helping verb from the chart.

1. ______________________ you like to be an explorer?
2. Today's explorers ______________________ venture beneath the sea or into space.
3. In the past, Arctic explorers ______________________ take many risks.
4. These brave men and women ______________________ not shelter in warm buildings.
5. By contrast, today's explorers ______________________ control temperatures even in space.
6. Next year, a new expedition ______________________ set out for the deep sea.
7. In this century, travelers ______________________ vacation at the South Pole!

Name ______________________ Date ____________

Antarctic Journal
Writing: Opinion Writing

Focus Trait: Evidence

Using Tone to Persuade

Writers of persuasive letters take care to use a formal, polite tone to better convince readers to do or think something. Additional details and information also help to convince readers.

Inappropriate Tone	Formal, Polite Tone
You should go see the snowmen and ice sculptures.	I'd like to invite you to see the snowmen and ice sculptures with me.

A. Read the parts of a letter below. On the line, rewrite each part using a more polite, formal tone.

Inappropriate Tone	Formal, Polite Tone
1. Hey Maria,	____________
2. Want to go to the museum?	I hope you will join ____________
3. There's a thing about Antarctica.	____________ on Antarctica.

B. Rewrite each sentence using a more formal, polite tone. Add or take out details, use synonyms, or provide additional evidence.

Pair/Share **Work with a partner to come up with reasons to go to the museum.**

Inappropriate Tone	Formal, Polite Tone
4. You enjoy penguins. There are some at the museum.	
5. I heard there'll be a slide for the penguins on the first day.	

Name ______________________ Date __________

The Life and Times of the Ant

What's the Purpose?

Suppose you are an illustrator hired to create an illustration for one of the pages of *The Life and Times of the Ant*. Study the illustrations on pages 416–417 and answer the questions to help you create your illustration.

Reread page 416. What is the main idea of each paragraph?

____

____

Describe the illustration on pages 416–417. What does it show? How are the ants dressed?

____

____

How does the illustration on these pages help you understand the main idea of the section?

____

____

What is the author's purpose in showing this illustration?

____

____

Name ______________________ Date __________

Draw an illustration that demonstrates the author's main purpose in writing *The Life and Times of the Ant.* Label important parts of the illustration and write a caption for it.

Name ______________________ Date ____________

Suffixes *-able, -ible*

edible	changeable	collapsible
agreeable	visible	breakable

Each sentence below includes a word with the suffix *-ible* or *-able*. Complete each sentence.

1. A plastic apple is not edible because

____

2. One thing that can be described as collapsible is

____

3. The most agreeable people are the ones who

____

4. One example of changeable weather is snow on one day and

____

5. Something that is visible in the night sky is

____

6. One thing that is breakable is

____

Name ______________________ Date __________

Final Long *e*

Basic 1–10. Complete the puzzle by writing the Basic Word for each clue.

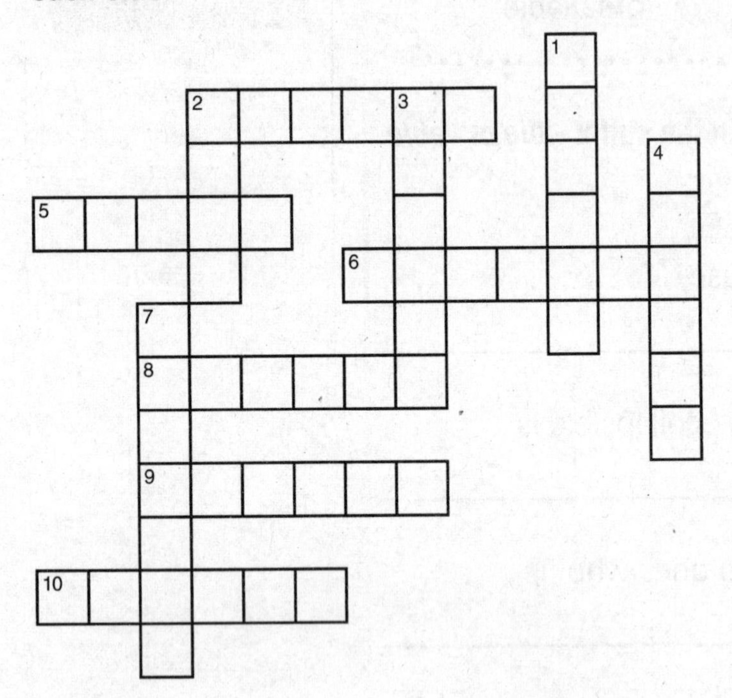

Across

2. sleepy
5. unoccupied
6. grassland
8. starving
9. music
10. constant

Down

1. a hurt or wound
2. responsibility
3. full of stars
4. a lot
7. smokestack

Challenge 12–14. Write a story about a detective working on a case. Use three of the Challenge Words. Write on a separate sheet of paper.

Spelling Words

1. turkey
2. lonely
3. colony
4. steady
5. hungry
6. valley
7. hockey
8. starry
9. melody
10. movie
11. duty
12. drowsy
13. chimney
14. plenty
15. daily
16. alley
17. fifty
18. empty
19. injury
20. prairie

Challenge

envy
fiery
mercy
discovery
mystery

Name ______________________ Date ____________

The Life and Times of the Ant
Spelling: Final Long *e*

Spelling Word Sort

Write each Basic Word beside the correct heading.

Final /ē/ spelled *y*	**Basic Words:** **Challenge Words:** **Possible Selection Words:**
Final /ē/ spelled *ey*	**Basic Words:**
Other spellings for final /ē/	**Basic Words:**

Challenge Add the Challenge Words to your Word Sort.

Connect to Reading Look through "The Life and Times of the Ant." Find words that have the final /ē/ spelling patterns on this page. Add them to your Word Sort.

Spelling Words

1. turkey
2. lonely
3. colony
4. steady
5. hungry
6. valley
7. hockey
8. starry
9. melody
10. movie
11. duty
12. drowsy
13. chimney
14. plenty
15. daily
16. alley
17. fifty
18. empty
19. injury
20. prairie

Challenge

envy
fiery
mercy
discovery
mystery

Name ______________________ Date ____________

Proofreading for Spelling

Find the misspelled words and circle them. Write them correctly on the lines below.

How would you like to share your bedroom with not one but fiftie or more of your closest friends? It might be crowded, but one thing is for sure—you wouldn't be lonelie. The underground nest of some ants can house up to 10 million ants. A colonie of ants can be found in many places—in an allie or in a valey. Ants love to feed on dead termites, caterpillars, and insects. They will eat the crumbs from your turky sandwich. These are some of the useful functions in the environment that hungery ants perform dayily. The next time you have some free time, instead of watching football or hocky on TV, try watching a movey about ants to learn more about these fascinating creatures!

1. ____________ 6. ____________
2. ____________ 7. ____________
3. ____________ 8. ____________
4. ____________ 9. ____________
5. ____________ 10. ____________

Spelling Words

1. turkey
2. lonely
3. colony
4. steady
5. hungry
6. valley
7. hockey
8. starry
9. melody
10. movie
11. duty
12. drowsy
13. chimney
14. plenty
15. daily
16. alley
17. fifty
18. empty
19. injury
20. prairie

Challenge

envy
fiery
mercy
discovery
mystery

Name ______________________ Date ______________

Present Participles

The **present participle** of regular verbs is formed by adding *-ing* to the verb. If the verb ends in *e*, drop the *e* before adding *-ing.*

walk + ing = walking

move + ing = moving

The **participle** form of a verb can be used as an adjective.

The crawling ants look very busy.

Their scurrying bodies are all over the grass.

Thinking Question
Which verb form ending in -ing describes a noun?

1–8. On the line, write the present participle form of the verb shown in parentheses.

1. The (forage) ______________ ants ran for cover from the rain.
2. Their (shelter) ______________ nest keeps the rain out.
3. The (tower) ______________ anthill is really something to see!
4. The (shift) ______________ walls of the nest are not sturdy.
5. Last week, a (feast) ______________ armadillo ate many ants.
6. Its (project) ______________ nose dug them out.
7. Today, (harvest) ______________ ants are gathering leaves.
8. Their (slice) ______________ jaws cut leaves.

Name ______________________ Date ____________

Past Participles

Form the **past participle** of regular verbs by adding *-ed* to the verb. If the verb ends in *e*, drop the *e* before adding *-ed*. If the verb ends in *y*, drop the *y* and add *-ied*.

present	past participle
mix	mixed
store	stored
study	studied

Remember that the participle form of a verb can be used as an adjective.

Workers move stored eggs each day.
The ants must move to an expanded nest.

Thinking Question
Which verb form that tells about a past action modifies a noun?

1–8. On the line, write the past participle form of the verb shown in parentheses.

1. (chew) ______________ dirt and saliva form little bricks for ant tunnels.
2. (pack) ______________ dirt outside the tunnels forms an anthill.
3. Its (curve) ______________ roof traps heat from the sun.
4. (exchange) ______________ food bonds the ants of the colony.
5. A (damage) ______________ nest calls for extra work.
6. The (tire) ______________ ants keep working.
7. A totally (ruin) ______________ nest means starting over.
8. Workers can put any (rescue) ______________ larvae in the new nest.

Name ____________________ Date __________

Participial Phrases

A **participial phrase** begins with a participle and describes a noun.

Participial phrases are formed using past and present participles.

The children playing with the puppy leaped for joy.
Mariella returned to find her picnic lunch covered with ants.

Thinking Question
Which phrase contains a participle that tells about a subject?

1–5. Underline the participial phrase in each sentence.

1. Ants scurrying through the grass are in search of food.
2. Ants chewing on dirt are expanding their nest.
3. Ants working on their nest are ignored by the people above them.
4. Leafcutter ants have jaws adapted for cutting leaves.
5. Leaf parts carried in their jaws arrive back at the nest.

6–8. Write a participle based on the word in the parentheses to complete each participial phrase.

6. Ants (nest) ____________ beneath the rocks were left alone.
7. Ants often do not escape alive from a nest (disturb) ____________ by an anteater.
8. A picnic (invade) ____________ by ants is an unhappy scene.

Frequently Confused Words

Some words sound the same but have very different meanings. These similar-sounding words are often confused.

ant, aunt	My **aunt** saw an **ant** crawling through her kitchen.
feat, feet	Jumping twelve **feet** in the air would be an amazing **feat**.
flea, flee	The dog tried to **flee** from the **flea** that was biting it.
knew, new	Bill **knew** the ants would build a **new** nest.
wait, weight	I can't **wait** until I am strong enough to lift a hundred-pound **weight**.
weather, whether	**Whether** we go camping depends on the **weather**.

1–5. Circle the correct word in parentheses to complete the sentence.

1. I never (knew, new) until now that some insects are like superheroes.
2. A (flea, flee) can jump over 100 times its height!
3. The tiny ant can carry an object with a (wait, weight) five times its own.
4. How does such a tiny insect perform such a (feat, feet)?
5. These insects change the Earth (weather, whether) we observe them or not.

6–11. Circle the words that are incorrect. Write the correct words on the blanks at the right.

Their is probably no insect more amazing than the aunt. They make up only about 1.3 percent of the known insect species, but they account for half the total wait of all insects on Earth. They carry most of the dead bodies of tiny animals back too their nests. They move more soil than earthworms. Its true that we need ants more than they need us, weather we admit it or not.

____
____
____
____
____
____

Name ______________________ Date __________

Sentence Fluency

You can combine sentences with participles to make them more varied and interesting.

The people were watching the ants. They were curious.
The people <u>watching</u> the ants were curious.

Rosa stood up. Her arm was covered with ants.
Her arm <u>covered</u> with ants, Rosa stood up.

1–5. Combine the sentences using participles. Use correct punctuation and capitalization. Write the sentence on the line.

1. We are learning about ants. We find them interesting.

____

2. The ant is one of the strongest creatures on Earth. It can lift five times its weight.

____

____

3. We created a proposal. We hope to buy an ant farm for our class.

____

4. We will become keen observers. We will improve our science skills.

____

5. We will properly care for our ant farm. It will be a great addition to our class.

____

Name ______________________ Date ____________

Focus Trait: Purpose

Using and Ordering Important Details

Unordered Details	Ordered Details
A honeybee's legs carry pollen to the plants that the bee visits. The legs of a honeybee allow it to do much more than walk. Like all insects, a honeybee has six legs.	Like all insects, a honeybee has six legs. The legs of a honeybee, however, allow it to do much more than walk. Its legs also carry pollen to the plants that the bee visits.

Read each main idea. Number the details below to show the order that best supports the main idea. Write the number on the line.

Main idea: It is easy to identify a honeybee.

_____ A honeybee's body is about half an inch long.

_____ A honeybee's body has three parts.

_____ Its body is hairy, and it is yellow and black in color.

_____ Like many insects, honeybees have four wings.

Main idea: Honeybees are important insects.

_____ Pollen must move from plant to plant so new plants can grow.

_____ Honeybees help farmers produce billions of dollars worth of crops.

_____ Honeybees help plants grow by carrying pollen from one plant to another.

_____ Honeybees pollinate many food crops, such as apples, nuts, cucumbers, and cherries.

Name ______________________ Date ____________

Ecology for Kids
Independent Reading

Ecology for Kids

Eco-Friendly Lodge Brochure

Take a close look at this paragraph from page 450. What words help you understand the author's argument? Circle the words that are powerful. For example, *protect* is a much stronger word than *help*. Circle the word *protect*.

One important way to protect the environment is to help stop pollution. Here are a few ideas:

Put trash in its place. Trash does not belong in the streets, rivers, or the oceans. Trash and other kinds of pollution harm all living things.

Use solar-powered clocks and calculators when you can. If you use battery-power, recycle used batteries.

When you leave a room, turn off the light. When you are not using televisions, radios, and computers, turn them off, too. That way, your family will use less electricity and save money.

Evaluate the author's word choice. How could he have made his argument even more powerful?

____

____

Name ______________________________ Date ____________

Now fill in this travel brochure for an Eco Lodge. Make sure you use words that will convince an eco-wise traveler that the lodge uses environmentally friendly practices.

Welcome! 

Paradiso Rio Rainforest Lodge is located in a protected rainforest area one hour from the capital. Our lodge offers hiking, mountain biking, horseback riding, and rainforest tours. Our rooms come with ______________ faucets and showers. Our lodge has solar panels to collect ______________ from the sun and convert it to ___________. Our chef prepares dinners with locally grown, organic ingredients to ______________ your health and the environment's. All of our practices help to make sure that your stay has no ______________ on the environment!

Paradiso Rio Rainforest Lodge

Name ______________________ Date ____________

Using Context

crash channel shape tire
track place thunder

Read each sentence. Circle the correct definition for each underlined word using the context of the sentence.

1. The glass fell off the table with a crash.
   a. a loud noise **b.** a collision, a wreck
2. Everyone cheered as he ran around the track.
   a. a mark, as a footprint **b.** a course set up for racing
3. The boat sailed down the channel.
   a. a waterway **b.** a means of communicating
4. She didn't want anyone to take her place as she waited to buy tickets.
   a. an area or region **b.** a position in line
5. The football player was in great shape.
   a. the outline of something **b.** physical condition
6. After we saw the lightning, we heard some thunder.
   a. to speak loudly **b.** a loud noise from the sky
7. I could not ride my bike because there was a hole in the tire.
   a. rubber covering a wheel **b.** to run out of energy

Name _______________ Date __________

Changing Final *y* to *i*

Basic 1–10. Write the Basic Word to complete each analogy.

1. *Trees* are to *forests* as *cities* are to _____ .
2. *Biggest* is to *largest* as *smallest* is to _____ .
3. *Weakest* is to *strongest* as *liveliest* is to _____ .
4. *Seeds* are to *plants* as *caterpillars* are to _____ .
5. *Smoother* is to *rougher* as *tougher* is to _____ .
6. *Happier* is to *merrier* as *windier* is to _____ .
7. *Better* is to *best* as _____ is to *noisiest.*
8. *Lightest* is to *darkest* as *ugliest* is to _____ .
9. *Cleaning* is to *chores* as *photography* is to _____ .
10. *Cold* is to *colder* as *busy* is to _____ .

1. _______________ 6. _______________
2. _______________ 7. _______________
3. _______________ 8. _______________
4. _______________ 9. _______________
5. _______________ 10. _______________

Challenge 11–14. You helped out at the community garage sale. Tell how you sorted items for sale. Use four of the Challenge Words. Write on a separate sheet of paper.

Spelling Words

1. tiniest
2. hobbies
3. copied
4. countries
5. pitied
6. easier
7. laziest
8. families
9. spied
10. happiest
11. ladies
12. friendlier
13. studied
14. busier
15. breezier
16. prettiest
17. noisier
18. healthier
19. butterflies
20. funniest

Challenge

heaviest
categories
communities
multiplied
qualities

Name ______________________ Date ____________

Spelling Word Sort

Write each Basic Word beside the correct heading.

Adding *-es* to a consonant + *y* word	**Basic Words:** **Challenge Words:** **Possible Selection Words:**
Adding *-ed* to a consonant + *y* word	**Basic Words:** **Challenge Words:**
Adding *-er* to a consonant + *y* word	**Basic Words:**
Adding *-est* to a consonant + *y* word	**Basic Words:** **Challenge Words:**

Challenge Add the Challenge Words to your Word Sort.

Connect to Reading Look through "Ecology for Kids." Find words that change the final *y* to *i* before adding *-es, -ed, -er,* or *-est*. Add them to your Word Sort.

Spelling Words

1. tiniest
2. hobbies
3. copied
4. countries
5. pitied
6. easier
7. laziest
8. families
9. spied
10. happiest
11. ladies
12. friendlier
13. studied
14. busier
15. breezier
16. prettiest
17. noisier
18. healthier
19. butterflies
20. funniest

Challenge

heaviest
categories
communities
multiplied
qualities

Proofreading for Spelling

Ecology for Kids
Spelling: Changing Final *y* to *i*

Find the misspelled words and circle them. Write them correctly on the lines below.

Observing nature can be entertaining and informative. Nature has been speid upon and studyed through the ages and has taught ladys, gentlemen, and familes many lessons. We have coiped things we see happening in nature to make us healthyer and friendlyer. We have pityd people who take no notice of nature. Some of the prettyiest and funnieste things can be found in nature—look at a sunset, or look at baby birds, each noiser than the other, opening their mouths wide to be fed. Many people have found that some of their happist times have been spent observing nature.

1. ______________ 7. ______________
2. ______________ 8. ______________
3. ______________ 9. ______________
4. ______________ 10. ______________
5. ______________ 11. ______________
6. ______________ 12. ______________

Spelling Words

1. tiniest
2. hobbies
3. copied
4. countries
5. pitied
6. easier
7. laziest
8. families
9. spied
10. happiest
11. ladies
12. friendlier
13. studied
14. busier
15. breezier
16. prettiest
17. noisier
18. healthier
19. butterflies
20. funniest

Challenge

heaviest
categories
communities
multiplied
qualities

Name ____________________ Date ____________

Irregular Verbs

Verbs that do not add *-ed* to show past action are called **irregular verbs**. You must remember the spellings of irregular verbs.

present tense verb: give
irregular past tense verb: gave

Thinking Question
What verb does not add -ed *to show past action?*

1–8. Write the correct form of the verb in parentheses to show past action.

1. The scientist (know) how to protect the environment.

____

2. Our science teacher (brings) photographs of various ecosystems to class. ____________

3. She (tells) us that one way to protect the environment is to stop pollution. ____________

4. It would also help the environment if we (grow) our own vegetables. ____________

5. We (take) very long showers. ____________

6. We (leave) the lights on in empty rooms.

____

7. We (drive) everywhere instead of walking or riding bikes.

____

8. My family and I (make) a plan for how to save water, electricity, and gasoline. ____________

Name ______________________ Date __________

The Special Verb *be*

Ecology for Kids
Grammar: Irregular Verbs

The verb *be* tells what someone or something is or is like. It does not show action. It can be used as a main verb or a helping verb. The verb *be* has special forms for different tenses and different subjects.

forms of the verb *be*

subject	present tense	past tense
I	am	was
he, she, it	is	was
we, you, they	are	were

past participle with form of helping verb *have*

I, we, you, they	have been
he, she, it	has been

Thinking Questions
What is the subject? What is the tense? What form of be *is correct?*

1–6. Write the form of the verb *be* in parentheses that correctly completes each sentence.

1. Last week, the students (are, were) learning about ecosystems. ________
2. An ecosystem (is, are) a place where groups of living and nonliving things interact with their environment. ________
3. Forests, lakes, and deserts (is, are) examples of ecosystems. ________
4. Yesterday, I (am, was) working on a project about the ocean. ________
5. Today, I (am, was) presenting my project about the ocean to my classmates. ________
6. I (been, have been) enjoying learning about the ocean. ________

Name ____________________ Date __________

Helping Verbs

Many **irregular verbs** change spelling when they are used with **helping verbs**. Often the new spelling uses *-n* or *-en* to show past tense.

Irregular verb: grow
Past tense: grew
Past tense form with helping verb: had grown

1–5. On the line, write the correct form of the verb in parentheses.

1. My class had (drive) __________ all morning to get to the seashore.
2. Then we had (ride) __________ in a boat to get to a mangrove swamp.
3. It was the first time I had (see) __________ such a unique ecosystem.
4. When it heard us coming, a heron had (hide) __________ among the trees.
5. Afterwards, a scientist had (speak) __________ to us about preserving mangrove swamps.

Name ______________________ Date ____________

Progressive Verb Tenses

Progressive verb tenses show action that is ongoing.

present progressive	is learning, are learning
past progressive	was learning, were learning
future progressive	will be learning

1–7. Complete each sentence with the correct progressive form of the verb in parentheses ( ).

1. Our planet ______________ more polluted every year. (become)
2. Tropical rainforests ______________ rapidly now. (disappear)
3. Two hundred years ago, these forests ______________ on four different continents. (thrive)
4. But the need for land to settle ______________ rapidly. (grow)
5. Settlers ______________ forests to raise crops. (clear)
6. Now people ______________ trees to replace some of our lost forests. (plant)
7. The students at our school ______________ Earth Day next April. (celebrate)

Name ________________________ Date ____________

Conventions

Incorrect Form of Verb
They dove into the bay and taked a look at its ecosystem.
Correct Form of Verb
They dove into the bay and took a look at its ecosystem.

1–5. Choose the correct form for the verb in the parentheses. Rewrite the sentences to make the author's meaning clear.

1. Yesterday, the scientists (find, found) an unfamiliar creature in the bay.

   ____

   ____

2. When they returned to shore, they (brung, brought) it to the laboratory.

   ____

   ____

3. They now (know, knew) some of the changes that happened as a result of pollution in the bay.

   ____

   ____

4. The scientists (writed, wrote) a report about their findings.

   ____

   ____

5. They (gived, gave) a talk about their discoveries.

   ____

   ____

Focus Trait: Conventions

Focusing on the Main Idea

Good writers keep readers engaged by using correct grammar, spelling, and punctuation. They also make sure all details and ideas support the main idea. This writer followed writing conventions and deleted a sentence that did not support the main idea.

> Lightning is caused by electric charges. Ice and raindrops move quickly in a storm cloud and create a charge at the bottom of the cloud. At the same time, an opposite charge is created on the ground. When sparks from the cloud meet sparks from the ground, they create a bolt of lightning. ~~A tree hit by a bolt of lightning can sometimes survive.~~
>
> **Main idea:** *Lightning is caused by electric charges.*

Read the paragraph and write the main idea. Then cross out the sentence that does not support the main idea.

1. A fulgarite is a long tube in the ground created by lightning. First, lightning hits the ground and goes deep into the soil. A bolt of lightning has as much power as all the power plants in the United States can make in the same amount of time! The heat from the lightning melts sand in the ground, forming a fulgarite. This crusty tube shows the shape of the lightning bolt.

Main idea: ____

2. There is a story told about Benjamin Franklin that he performed an experiment that is now famous. He flew a kite in a big storm. A key was tied to the bottom of the kite string. Lightning struck, and sparks flew from the key! You can estimate how far lightning is by listening to thunder. A silk ribbon on the string kept Franklin's hand from getting hurt.

Main idea: ____

Name _______________________ Date ____________

Riding Freedom

You're Hired!

Authors use personification to help readers see, feel, and hear what is being described and give color to the description. Answer the questions below about personification in "Riding Freedom."

Reread page 480. Find an example of personification. List it below.

____

____

____

What nonliving thing is the author describing? What human characteristics does the author give to it?

____

____

____

How does the author's use of personification help you better see, feel, or sense the object? How does it help you understand it?

____

____

____

____

Imagine that Charley asks James to write a job recommendation for a driving position with a new company. Follow the steps below to help James write the recommendation.

- Reread pages 478–483.
- Think about Charley/Charlotte's performance. In what difficult circumstances did Charlotte find herself? How did she still manage to do her job? Include personification to describe how Charley prevailed.

Name ______________________ Date ____________

Figurative Language

Figurative language describes something by comparing it to something else that seems to be unlike it.

A **simile** is figurative language that compares two things using *like* or *as*.
examples: The horse runs like the wind. The rider is as skinny as a rail.

A **metaphor** is figurative language that makes a comparison without *like* or *as*.
examples: That storm was a monster. Each snowflake is a sculpted gem.

An **idiom** is figurative language that uses words in a way other than their usual meaning.
examples: under the weather (feeling sick); to be all wet (to be totally wrong)

1–3. Circle the words that best complete each metaphor or simile. Then, on the line, write *S* if the comparison is a simile. Write *M* if it is a metaphor.

1. When the passengers changed places it was like ____________.
   a. a game of musical chairs **b.** a steep cliff
2. When the children became tired, they fought like ____________.
   a. a sleeping kitten **b.** cats and dogs
3. The rough, winding road was ____________.
   a. a puzzle to solve **b.** a field of trees

Figure out the meaning of the underlined idiom. Write the meaning on the line.

4. The passengers were <u>on edge</u> because they feared the stagecoach would be robbed. ____________

Name ______________________ Date ____________

Words with /k/, /ng/, and /kw/

Basic 1–11. Write the Basic Word that best replaces the underlined word or words in each sentence.

1. Some students love the subject of gymnastics.
2. We avoid dangerous gymnastic exercises.
3. Some fear making a blunder while performing.
4. A gymnast accidentally hit her feet on the balance beam.
5. Her feet will hurt until they're iced.
6. She will present a query to her coach about safety.
7. These two gymnasts have the same ability on the parallel bars.
8. Young gymnasts perform for the community audience.
9. Soon the empty scoreboard will show our score.
10. The scoreboard is flashing now in charged lights!
11. Let's have our outdoor party after practice.

1. ______________ 7. ______________
2. ______________ 8. ______________
3. ______________ 9. ______________
4. ______________ 10. ______________
5. ______________ 11. ______________
6. ______________

Challenge 12–14. Write about the headline below. Use three Challenge Words. Write on a separate sheet of paper.

IMPORTANT ARCHAEOLOGICAL DISCOVERY MADE

Spelling Words

1. risky
2. track
3. topic
4. blank
5. question
6. pocket
7. monkey
8. junk
9. equal
10. ache
11. public
12. attack
13. struck
14. earthquake
15. picnic
16. banker
17. electric
18. blanket
19. mistake
20. stomach

Challenge

request
skeleton
peculiar
attic
reckless

Name ________________________ Date ____________

Spelling Word Sort

Riding Freedom
Spelling: Words with /k/, /ng/, and /kw/

Write each Basic Word beside the correct heading.

/k/ spelled *ck*	Basic Words: Challenge Words: Possible Selection Words:
/k/ spelled *k* or *c*	Basic Words: Challenge Words: Possible Selection Words:
Other spellings for /k/	Basic Words:
Spellings for /kw/	Basic Words: Challenge Words:
/ng/ before *k*	Basic Words:

Challenge Add the Challenge Words to your Word Sort.

Connect to Reading Look through "Riding Freedom." Find words that have the /k/, /ng/, and /kw/ spelling patterns on this page. Add them to your Word Sort.

Spelling Words

1. risky
2. track
3. topic
4. blank
5. question
6. pocket
7. monkey
8. junk
9. equal
10. ache
11. public
12. attack
13. struck
14. earthquake
15. picnic
16. banker
17. electric
18. blanket
19. mistake
20. stomach

Challenge
request
skeleton
peculiar
attic
reckless

Name ______________________ Date ____________

Proofreading for Spelling

Riding Freedom
Spelling: Words with /k/, /ng/, and /kw/

Find the misspelled words and circle them. Write them correctly on the lines below.

The stagecoach driver was glad to pull into the station yard. It had been a riskey ride. There was always the threat that outlaws would attak them. There was an eqal threat of the area being struk by an earthkwake. The driver had to leave her seat to remove some junck that obstructed the trak. She thought it might be an ambush—but all was well.

She was carrying a special passenger—a bankar who carried a lot of money in his pockit. This passenger was very demanding—he even asked for an extra blankit. It all was enough to make the driver's stomak acke!

1. ______________
2. ______________
3. ______________
4. ______________
5. ______________
6. ______________
7. ______________
8. ______________
9. ______________
10. ______________
11. ______________
12. ______________

Spelling Words

1. risky
2. track
3. topic
4. blank
5. question
6. pocket
7. monkey
8. junk
9. equal
10. ache
11. public
12. attack
13. struck
14. earthquake
15. picnic
16. banker
17. electric
18. blanket
19. mistake
20. stomach

Challenge

request
skeleton
peculiar
attic
reckless

Name ________________________ Date __________

Adjectives

An **adjective** is a word that gives information about a noun or pronoun. An adjective can tell *what kind* or *how many*.

A sudden boom of thunder scared the six horses.
drinking fountain (fountain for drinking)

Thinking Question
What words describe a noun?

1–3. Write the adjectives that describe the underlined nouns. Then write *what kind* or *how many* for each adjective.

1. We saw several flashes of bright lightning across the sky.

   ____

2. The frightened horses bolted down the steep hill.

   ____

3. The cold, hard rain soaked the driver.

   ____

4–6. Write each adjective and circle the noun that it describes.

4. Today, heavy traffic often clogs the streets of big cities.

   ____

5. Drivers tied their horses to hitching posts while they ate a hot meal.

   ____

6. The rough, dirt roads of the past have been replaced by smooth highways.

   ____

Name ____________________ Date __________

Adjectives After *Be*

Adjectives describe nouns and pronouns such as *I*, *it*, and *we*.
An adjective can follow the word it describes. This usually happens when an adjective follows a form of the verb *be*.

She was proud.

Thinking Questions
What adjective follows a form of be? What word does it describe?

1–8. Underline each adjective. Then write the word that it describes on the line.

1. The river was deep. ____________
2. I am warm under the blanket. ____________
3. The driver is calm. ____________
4. The valley is foggy. ____________
5. We were tired from the journey. ____________
6. The horses are strong. ____________
7. The coach was confident. ____________
8. The ride is bumpy. ____________

Order of Adjectives

If more than one adjective tells about a noun, those adjectives must be in the correct order. Use this order for lists of adjectives:

Opinion	Size/Shape	Age/Color	Material	Purpose	Noun
gorgeous	long	old	woolen	winter	coat
skillful		young		horse	trainer

Read the sentences. Combine the adjectives in the correct order and write them on the line.

1. The jockey is an athlete.
   She is slim.
   The jockey is skillful.
   The jockey is a ________________ athlete.
2. Seabiscuit was a racehorse.
   He was a thoroughbred.
   He was remarkable.
   Seabiscuit was a ________________ racehorse.
3. He had a body that looked unfit for speed.
   His build was thick.
   He was awkward.
   He had a(n) ________________ body that seemed unfit for speed.
4. This small horse would become the champion of all time.
   He was the greatest.
   He was beloved.
   This small horse would become one of the ________________ champions of all time.

Name ____________________ Date __________

Modal Auxiliaries

Helping verbs are used with main verbs. Some helping verbs help express whether the action is possible, certain to happen, or should happen.

Thinking Question
What type of action is being expressed in the sentence?

Helping Verb	Expresses	Example
may, can	action is possible	That horse *can* run fast. It *may* win the race.
could, might	action is possible but not certain	If it were younger, I *could* train it to jump. The vet *might* repair the horse's broken leg.
will, must	action has to occur	Your horse *will* run, but you *must* train it.
should	opinion: what ought to happen	You *should* feed and water your horse before you rest.

Write a helping verb from the chart to complete each sentence.

1. I will show that I ____________ drive a team again.
2. Frank and James believe that Charley ____________ not drive again.
3. Charlotte ____________ prove that she is capable or give up her work.
4. If she learns new ways of sensing the road, she ____________ succeed in her goal.
5. She knows that the bridge ____________ fall with heavy weight on it.

Name ______________________ Date ____________

Sentence Fluency

Short, Choppy Sentences	Combined Sentences with Adjective
The stagecoach pulled up to the inn. The stagecoach was crowded.	The crowded stagecoach pulled up to the inn.

1–2. Combine each pair of sentences by moving an adjective before a noun.

1. The seats inside the coach softened the bumpy ride. The seats were leather.

____

____

2. The door rattled the entire ride. The door was creaky.

____

____

Short, Choppy Sentences	Combined Sentences with Adjectives
The travelers were tired. They were hungry.	The travelers were tired and hungry.

3–4. Combine each pair of sentences by joining adjectives with the word *and*.

3. The old stagecoach was leaky. It was damp.

____

____

4. The scenery was beautiful on their journey west. The scenery was wild.

____

____

Name ______________________ Date ____________

Focus Trait: Development

Describing with Similes

Description	Description with Simile
The passengers huddled together.	The passengers huddled together like a bunch of grapes.

A. Read each description. Make it more vivid by adding a simile. Remember to use *like* or *as*.

Description	Description with Simile
1. The river water was cold.	The river water was ______________ ______________
2. The dark clouds moved quickly.	The dark clouds moved ______________ ______________

B. Read each sentence. Add a simile to each sentence to make the description more vivid. Write your new sentences.

Pair/Share **Work with a partner to brainstorm similes to add.**

Description	Simile Added
3. The river had risen.	
4. The wood of the bridge moaned.	
5. The bridge timbers swayed.	

Name ______________________ Date ____________

The Right Dog for the Job: Ira's Path from Service Dog to Guide Dog

Guide Dog Timeline

Complete the timeline using details from the article.

Read page 503. Where does Ira go first?

____

____

Read page 508. Where does Ira go next?

____

____

Read page 509. Who does Ira work with next?

____

____

What is Ira finally ready to do?

____

____

Name ____________________ Date __________

The Right Dog for the Job: Ira's Path from Service Dog to Guide Dog

Independent Reading

Why was it important for Ira to take these steps to become a service dog? Tell why each step was important, and why the order the steps were taken is important.

Name ______________________________ Date ____________

Suffixes *-ion*, *-ation*, *-ition*

information exhibition attention graduation
competition combination cooperation

Each sentence shows a word in parentheses that uses the suffix *-ion*, *-ation*, or *-ition*. Complete the sentence using the word in parentheses.

1. (information) When I read a newspaper ______________
____

2. (competition) She was excited about being ___________
____

3. (exhibition) He wanted to go see the paintings at ______
____

4. (combination) I think that ice cream and cake is ______
____

5. (attention) Yelling very loud will get you ____________
____

6. (cooperation) When you're working in a group at school
____

7. (graduation) After you finish school, ______________
____

Name ______________________ Date ____________

Words with Final /j/ and /s/

Basic 1–11. Write the Basic Word that best completes each group.

1. preparation, training, ____________________
2. workplace, department, ____________________
3. buggy, coach, ____________________
4. destruction, wreckage, ____________________
5. observe, see, ____________________
6. twofold, double, ____________________
7. possibility, likelihood, ____________________
8. bundle, carton, ____________________
9. wedlock, matrimony, ____________________
10. supervise, guide, ____________________
11. look, peep, ____________________

Challenge 12–14. Describe costumes and sets you might design for a school play that takes place in medieval times. Use three Challenge Words. Write on a separate sheet of paper.

Spelling Words

1. glance
2. judge
3. damage
4. package
5. twice
6. stage
7. carriage
8. since
9. practice
10. marriage
11. baggage
12. office
13. message
14. bridge
15. chance
16. notice
17. ridge
18. manage
19. palace
20. bandage

Challenge

fringe
average
fleece
fragrance
excellence

Name ______________________ Date ____________

Spelling Word Sort

Write each Basic Word beside the correct heading.

/j/ in one-syllable words	**Basic Words:** **Challenge Words:**
/ĭj/ in two-syllable words	**Basic Words:**
/ĭj/ in words with more than two syllables	**Challenge Words:**
Final /s/ spelled *ce*	**Basic Words:** **Challenge Words:** **Possible Selection Words:**

Spelling Words

1. glance
2. judge
3. damage
4. package
5. twice
6. stage
7. carriage
8. since
9. practice
10. marriage
11. baggage
12. office
13. message
14. bridge
15. chance
16. notice
17. ridge
18. manage
19. palace
20. bandage

Challenge

fringe
average
fleece
fragrance
excellence

Challenge Add the Challenge Words to your Word Sort.

Connect to Reading Look through "The Right Dog for the Job." Find words that have the final /j/ and /s/ spelling patterns. Add them to your Word Sort.

Name ______________________ Date __________

The Right Dog for the Job
Spelling: Words with Final /j/ and /s/

Proofreading for Spelling

Find the misspelled words and circle them. Write them correctly on the lines below.

My sister Jenny's new guide dog, Goldie, is now a welcome member of our household. She came with very little bagage—just one squeaky toy. We've been to the pet store tweice sinse then, so now Goldie has a big basket of dog toys in Jenny's offise.

Goldie's a hero, too! A few weeks ago, she and Jenny walked along the rige behind our house. Jenny tripped and sprained her ankle. Goldie barked for help, and a police officer on a nearby brige heard her. He came, put a bandag on Jenny's ankle, and helped her home.

Last week there was a guide-dog award ceremony. The judje called Goldie and Jenny up on staje. He read a mesage Jenny had sent describing Goldie's actions. Then he gave Goldie a medal and Jenny a pakage with dog treats. Goldie looked like the queen of the palase.

1. ______________ 7. ______________
2. ______________ 8. ______________
3. ______________ 9. ______________
4. ______________ 10. ______________
5. ______________ 11. ______________
6. ______________ 12. ______________

Spelling Words

1. glance
2. judge
3. damage
4. package
5. twice
6. stage
7. carriage
8. since
9. practice
10. marriage
11. baggage
12. office
13. message
14. bridge
15. chance
16. notice
17. ridge
18. manage
19. palace
20. bandage

Challenge

fringe
average
fleece
fragrance
excellence

Name ______________________ Date ____________

Adverbs that Tell *How, When,* and *Where*

An **adverb** is a word that tells something about a verb. Some adverbs tell *how*, *when*, or *where*. An adverb can come before or after the verb. Most adverbs that tell *how* end in *-ly*.

The adverbs in this sentence tell about the verb *played*:

when **how** **where**
Yesterday, our puppy played happily outside.

Thinking Questions
What is the verb? What word tells how *about the verb?*

1–5. The verb in each sentence is underlined. Write the adverb. Then write whether it tells *when*, *how*, or *where*.

1. Leon talked softly to the new puppy. ______________
2. Robo licked Leon's face excitedly. ______________
3. Suddenly, Leon hugged Robo. ______________
4. Now the family plays with Robo. ______________
5. Leon taught Robo to sit there. ______________

6–10. Underline each adverb. Write the verb it describes.

6. Someday Robo will learn how to behave. ______________
7. He secretly chewed Dad's new slippers. ______________
8. Mom put the puppy outside. ______________
9. Robo wagged his tail innocently. ______________
10. Everyone immediately laughed at the dog's expression. ______________

Name ______________________ Date __________

Adverbs of Frequency and Intensity

An **adverb** is a word that tells something about a verb.
Some adverbs tell how often something happens.
We usually walk in the park.
Ralph sometimes barks at birds.

Some adverbs tell how much of something is done.
He ate enough, but he hardly slept.
She almost won the race.

Thinking Questions
Which word is the verb? Which word tells how often *or* how much?

1–5. The verb in each sentence is underlined. Write the adverb that tells *how often*.

1. I always take my dog, Pal, for a walk. ______________
2. Pal and I visit the dog park often. ______________
3. I usually make him wear his leash in the park. ______________
4. One little black dog seldom barks. ______________
5. Pal never barks or bites. ______________

6–10. Underline each adverb. Write the verb it describes.

6. We sometimes swim with our dogs. ______________
7. Pal scarcely stopped at the water's edge. ______________
8. I almost won a race with Pal. ______________
9. My good dog, Pal, nearly lost that race! ______________
10. Pal follows me a lot. ______________

Name ______________________ Date ____________

Adverbs in Different Parts of Sentences

An **adverb** is a word that tells something about a verb. Adverbs often follow the verb, though some adverbs can be used at the beginning, middle, or end of a sentence.

adverb: carefully
Carefully, Mrs. Marsh trained her service dog.
Mrs. Marsh carefully trained her service dog.
Mrs. Marsh trained her service dog carefully.

Thinking Questions
What is the adverb that tells about the verb? In what part of the sentence is the adverb?

1–5. The verb in each sentence is underlined. Write the adverb.

1. Often a dog trainer makes careless mistakes. ____________
2. Puppies in their first year of life learn best. ____________
3. A trainer repeats the commands again. ____________
4. Our teacher usually knows every dog. ____________
5. I think about my dog a lot. ____________

6–10. Underline each adverb. Write the verb it describes.

6. Once, five of the guide dogs got an award. ____________
7. Three of the dogs had won before. ____________
8. He quickly drank all the water in his bowl. ____________
9. The best guide dog works for Mrs. Hatcher now. ____________
10. Spot, please come here. ____________

Name ______________________ Date ____________

Progressive Verb Tenses

Progressive verb tenses express continuing action. Each progressive tense is formed by joining a form of *be* with the *-ing* form of a verb.

Present Progressive: is teaching, are teaching (now)
Past Progressive: was teaching, were teaching (earlier)
Future Progressive: will be teaching (at a later time)

1–9. Complete each sentence using the verb and progressive form in parentheses ( ).

1. The trainers ______________ a new guide dog to Alisha. (giving, future)
2. Alisha ______________ excitedly for the new dog. (waiting, present)
3. Her old dog ______________ her until he became ill. (guiding, past)
4. The trainers ______________ the new dog now. (evaluating, present)
5. They ______________ sure to prepare the dog for its tasks. (make, future)
6. The dog ______________ very quickly. (learn, present)
7. He already ______________ for red lights. (stop, present)
8. Yesterday, Alisha ______________ the application to get the dog. (filling out, past)
9. She hopes the new dog ______________ her for many years. (serve, future)

Name _______________ Date _______________

Word Choice

Good writers choose precise **adverbs**. An adverb can change the meaning of a sentence.

She walked painfully across the street.

She walked lazily across the street.

She walked proudly across the street.

Read the story. Then fill in the blanks with precise adverbs. Create a story that makes sense.

My aunt Remedios is ninety years old. _______________ we visited her in Arizona. Her canine companion, Charles, whined _______________ when we arrived. Aunt Remy sat _______________ in her wheelchair. My mother told us that she could _______________ walk.

During our visit, we saw that Charles helped Remy _______________. That good dog _______________ left my aunt's side. When Remy accidentally dropped something, Charles _______________ picked it up in his mouth. When she rolled her chair _______________, Charles followed.

I know that Aunt Remy would be lonely without her dog. I _______________ miss Charles, too.

Focus Trait: Purpose

Using Informal Language

A friendly letter is written to tell a person you know well about something interesting that happened. Friendly letters are often written in informal language.

Heading	450 Bond Street Lakeside, OH 12345 June 1, 2014
Salutation	Dear Grandma,
Message	Hot dog! I just opened the birthday gift you sent me. It is awesome! I love the necklace and matching bracelet. How did you know blue gemstones are my favorite? I will think of you whenever I wear the pretty jewelry. Thank you very much.
Closing	Your loving granddaughter,
Signature	Alyssa

Write a message for a thank-you note on the lines below. State the reason you are writing the letter and connect ideas in an orderly way. Write your letter as a short narrative. Use words you would in regular speech.

Dear ______________

____

____

____

____

____

____

Name ______________________ Date ____________

Hercules' Quest

Zeus' Speech

At the end of the story, Zeus was so pleased with his son that he brought him to Mount Olympus to live with him and the other gods. Imagine Zeus wants to have an awards ceremony for his son, Hercules, to introduce him to the other gods and to his new home. Help Zeus write a speech introducing his son. Reread pages 532–536 and answer these questions to prepare you for writing the speech.

How does Hercules accomplish his first goal? What does this tell you about his character?

____

____

How does Hercules accomplish his second goal? What does this tell you about his character?

____

____

How does Hercules accomplish his third goal? What does this tell you about his character?

____

____

Reread the comment about the allusion "the wrath of Hera" on page 533. Think of a word that could be an allusion to Hercules. What would it mean?

____

____

Name ______________________ Date ____________

Hercules' Quest

Independent Reading

Write Zeus's speech below. In the speech, tell how Hercules earned his position among the gods because of his acts. Include your allusion for Hercules in your speech.

Please welcome my son, Hercules! Through his great acts of strength, he has proven he is a god.

Name ______________________ Date __________

Hercules' Quest
Vocabulary Strategies:
Adages and Proverbs

Adages and Proverbs

Practice makes perfect.
Look before you leap.
Honesty is the best policy.
The early bird gets the worm.
Seeing is believing.
There's no use crying over spilt milk.

Complete each sentence using one of the sayings from the box.

1. Hercules awoke at dawn because he knew that ______________________.

2. Hercules didn't lie to his father because he knew that ______________________.

3. As a boy, Hercules acted rashly and did not know that you should ______________________.

4. Zeus knew Hercules would someday learn to use his powers wisely because ______________________.

5. He didn't think Hercules could kill a lion. When he watched the boy fight the animal, he realized that ______________________.

6. Hercules didn't worry about what he had done in the past because ______________________.

Name ______________________ Date __________

Prefixes *re-*, *un-*, *dis-*

Basic 1–10. Read the paragraphs. Write the Basic Words that best complete the sentences.

"Look how (1) __________ this room is!" my dad said. I said that I had cleaned it earlier, but he told me that I needed to (2) __________ the whole thing. I didn't want to (3) __________ him, so I started to organize some of the (4) __________. I noticed right away that a shelf of books was sagging and (5) __________, so I decided that I would try to (6) __________ the whole bookcase. I started to (7) __________ all of the books onto the floor and took the bookcase apart. This (8) __________ task took longer than cleaning the room would have taken.

"George!" exclaimed my father. "I (9) __________ that I asked you an hour ago to clean your room!"

Now I remember why I (10) __________ cleaning so much!

Challenge 11–14. Your favorite store is going out of business. Write an e-mail to a friend about your last visit to the store. Use four Challenge Words. Write on a separate sheet of paper.

Spelling Words

1. unused
2. refresh
3. dislike
4. replace
5. unpaid
6. redo
7. disorder
8. unplanned
9. distrust
10. rewind
11. untrue
12. unload
13. recall
14. displease
15. uneven
16. rebuild
17. restart
18. uncover
19. untidy
20. discolor

Challenge

disband
rearrange
discontinue
refund
unusual

Name ____________________ Date __________

Hercules' Quest
Spelling:
Prefixes: *re-*, *un-*, *dis-*

Spelling Word Sort

Write each Basic Word beside the correct heading.

re- + base word	**Basic Words:** **Challenge Words:**
dis- + base word	**Basic Words:** **Challenge Words:**
un- + base word	**Basic Words:** **Challenge Words:**

Challenge Add the Challenge Words to your Word Sort.

Spelling Words

1. unused
2. refresh
3. dislike
4. replace
5. unpaid
6. redo
7. disorder
8. unplanned
9. distrust
10. rewind
11. untrue
12. unload
13. recall
14. displease
15. uneven
16. rebuild
17. restart
18. uncover
19. untidy
20. discolor

Challenge

disband
rearrange
discontinue
refund
unusual

Name ______________________ Date ____________

Proofreading for Spelling

Hercules' Quest
Spelling:
Prefixes: *re-*, *un-*, *dis-*

Find the misspelled words and circle them. Write them correctly on the lines below.

To the ancient Greeks, an earthquake or drought was not accidental or unplaned. Everything had a reason. So, how did they attempt to explain these events and replaise the unknown with the known? They did this by telling stories about their gods. Today we call these stories Greek myths.

Many of the Greek gods seemed to dislieke one another. There was a lot of distrussed as they competed for power. Humans had to be careful not to displeaze the gods, for doing so could bring chaos and dissorder. An uneaven relationship existed, as some gods were kind, while others were cruel.

Though the myths are untrew, historians use them to uncuver the truth about Greek life. Ancient stories help us recawl how people lived and rebild the story of their society. These ancient myths allow us to rewinde the human story and see how ancient people explained difficult ideas.

1. ____________ 7. ____________
2. ____________ 8. ____________
3. ____________ 9. ____________
4. ____________ 10. ____________
5. ____________ 11. ____________
6. ____________ 12. ____________

Spelling Words

1. unused
2. refresh
3. dislike
4. replace
5. unpaid
6. redo
7. disorder
8. unplanned
9. distrust
10. rewind
11. untrue
12. unload
13. recall
14. displease
15. uneven
16. rebuild
17. restart
18. uncover
19. untidy
20. discolor

Challenge

disband
rearrange
discontinue
refund
unusual

Prepositions

A **preposition** shows the connection between words in a sentence. Some prepositions describe time, such as *before*, *after*, or *during*. Others describe place, such as *over*, *in*, *on*, *above*, or *below*.

preposition
The runners raced on the track.

Thinking Question
What word shows a connection between other words in the sentence?

1–10. Find the preposition in each underlined phrase. Write the preposition on the line.

1. I read *Hercules the Mighty* long into the night. ____________
2. Hercules had to fight with many beasts and monsters. ____________
3. He had tremendous strength in his muscles. ____________
4. After my read-a-thon, I dreamed I had super strength. ____________
5. I could easily lift a house over my head. ____________
6. My older brother stood under the house giving me orders. ____________
7. When I awoke, he was beside my bed telling me to get up. ____________
8. I have noticed my dreams during the night are often silly. ____________
9. My brother does strength exercises before school. ____________
10. Maybe that is why he was featured in my crazy dream. ____________

Name ______________________ Date __________

Lesson 18
READER'S NOTEBOOK

Prepositional Phrases

Hercules' Quest
Grammar: Prepositions and Prepositional Phrases

A **prepositional phrase** begins with a preposition and ends with a noun or a pronoun. Both these words and all of the words in between them make up the prepositional phrase.

prepositional phrase
The girls have been best friends for a long time.

At school, they join many of the same clubs.

Thinking Question
What phrase begins with a preposition and ends with a noun or pronoun?

1–6. In each sentence below, underline the preposition. Write the prepositional phrase.

1. Myths say that Hercules once lived among ordinary humans.

   ____

2. Zeus watched Hercules from Mount Olympus.

   ____

3. Hercules completed impossible challenges on Earth.

   ____

4. Hercules only laughed at the dangerous tasks.

   ____

5. He showed that he was kind and helpful during his stay.

   ____

6. After his successes, Hercules could go home.

   ____

Name ______________________________ Date ____________

Prepositional Phrases to Provide Details

A prepositional phrase can also provide details to help describe a noun. The noun it helps describe is not part of the prepositional phrase.

noun described **preposition**
Our school (play) this year is about a female athlete.

Thinking Questions
What is the prepositional phrase in the sentence? What details does it give about the sentence?

1–6. Look at the underlined preposition. Write a detail on the lines below to complete each sentence. Then circle the noun being described.

1. "Hercules' Quest" is a story about
_______________________________.
2. It is a myth retold by _______________________________.
3. People of _______________________________ enjoy myths and tales.
4. In Greek myths, Zeus rules from his kingdom on
_______________________________.
5. We will be writing our own tales for
_______________________________.
6. I will write a myth about
_______________________________.

Name ______________________ Date __________

Sentence Fragments and Run-On Sentences

A sentence expresses a complete thought. It has a subject (the who or what) and a predicate (what the subject does or is). A sentence fragment lacks a subject or a predicate.

Complete sentence	Subject Predicate The goddess Hera did not like baby Hercules.
Sentence fragments	Many dangerous enemies. Lived in the kingdom.
Run-on sentence	Hercules fought a lion, later he killed the hydra.

To correct a sentence fragment, add the missing subject or predicate. One way to correct a run-on sentence is to put a period between the two sentences. Capitalize the first word in the second sentence.

1–5. Write *fragment* or *run-on* beside each group of words. Correct the sentence error on the line. Use periods and capital letters correctly.

1. Had to gather golden apples for the king. __________

____

2. A dragon guarded these apples it never slept. __________

____

3. Hercules made a plan he would ask Atlas for help. __________

____

4. tricked Atlas into getting the apples. __________

____

5. The giant Atlas. __________

____

Name ______________________ Date ____________

Ideas

Use prepositional phrases to add interesting or important details to your writing.

The hero fought the monster. The hero with supernatural strength fought the monster with two heads.

1–8 Add a prepositional phrase that provides descriptive detail to each sentence below.

1. The hero had to fight

   ____.

2. A serpent was hiding

   ____.

3. A lion frightened attackers

   ____.

4. A dragon stood guard

   ____.

5. The hero wanted to save the kingdom

   ____.

6. The hero carried a sword

   ____.

7. The hero's horse could fly

   ____.

8. The hero's horse had wings

   ____.

Name ______________________ Date ____________

Hercules' Quest
Writing: Narrative Writing

Focus Trait: Elaboration

Good writers elaborate on their narrative's events by adding more descriptive words and details.

Without Descriptive Words	With Descriptive Words
The hydra's heads turned toward Hercules.	The hydra's nine slimy heads spun around and bared their knife-sharp fangs at Hercules.

1–4 Rewrite the sentences to include descriptive adjectives, verbs, or phrases that add detail.

1. Hera was angry when Hercules killed the hydra.

____

____

2. The mountain of Atlas was huge.

____

____

3. Atlas grew tired and stiff from holding up the world.

____

____

4. As a boy, Hercules killed a lion.

____

____

Name ______________________ Date ____________

Harvesting Hope: The Story of Cesar Chavez

"Yes, It Can Be Done!"

Answer the questions below about Cesar Chavez's *La Causa*. Then, draw a sign for *La Causa* on the next page.

Reread the third paragraph on page 566. What do you think the idiom "die of embarrassment" means? How does it help you understand how Cesar feels?

____

____

____

Reread page 567. How did the members of *La Causa* choose to protest?

____

____

The Aztec eagle is a symbol of strength, patience, and courage. Why might Cesar have chosen a bold black eagle as the symbol for *La Causa?*

____

____

Design a sign that expresses the concerns and goals of *La Causa*. In your sign, include these ideas:

- **a symbol for *La Causa* that relates to its goals, and**
- **a slogan that uses an idiom relating to *La Causa*.**

Name ____________________ Date __________

Harvesting Hope: The Story of Cesar Chavez
Vocabulary Strategies:
Reference Materials

Reference Materials

blur	strike	belief
suspicious	harvest	right

Each sentence shows a word in *italics*. Use a dictionary to answer questions about the words or to help you use them in a sentence.

1. The word *blur* can be used as what parts of speech?

   ____

2. How many syllables does the word *suspicious* have?

   ____

3. Use the word *strike* with a different meaning in two sentences.

   ____

   ____

4. What guide words are found at the top of the page on which *harvest* appears?

   ____

5. According to your dictionary, which syllable of *belief* is the stressed syllable? How can you tell?

   ____

   ____

6. Use the word *right* with a different meaning in two sentences.

   ____

   ____

Name ____________________ Date ____________

Suffixes *-ful*, *-less*, *-ness*, *-ment*

Basic 1–11. Write the Basic Word that best fits each clue.

1. full of happiness ____________
2. without end ____________
3. a state of tidiness ____________
4. concrete surface ____________
5. unable to stay at rest ____________
6. the act of moving ____________
7. a state of having no strength ____________
8. using more than is needed ____________
9. sickness ____________
10. having bright colors ____________
11. affection ____________

Challenge 12–15. Your school newspaper is featuring a health article. Your job is to submit some first-aid tips. Use four of the Challenge Words. Write on a separate sheet of paper.

Spelling Words

1. colorful
2. weakness
3. movement
4. endless
5. truthful
6. illness
7. cheerful
8. useless
9. beautiful
10. restless
11. clumsiness
12. pavement
13. peaceful
14. fondness
15. neatness
16. speechless
17. statement
18. wasteful
19. penniless
20. treatment

Challenge

numbness
ailment
resourceful
cleanliness
appointment

Name ______________________ Date ____________

Harvesting Hope: The Story of Cesar Chavez
Spelling: Suffixes *-ful*, *-less*, *-ness*, *-ment*

Spelling Word Sort

Write each Basic Word beside the correct heading.

base word + *-ful*	**Basic Words:** **Challenge Words:** **Possible Selection Words:**
base word + *-less*	**Basic Words:**
base word + *-ness*	**Basic Words:** **Challenge Words:**
base word + *-ment*	**Basic Words:** **Challenge Words:** **Possible Selection Words:**

Spelling Words

1. colorful
2. weakness
3. movement
4. endless
5. truthful
6. illness
7. cheerful
8. useless
9. beautiful
10. restless
11. clumsiness
12. pavement
13. peaceful
14. fondness
15. neatness
16. speechless
17. statement
18. wasteful
19. penniless
20. treatment

Challenge

numbness
ailment
resourceful
cleanliness
appointment

Challenge Add the Challenge Words to your Word Sort.

Connect to Reading Look through "Harvesting Hope: The Story of Cesar Chavez." Find words that have the suffixes *-ful*, *-less*, *-ness*, or *-ment*. Add them to your Word Sort.

Name ______________________________ Date ____________

Harvesting Hope: The Story of Cesar Chavez
Spelling: Suffixes *-ful, -less, -ness, -ment*

Proofreading for Spelling

Find the misspelled words and circle them. Write them correctly on the lines below.

In 1948, Helen Fabela married Cesar Chavez, a man known for his endlest work to improve the treatmint of migrant farm workers in the United States. Though the couple endured rather peniles times and poor living conditions, Helen supported Cesar's work. She also made her own statment by starting a teaching program for Mexican farm workers.

Some dishonest people were not truthfil and started rumors about Mexican farm workers. Helen was spechles at the weekness of their values, and she thought it was uzeles to complain.

Helen had a chearful attitude, and she provided an environment for her husband and eight children that was beautyful and peaseful. Today Helen Chavez is an inspiration to her 31 grandchildren.

1. ____________________ 7. ____________________
2. ____________________ 8. ____________________
3. ____________________ 9. ____________________
4. ____________________ 10. ____________________
5. ____________________ 11. ____________________
6. ____________________

Spelling Words

1. colorful
2. weakness
3. movement
4. endless
5. truthful
6. illness
7. cheerful
8. useless
9. beautiful
10. restless
11. clumsiness
12. pavement
13. peaceful
14. fondness
15. neatness
16. speechless
17. statement
18. wasteful
19. penniless
20. treatment

Challenge

numbness
ailment
resourceful
cleanliness
appointment

Name ______________________ Date __________

Clauses

A **clause** is a group of words with a subject and predicate. If a clause can stand alone as a sentence, it is an **independent clause**. A **dependent clause** cannot stand alone. Many dependent clauses begin with a transition word such as *before, after, since, because, who, whose, that,* or *which.*

Dependent Clause	**Independent Clause**
Since they had no water for crops,	they had to leave the ranch.

Independent Clause	**Dependent Clause**
Chavez was the leader	that the workers chose.

Thinking Questions
What clauses can stand alone? Which clauses cannot stand alone?

1–6. Underline the dependent clause in each sentence. Circle the transition word that introduces the dependent clause.

1. After they worked long hours, migrant workers had little to eat.
2. Workers who complained to the owners were fired, punished, or even killed.
3. The farm workers suffered because their work was so hard.
4. Until Chavez organized the workers, they had no way to fight back.
5. After the workers began to march, other people learned about their cause.
6. A huge, cheering crowd met the marchers when they reached Sacramento.

Name ______________________ Date __________

Harvesting Hope: The Story of Cesar Chavez
Grammar: Relative Pronouns and Adverbs

Relative and Interrogative Pronouns

Some dependent clauses begin with a relative pronoun, such as *who, whom, whose, that,* or *which.* These clauses act as adjectives and answer the questions *Which one?* or *What kind?* about a noun or pronoun.

Interrogative pronouns introduce questions. *What, who,* and *which* are pronouns that ask questions.

Thinking Question
Which word introduces a dependent clause that tells about the noun that comes before it?

Dependent Clause: California is the state **that** produces the most fruit crops. [tells which state]

Question: **Who** will help me pick the crops today?

Thinking Question
Which word introduces a question?

1–5. Circle the interrogative or relative pronoun in each sentence. For sentences containing a relative pronoun, underline the dependent clause. Write the noun this clause describes on the line at the right.

1. There was a terrible drought that caused the Chavez family to lose their ranch. ____________
2. They moved to California, which offered jobs for migrant farm workers. ____________
3. What jobs are the hardest to do?
4. Migrant children, who move often, have difficulty keeping up in school. ____________
5. Which company opposed the strike?

Name ______________________________ Date ____________

Relative Adverbs in Clauses

Relative adverbs begin dependent clauses that tell *where, when* or *why*.

Dependent Clause

I can tell you **why** migrant workers loved Cesar Chavez.

California is the place **where** La Causa was born.

Do you know **when** Chavez was born?

Thinking Question
Which word introduces a dependent clause that tells about a place, a time, or a reason?

1–6. Underline the dependent clause in each sentence. Circle the relative adverb that begins the clause.

1. That Arizona ranch is where Chavez lived as a young boy.
2. The family had to move away when a drought ruined the crops.
3. Their sad mother told them why they had to leave their home.
4. The family had to live in a dirty shed when they arrived in California.
5. I wonder why the landowner treated workers so poorly.
6. An old theater in Fresno is where the first National Farm Workers meeting took place.

Name ____________________ Date ____________

Prepositions and Prepositional Phrases

Prepositions	Prepositional Phrases
from, to	The farm workers walked from Delano to Sacramento.

1–5. Underline the preposition twice and the rest of the prepositional phrase once in each sentence.

1. Most farms in the valley are large.
2. Many farms use modern equipment for plowing, planting, and harvesting.
3. However, tender fruit crops are harvested by hand.
4. Farm workers bend, pull, and sweat under the hot sun.
5. After a long day, they are ready to rest and enjoy themselves.

6–7. Combine each set of sentences, using prepositional phrases correctly. Write the new sentence on the line.

6. Our family is proud. We are proud of our good work.

____

____

7. Chavez was proud but humble. He was proud of his heritage. He felt humble about his achievements.

____

____

Name ______________________ Date ____________

Sentence Fluency

Transition words help writers combine ideas. They show readers how ideas and events are related.

1–6. Complete the sentences below by writing transition words from the box.

as a result	however	since
in short	because	finally

1. Many people lost their farms ____________ a terrible drought occurred.
2. ____________, there was work available on the rich farms in California.
3. ____________, they became migrant workers for large California farms.
4. ____________ their pay was so low, they couldn't afford decent housing.
5. ____________, they formed *La Causa* to fight against harsh conditions and low wages.
6. ____________, their goals were to increase wages and improve working conditions.

Name ______________________ Date ____________

Focus Trait: Organization

Planning a Personal Narrative

A personal narrative is a story about something that happened in your life.

A. For your personal narrative, choose an event that you remember well or that has special meaning to you. Then fill in the blanks below to help you plan your story.

Topic: I will write about ______________________

What happened first: ______________________

Next: ______________________

Last: ______________________

What I learned: ______________________

B. Think about how the ideas in your narrative are connected. Write transition words to show time or place, cause and effect, and how or what kind.

Pair/Share Work with a partner to brainstorm sample sentences with two clauses. Underline the transition words you use.

____

____

____

____

____

Name ______________________ Date ______________

Sacagawea

Sacagawea's Journal

Review the events of Sacagawea's time with Lewis and Clark during the summer of 1805. Answer the questions below to help write a journal entry by Sacagawea.

Reread pages 592–593. When the boat carrying their supplies tipped, how was Sacagawea's reaction different from her husband's? What does this tell you about Sacagawea?

____

____

Reread pages 594–595. Why was traveling so difficult for Sacagawea and the explorers in June and July of 1805?

____

____

List two details that tell the difficulties Sacagawea and the explorers faced during the summer of 1805.

____

____

What did Sacagawea do when she saw her people, the Shoshone? How does this compare with the way she acted until this point?

____

____

Name _______________ Date _______________

Sacagawea
Independent Reading

Write Sacagawea's journal entry retelling the events of the summer of 1805. In the journal entry, infer what Sacagawea may have been feeling while she was traveling with Lewis and Clark using the details you found.

Name ______________________ Date __________

Shades of Meaning

Sacagawea
Vocabulary Strategies: Shades of Meaning

Synonyms are words that have similar meanings. They do not mean exactly the same thing. Synonyms may give us different feelings about the subject. For example, if a boat is **winding** upstream, it is traveling that way somewhat slowly. However, if the boat is **wandering** upstream, the journey is even slower and less direct.

Circle the synonym that best fits the context for each sentence. On the line, write why you chose this word.

1. I love to read about explorers and imagine I'm along on their (wild, crazy) adventures.

   ____

   ____

2. Sacagawea made the (bold, brash) decision to join the Corps of Discovery.

   ____

   ____

3. The crew had not eaten for days and (yearned, wished) for a meal.

   ____

   ____

4. The Corps would never have made it to the Pacific without their (strong-willed, pig-headed) leaders.

   ____

   ____

5. Sacagawea became (important, invaluable) to the mission.

   ____

   ____

Name ______________________ Date __________

Words with VCCV Pattern

Basic 1–10. Write the Basic Word that completes each analogy.

1. *Happily* is to *joyously* as *rarely* is to ______________ .
2. *Shoe* is to *sneaker* as *spice* is to ______________ .
3. *Omelet* is to *eggs* as *house* is to ______________ .
4. *Give* is to *receive* as *lend* is to ______________ .
5. *Puddle* is to *ocean* as *dollar* is to ______________ .
6. *Quarterback* is to *football* as *goalie* is to ______________ .
7. *Carpenter* is to *house* as *photographer* is to ______________ .
8. *Mountain* is to *peak* as *ravine* is to ______________ .
9. *Dentist* is to *teeth* as *mechanic* is to ______________ .
10. *Safety* is to *security* as *peril* is to ______________ .

Challenge 11–14. Write an e-mail to a friend about a movie you have seen recently. Describe a scene that you liked. Use four Challenge Words. Write on a separate sheet of paper.

Spelling Words

1. million
2. collect
3. lumber
4. pepper
5. plastic
6. borrow
7. support
8. thirty
9. perfect
10. attend
11. canyon
12. traffic
13. fortune
14. danger
15. soccer
16. engine
17. picture
18. survive
19. seldom
20. effort

Challenge

occur
venture
challenge
rascal
splendid

Name ______________________ Date ____________

Spelling Word Sort

Sacagawea
Spelling: Words with VCCV Pattern

Write each Basic Word beside the correct heading.

VCCV Pattern: Double consonants	**Basic Words:** **Challenge Words:** **Possible Selection Words:**
VCCV Pattern: Different consonants	**Basic Words:** **Challenge Words:** **Possible Selection Words:**

Spelling Words

1. million
2. collect
3. lumber
4. pepper
5. plastic
6. borrow
7. support
8. thirty
9. perfect
10. attend
11. canyon
12. traffic
13. fortune
14. danger
15. soccer
16. engine
17. picture
18. survive
19. seldom
20. effort

Challenge

occur
venture
challenge
rascal
splendid

Challenge Add the Challenge Words to your Word Sort.

Connect to Reading Look through "Sacagawea." Find words that have the VCCV pattern. Add them to your Word Sort.

Name ______________________ Date __________

Sacagawea
Spelling: Words with VCCV Pattern

Proofreading for Spelling

Find the misspelled words and circle them. Write them correctly on the lines below.

On their trip west, Lewis and Clark hired a French trader for his knowledge of Indian languages. Then they discovered that the trader's wife, Sacagawea, gave the crew more language suport than the trader. She was perfec for the job. Sacagawea would atend meetings between the explorers and Indians to be the interpreter. Even though the group did not meet much trafic on the trail, Sacagawea did not have time to be lonely. She would walk down the canyonn to colleck any food she could find for the more than thirte men to eat. When Sacagawea found a bush with what seemed like a milion berries on it, she couldn't pickure a better forchun. Her extra effert helped the crew servive the long journey. Lewis and Clark owed a lot to Sacagawea.

1. ____________ 7. ____________
2. ____________ 8. ____________
3. ____________ 9. ____________
4. ____________ 10. ____________
5. ____________ 11. ____________
6. ____________ 12. ____________

Spelling Words

1. million
2. collect
3. lumber
4. pepper
5. plastic
6. borrow
7. support
8. thirty
9. perfect
10. attend
11. canyon
12. traffic
13. fortune
14. danger
15. soccer
16. engine
17. picture
18. survive
19. seldom
20. effort

Challenge

occur
venture
challenge
rascal
splendid

Abbreviations for People and Places

An **abbreviation** is a short form of a word. Most abbreviations begin with a capital letter and end with a period. Both letters of state name abbreviations are capital letters, and no period is used.

Person	Mr. Hideki Nomo
Place	55 Porter Blvd.
Place	Shoreline, WA 98155

Thinking Question
What parts of the address are shortened forms of words?

1–8. Write each group of words. Use an abbreviation for the underlined word or words.

1. Shoshone Trading Company ____________
2. Charles Pompy, Junior ____________
3. 92 Mountain Road ____________
4. Doctor May Dawson ____________
5. 195 Water Street ____________
6. Mister Robert Woods, Senior ____________
7. 16 Muddy Creek Drive ____________
8. Beavercreek, Oregon 97004 ____________

Name ______________________ Date ____________

Abbreviations for Mailing Addresses

An **abbreviation** is a short form of a word. Use abbreviations when writing street names and states in a mailing address. Abbreviate words such as *road* or *avenue* with a capital letter and end with a period. Write both letters of state name abbreviations with capital letters and do not use periods.

Road	Rd.	Court	Ct.
Street	St.	Post Office	P.O.
Avenue	Ave.	Boulevard	Blvd.

Thinking Questions
What parts of an address can I make shorter? How can I shorten the whole word?

Write each mailing address using abbreviations.

Full Address	Abbreviated Address
1. Mister Pedro Saravia The Total Pet Supply Company 9302 Riverside Drive Toledo, Ohio 43601	
2. Miss Alexis Parker The Press Building 14 Paper Lane Seattle, Washington 98104	
3. Gregory Nulman President, Choice Restaurants Post Office Box 269 Brooklyn, New York 11216	

Name ____________________ Date ____________

Abbreviations for Time and Measurement

An **abbreviation** is a short form of a word. The abbreviations for days and months begin with a capital letter and end with a period. Some other abbreviations for time and measurements begin with a lowercase letter and end with a period.

time	**measurement**
Wed., Aug. 26	165 mi., 4 yd.

Thinking Questions
What parts can I make shorter? How can I shorten the whole word?

1–10. Write these groups of words, using correct abbreviations.

1. 8,000 feet ____________
2. 1 hour, 45 minutes ____________
3. Tuesday, January 7, 1806 ____________
4. Monday–Friday ____________
5. 3 yards, 11 inches ____________
6. April 30, 1803 ____________
7. November 24, 2014 ____________
8. Thursday, February 27, 1805 ____________
9. 7 hours, 15 minutes ____________
10. March 10, 1922 ____________

Name ______________________ Date ____________

Frequently Confused Words

These words sound the same, but their meanings and spellings are different.

ate/eight	The hungry men caught **eight** fish and **ate** every one for supper.
core/corps	Expert craftsmen were the **core** of the **Corps** of Discovery.
horse/hoarse	A tired man spoke in a **hoarse** voice about the **horse** he had lost.
meat/meet	When they would **meet** with Shoshone leaders, they would feast on **meat.**
their/there	**Their** goal was to reach the Pacific Ocean and return home from **there.**
threw/through	Traveling **through** the wilderness, they **threw** nothing useful away.

1–8. Circle the correct word in parentheses ( ).

1. Lewis and Clark's (core, corps) of men was united by a vital, exciting mission.

2. Since they set out traveling on a keelboat, the men had not a single (hoarse, horse) with them.

3. (Their, There) 55-foot boat carried 12 tons of supplies and gifts to give the Shoshone.

4. They would hunt for the (meat, meet) to feed the crew as they traveled.

5. In the mountain passage, the explorers (ate, eight) very little. In fact, they almost starved.

6. For over two years, the group traveled (threw, through) American wilderness.

7. The success and discoveries of the expedition (threw, through) Americans into a fever of excitement.

8. Sacagawea never dreamed she would (meat, meet) her brother, who had become a Shoshone chief.

Conventions

Each group of words has two incorrect abbreviations. Use proofreading marks to correct the abbreviations.

1. Mr. and mrs Tom Charbonneau, Jr.

1804 Hidatsa Dr.

Sioux City, Ia., 51101

2. Frid., Febr'y. 14

3. 55 mls per hour on the Fort Mandan expy

4. mond., octob 22

5. Doc. Michelle Mitchell

431 Expedition boulv'd

Bethel, ME 04217

6. 17 In, 3 ft., 4 yrd.

Name ______________________ Date ____________

Focus Trait: Conventions

Choosing Interesting, Important Details

Good writers use correct conventions so readers do not get confused. They also use details that will interest readers.

With Dull, Unimportant Details	With Interesting, Important Details
Newborn Jean-Baptiste Charbonneau began life with a grand adventure. **He became a favorite of William Clark. (not important)** Carried on his mother's back, the infant rode the whitewater of rivers. **He saw a lot of wildlife. (dull)**	Newborn Jean-Baptiste Charbonneau began life with a grand adventure. Carried on his mother's back, the infant rode the whitewater of rivers. He saw buffalo, wolves, bighorn sheep, and fierce grizzly bears.

Read the sets of sentences. Cross out details that are dull or not important. Then rewrite the sentences on the lines.

1. Jean-Baptiste became very ill in 1806 on the return journey. He had a fever. His neck and throat swelled up. A mixture of bear oil, pine resin, and wild onions helped him recover. The boy went on to have an interesting life.

____

____

____

____

Rewrite the next sentences on a separate sheet of paper. Replace the underlined words with more interesting, important details. Then edit for incorrect conventions.

2. <u>It would be cool</u> to have an adventure like jean-Baptiste Tomorrow's child might be born on the moon or journey to mars. <u>It might be dangerous. It would always be interesting.</u>

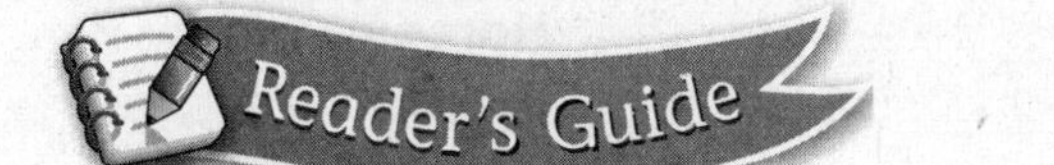

Horses

A Horse and a Human

Horses and humans have a unique history. In each square, draw and label a horse and rider in history. Use what you read on pages 2–3 to help you. Leave one square to draw yourself and horses.

Name ______________________ Date ____________

A Horse History

Read page 4. Use what you have read to make a timeline to describe horses and their ancestors.

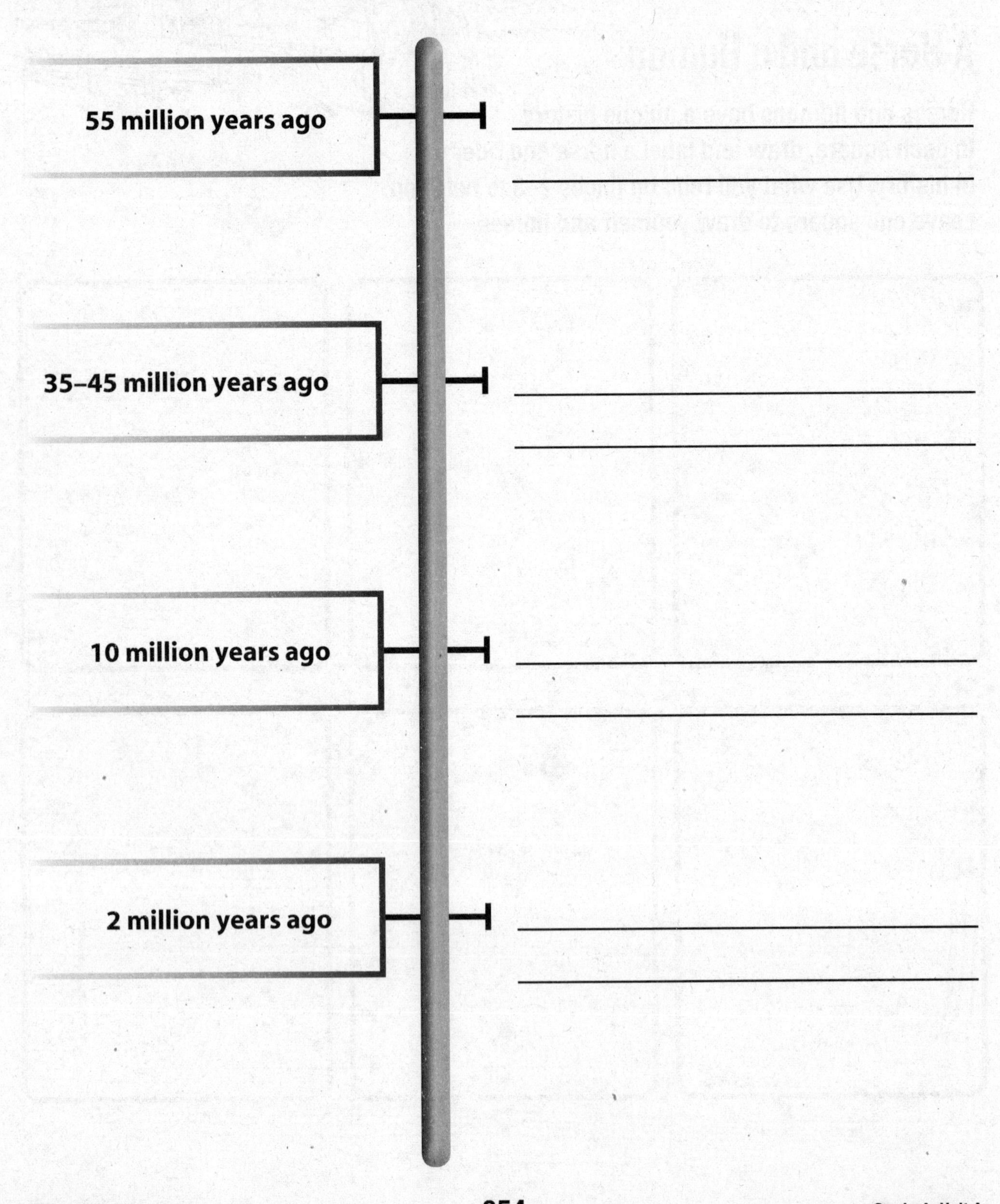

Name ______________________ Date ____________

What Big Teeth You Have!

Horses have changed a lot in 55 million years. One change has been what they eat.

Read pages 4–5, and then imagine that you are a scientist studying the changes of horses over time. In your own words, write a summary of horses, their diets, and their teeth.

Name ______________________ Date ____________

Besides grasses, horses today eat other things. Now imagine that you are in charge of the diets of the horses at Blue Ridge Farms. What will you serve?

Read pages 5–9. Design a menu for the horses. Think about menus you have seen and use your imagination to create a fun menu for the farm. Illustrate your menu.

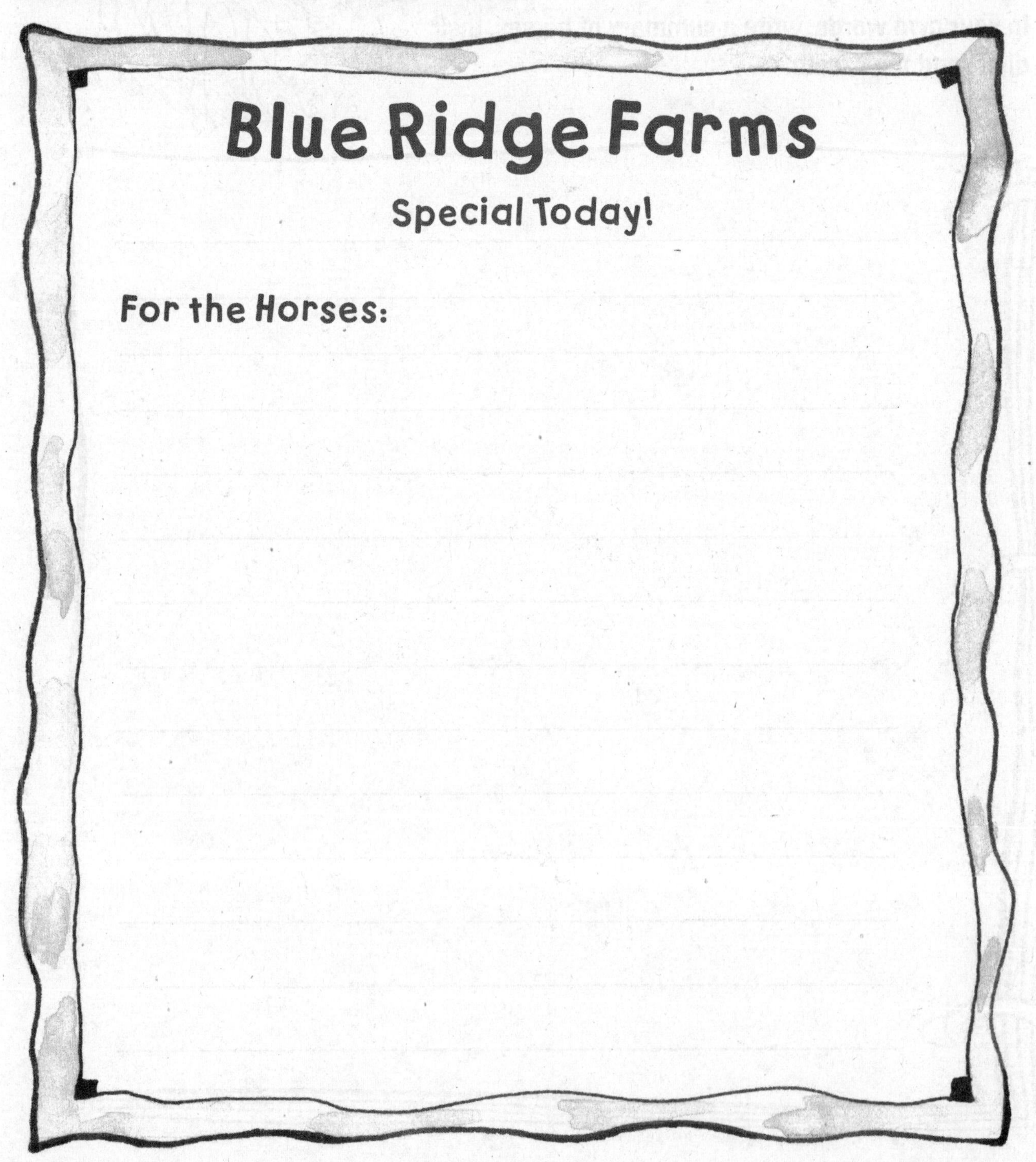

Name ______________________ Date ____________

Alike and Different

Horses and people have the same senses, but they do not work the same way. Read page 9. For each sense, create a diagram to show the differences and similarities between horse senses and human senses. Label your diagram with information from the book.

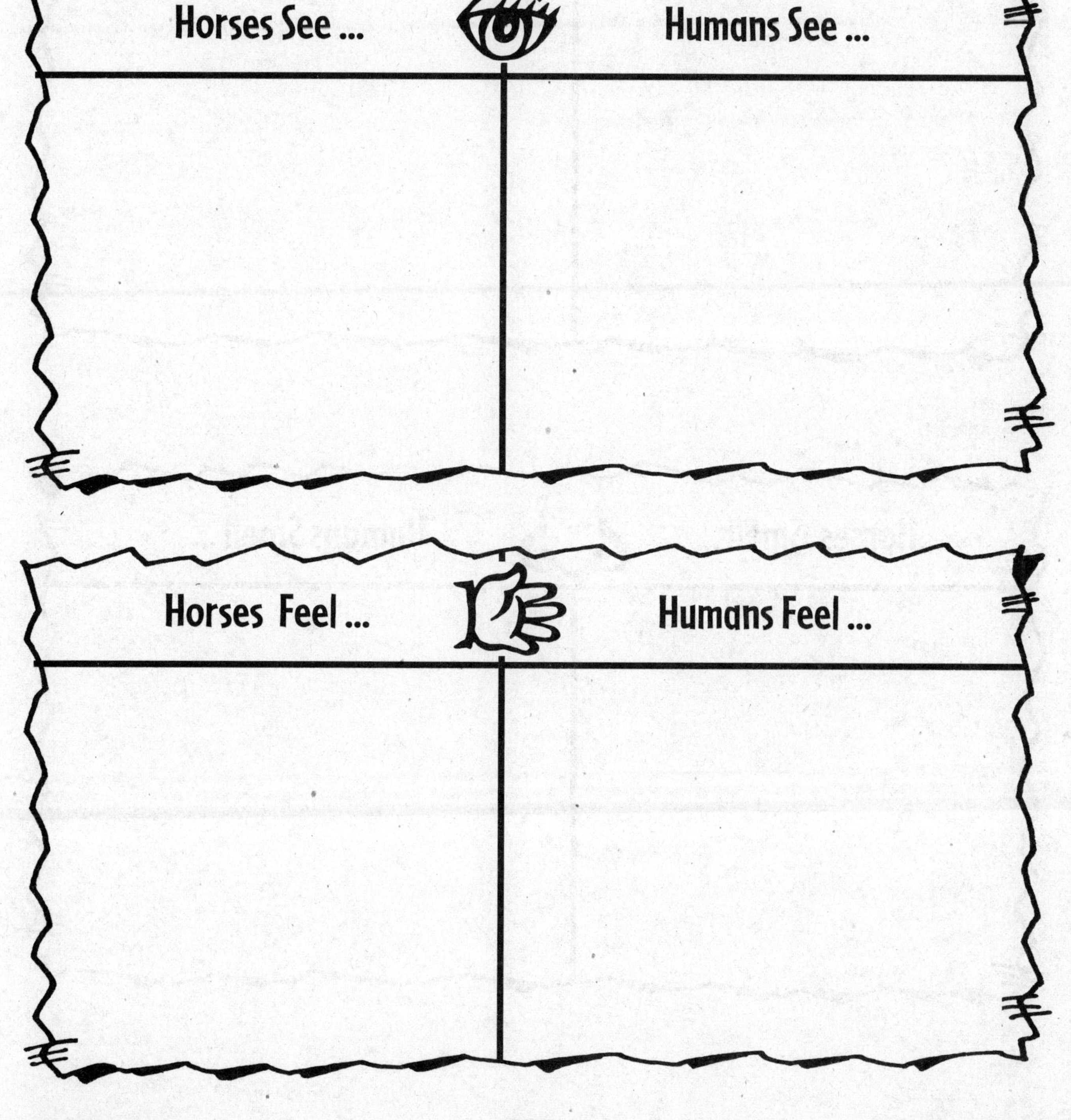

Name ______________________ Date __________

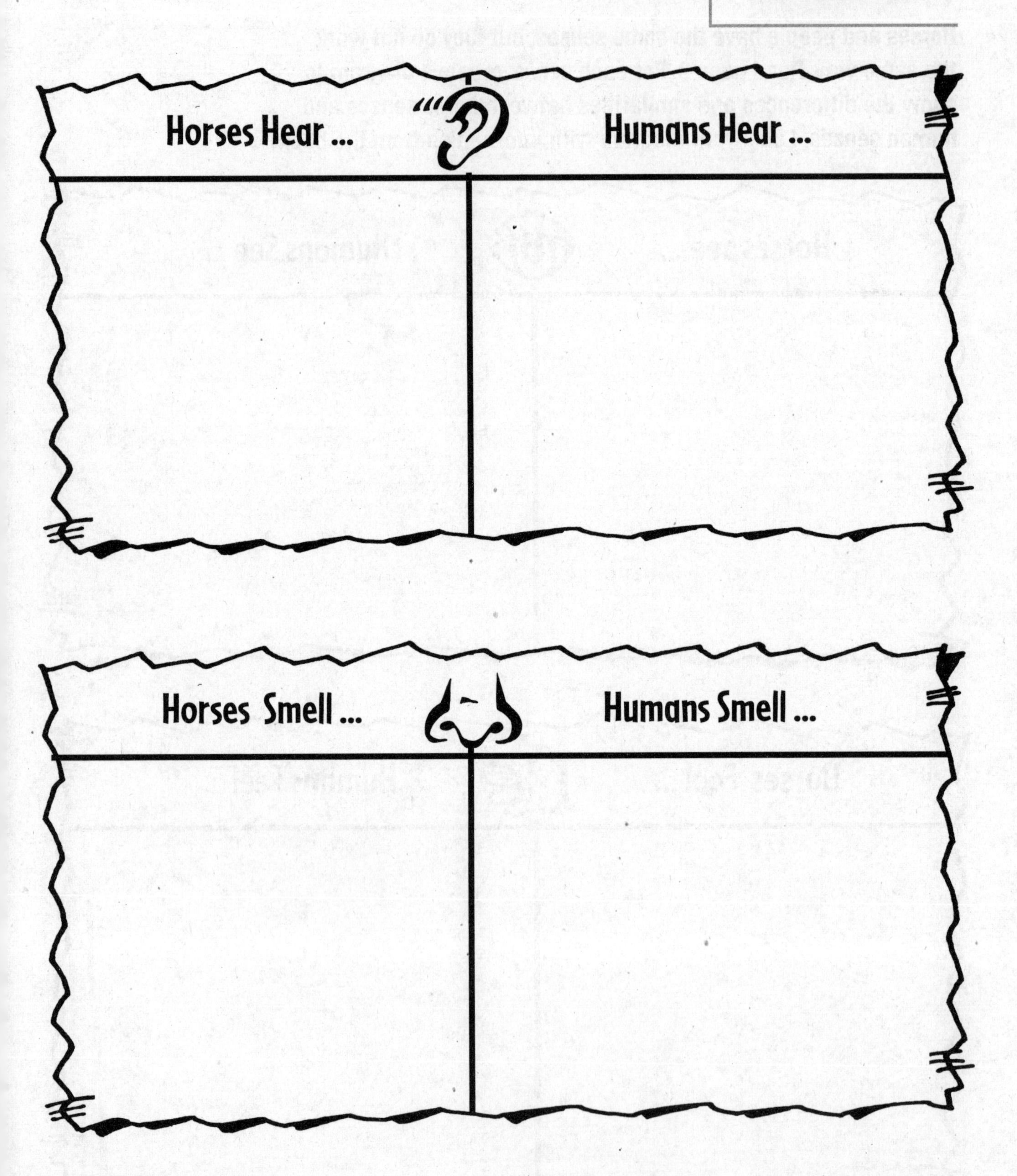

Horses

A Horse Family

You have read about the different names horses have that describe their age and whether they are male or female. Design a horse photo album. In each square, draw a portrait of a horse. Then label each portrait with a name. Describe what each name means. Use the names you read on page 11.

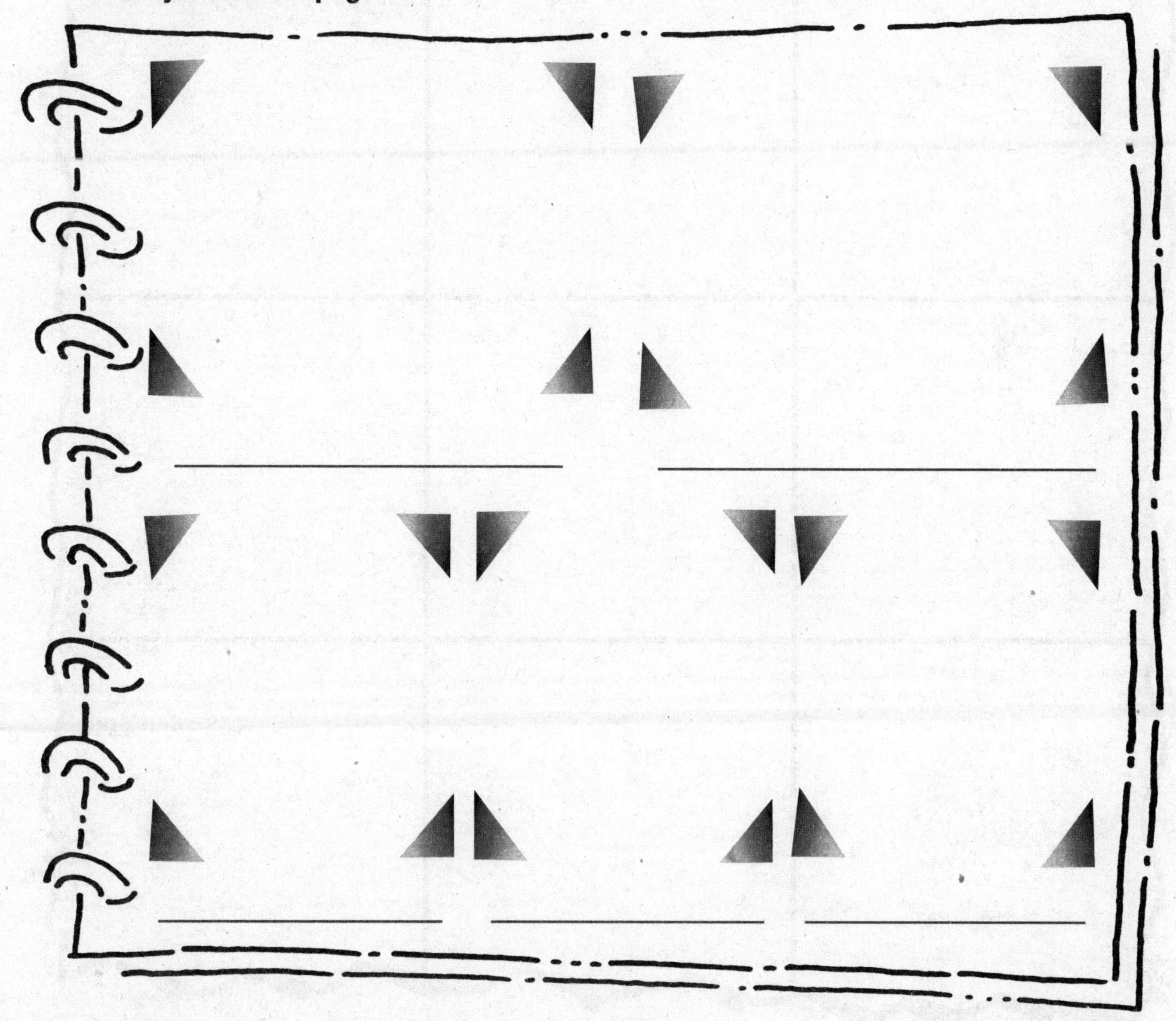

Name ______________________ Date ____________

Communication

Horses cannot talk like humans, but they can communicate. Use what you have read on page 12. In the left column, describe three things you might see horses do. In the middle column, describe what it means. In the right column, explain what you might do if you saw a horse trying to communicate.

What Horses Do	What It Means	What You Can Do

Name ______________________ Date ____________

Move Like a Horse

Horses walk, cantor, trot, and gallop. Read page 15. In each box, draw a horse in a different gait. Begin with the fastest gait and end with the slowest gait. Explain in your own words how people can identify at what speed a horse is moving.

Name ______________________ Date ____________

Horses
Segment 2
Independent Reading

Name ______________________________ Date ____________

Horses in the Zoo

You have learned many different things about horses. As a horse expert, a zoo has called you to make a plaque to inform visitors about the horses.

Think about the most important information you have read through page 15. Think about interesting information zoo visitors might want to read. Create a plaque to tell about horses.

Name ______________________ Date ____________

Horses
Segment 2
Independent Reading

A New Baby in the Zoo

When babies are born in the zoo, the zookeepers often send announcements to local newspapers. Write a press release for a new baby horse! Do not forget to give the baby a unique name.

Press Release

Name:

____

Date of birth:

____

____

Will I be a filly or a colt? Why?

____

____

____

How can you tell which mare is my mother?

____

____

____

____

Name ______________________ Date ____________

Horses

A Picture Dictionary

There are many names for the colors of horses. Use what you have read to create a picture dictionary to show the differences between the words.

Read pages 16–17. Use crayons or colored pencils to color the horses according to their names.

Bay

Palomino

Name ______________________ Date ____________

The names for horse colors may be hard to remember. Think of a trick that can help you remember the meaning of one of the color names and write it below.

____

____

____

____

Name ______________________ Date __________

Horse Riddles

In this book about horses, there are many new words. Read the following riddles and see if you can figure out what new word the riddle describes. If you need a hint, read the page shown under the riddle.

I am an ancestor of the modern horse. I was the size of a large dog. I ate grasses and leaves.

Which ancestor am I?

____

____

____

Need a clue? Read page 4.

I am the word that describes the way horses move. If you spell me differently, I mean an opening in a wall or fence.

What word am I?

____

____

____

Need a clue? Read page 15.

I am a word to describe the color of many horses. If I am light, I am called dun. If I am dark, I am called chestnut.

What color am I?

____

____

____

Need a clue? Read page 16.

I am a word to describe the color of a horse. I am the word to describe a horse that is black and white.

What color word am I?

____

____

Need a clue? Read page 17.

Name ______________________ Date __________

Write two riddles about words you have learned about horses. Give your readers clues to solve the riddles using what you have read. Write the page from *Horses,* where your reader can find more clues if he or she needs some.

Now turn your paper upside down.
Write the answers to your riddles on this line.

Name ______________________ Date ___________

Horses: Hotbloods, Coldbloods, Warmbloods

In this section, you have read about the three groups of horse breeds. Use what you learned to take notes. Then follow the directions to write an online encyclopedia article.

First, take notes on the three types of horse breeds. Reread pages 19–23 to review the similarities and differences. Include examples of each type, where each type lives, and how humans use each type.

Name ______________________ Date ____________

Now use your notes to create an online encyclopedia article. Remember to include headings. After each heading, include specific examples and details of each breed.

File Edit View Favorites Tools Help

Address

Go

Horse Breeds

Heading 1: ______________________

____

____

____

Heading 2: ______________________

____

____

____

Heading 3: ______________________

____

____

____

Internet

Name ______________________ Date ____________

Horses

Pony Wanted

You would like to buy a pony. Think about why a person might need a pony and then write a want ad for a newspaper. How will you take care of the pony? What makes you the best owner for this pony? Use persuasive words to convince the person to sell you the pony. Read pages 24–25 for more information.

WANTED: PONY

____

____

____

____

____

____

____

____

____

____

____

Name ______________________ Date ____________

Be a Photojournalist

Look at the photographs throughout *Horses*. You should notice that some of the pictures show how strong workhorses are. Others show off the beautiful colors. The photos on pages 26–27 show the wildness of feral mustangs. Imagine that you want photos of the feral ponies in Britain. Write a note describing the type of photo that you would want to show off the ponies' unique qualities. Be sure to note what the background should look like and what the photo should show the ponies doing.

Assignment: Feral Ponies of Britain

Notes: ______________________

____

____

____

____

____

____

Name ______________________ Date ____________

Today and Yesterday

In *Horses*, you have read many different ways in which humans have used horses. Some of these examples are from the present. Some of these examples are from the past.

Draw and label three ways people used horses years ago.

Name ________________________ Date ____________

Draw and label ways people use horses today.

Dear Editor

Look at the drawings you created about horses and people yesterday and today on pages 273–274. Pretend that you visited a farm that used horses. Write a letter to the editor of your school newspaper about your experience. Explain why you think the school should go to this farm for a field trip.

Dear Editor,

____

____

____

____

____

____

____

____

____

____

____

Sincerely,

____

Name ______________________ Date ____________

My Library

Write a review of *Horses*. Fill in from one to five stars to rate the book. Explain one thing you learned that was interesting. Then explain what you thought of the book. Use examples from the book to support the ideas in your review.

Horses

I rate this book: ☆ ☆ ☆ ☆ ☆

____

____

____

____

____

____

____

____

____

____

____

Name ______________________ Date ____________

The World According to Humphrey

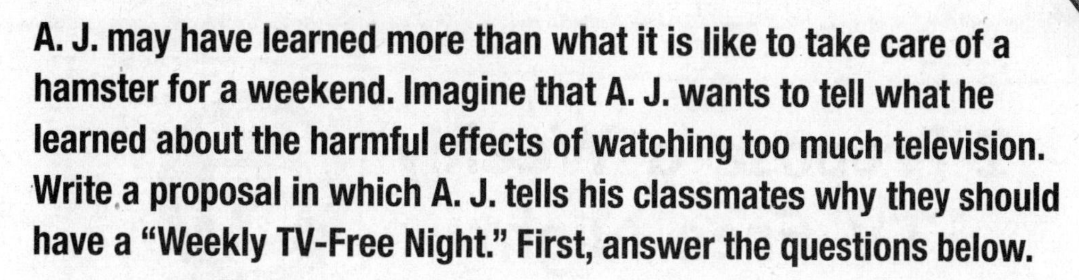

A. J.'s Proposal

A. J. may have learned more than what it is like to take care of a hamster for a weekend. Imagine that A. J. wants to tell what he learned about the harmful effects of watching too much television. Write a proposal in which A. J. tells his classmates why they should have a "Weekly TV-Free Night." First, answer the questions below.

Reread pages 628 and 632–633. How have A. J.'s nighttime activities changed?

____

____

____

Look at the illustrations on pages 628 and 633. How does the family look in each illustration?

____

____

____

How can too much television affect a family?

____

____

Write A. J.'s proposal for a "Weekly TV-Free Night" to his fellow classmates. What might A. J. say about watching too much television based on what happened over the weekend? Give A. J.'s argument about why it would be good for everyone to turn off the television at least one night a week. Use details from the story to support A. J.'s argument.

I Propose a Weekly TV-Free Night

TV

____

____

____

____

____

____

____

____

____

____

____

Name ______________________ Date ____________

The World According to Humphrey
Vocabulary Strategies: Using Context

Using Context

figure	might	cover	racket
block	corner	pet	combination

Each sentence below contains a multiple-meaning word. Read each sentence. Fill in the circle next to the definition that fits the way the word is used in the sentence.

1. Alma was able to figure out a hard math problem.
   ○ **A.** understand ○ **B.** a shape
2. The two friends lived on the same block.
   ○ **A.** get in the way of ○ **B.** a section of a street
3. He used all his might to pick up the heavy box.
   ○ **A.** maybe ○ **B.** strength
4. I will put my desk in the corner of the room.
   ○ **A.** place where two walls meet ○ **B.** to trap
5. The music was a combination of rock and jazz styles.
   ○ **A.** numbers used to open a lock ○ **B.** a mix or blend of things
6. You should cover your head with a hat when it is cold.
   ○ **A.** a blanket ○ **B.** to put something on top of something else
7. My friend asked if he could pet my dog.
   ○ **A.** stroke an animal ○ **B.** an animal kept by humans
8. I left my racket at a friend's house.
   ○ **A.** something used to play tennis ○ **B.** a loud noise

Name ______________________ Date __________

Words with VCV Pattern

Basic 1–10. Read the paragraph. Write the Basic Word that best replaces the underlined word or words in each sentence.

Moving to a new place was an (1) important occasion in my life. I was only a (2) person who studies when my family shot into space. We flew to the (3) heavenly body Zondora. The shuttle flight from Earth to Zondora was very (4) fast. We stayed in a hovering (5) resort. The workers there were (6) respectful and helpful. Zondora has large lava pits and (7) icy plains. It has a large shield to (8) protect against anything that could harm the planet. If the shield is threatened, a (9) device that makes a loud noise blares. The people (10) join together to keep Zondora safe.

1. ______________ 6. ______________
2. ______________ 7. ______________
3. ______________ 8. ______________
4. ______________ 9. ______________
5. ______________ 10. ______________

Challenge 11–14. Your brother and your best friend are on opposing teams of a football game. Write a journal entry that tells how you cheered for both teams. Use four of the Challenge Words. Write on a separate sheet of paper.

Spelling Words

1. event
2. humor
3. rapid
4. music
5. relief
6. planet
7. detail
8. unite
9. frozen
10. figure
11. siren
12. polite
13. hotel
14. protest
15. punish
16. defend
17. relay
18. habit
19. student
20. moment

Challenge

rumor
jealous
license
image
rival

Name ____________________ Date __________

Spelling Word Sort

The World According to Humphrey
Spelling: Words with VCV Pattern

Write each Basic Word beside the correct heading.

VC/V: Divide after the consonant	**Basic Words:** **Challenge Words:** **Possible Selection Words:**
V/CV: Divide before the consonant	**Basic Words:** **Challenge Words:** **Possible Selection Words:**

Spelling Words

1. event
2. humor
3. rapid
4. music
5. relief
6. planet
7. detail
8. unite
9. frozen
10. figure
11. siren
12. polite
13. hotel
14. protest
15. punish
16. defend
17. relay
18. habit
19. student
20. moment

Challenge

rumor
jealous
license
image
rival

Challenge Add the Challenge Words to your Word Sort.

Connect to Reading Look through "The World According to Humphrey." Find words that have the VC / V and V / CV spelling pattern on this page. Add them to your Word Sort.

Name ______________________________ Date ____________

Proofreading for Spelling

Find the misspelled words and circle them. Write them correctly on the lines below.

What a releef to be back at school! If only I could talk, I would ask Mrs. Brisbane for a momint of her time to protes the weekend's arrangement at the Thomases' house. Don't get me wrong now. The family treated me nicely, and they did not punich me when water spilled inside my cage. They actually thought it was an exciting ivent! Mr. Thomas thinks he has a great sense of humer, but here's a small deteil that I'll only share with Mrs. Brisbane: his jokes are the corniest on the planit. Mrs. Thomas is very pollite, but her taste in muzic is simply awful. She also has a very bad habet of serving frozin pizza that isn't cooked through. "Look at our little hamster go!" Mrs. Brisbane said. "He's running a relae race on his wheel. I think he's glad to be back."

1. ______________________
2. ______________________
3. ______________________
4. ______________________
5. ______________________
6. ______________________
7. ______________________
8. ______________________
9. ______________________
10. ______________________
11. ______________________
12. ______________________
13. ______________________

Spelling Words

1. event
2. humor
3. rapid
4. music
5. relief
6. planet
7. detail
8. unite
9. frozen
10. figure
11. siren
12. polite
13. hotel
14. protest
15. punish
16. defend
17. relay
18. habit
19. student
20. moment

Challenge

rumor
jealous
license
image
rival

Name ______________________ Date ____________

Comparative Forms of Adjectives

A **comparative adjective** compares one person, place, or thing to another. To form a comparative adjective, you can usually add *-er* to the adjective. If the adjective ends in *y*, change the *y* to *i* before adding *-er*.

adjective	**comparative adjective**
Josh is tall.	Jacob is taller than Josh.
The weather is dry today.	The weather is drier today than yesterday.

Thinking Questions
Are there two persons, places, or things being compared? Does the adjective end in -er *or use* more?

1–4. Write the comparative form of the adjective in each sentence.

1. I think that spring feels (warm) ____________ than winter.
2. My dog seems hungry, but your dog looks ____________ .
3. Maddie is short, but Cindy is ____________ .
4. Her song is lovely, but I think your song sounds ____________ .

Some comparative adjectives are formed by adding the word *more*. Usually longer adjectives form the comparative this way.

Joe is more polite than Henry.

5–8. Write the comparative form of each adjective.

5. Sally felt (miserable) ______________ when she knew she had the flu.
6. That company is (efficient) ______________ than its competitor.
7. Will you feel (comfortable) ______________ sitting here?
8. Tonight's dinner tastes (delicious) ______________ than last night's.

Name ____________________ Date ____________

Superlative Forms of Adjectives

When we use adjectives to compare more than two persons, places, or things, we use the superlative form of the adjective. To form a **superlative adjective**, add *-est* or write *most* before the adjective.

Adjective	Comparative	Superlative
happy	happier	happiest
complex	more complex	most complex

Emily is luckier than Mary, but Alyssa is the luckiest of all.

Without a map, Gregory is more confused than Lew, but Edwin is the most confused.

Thinking Questions
Are there more than two persons, places, or things being compared? Does the adjective end in -est *or use* most*?*

1–5. Write the correct form of the adjective in parentheses to complete the sentence.

1. A rose is pretty, but Tom thinks an orchid is (pretty) ____________
2. Susan says that of all the flowers, the peony is the (pretty) ____________
3. This tulip is the (bright) ____________ shade of red I've ever seen.
4. Carrie told him that lavender smells (wonderful) ____________
5. Trees grow the (tall) ____________ of all plants.

Name ______________________ Date ____________

Comparative and Superlative Forms of Adverbs

Adverbs often work with verbs and tell how, when, or where an action happens. They are used with action verbs, and many end with *-ly*. A **comparative adverb** compares the action of two or more things. The word *more* is often used. A **superlative adverb** compares the action of more than two things. The word *most* is often used.

Adverb	**Comparative**	**Superlative**
slowly	more slowly	most slowly
soon	sooner	soonest
promptly	more promptly	most promptly

Thinking Questions
Does the adverb end in -ly*? Is the word* more *or* most *added?*

Use a comparative or superlative adverb for each blank below. Use the list on the right to help you complete the sentences.

louder
loudest
more quickly
most quickly
more completely
most completely
closer
closest
harder
hardest
faster
fastest

1. Although many musicians were loud, Donald played the trumpet __________.
2. Sarah could add numbers __________ than her brother.
3. Jerry ran __________ than his best friend.
4. Of all my friends, Carmin lives __________.
5. Marty worked __________ on the project than his partner.
6. Jeremy answered the question __________ of the three contestants.

Name ______________________ Date ____________

Prepositions and Prepositional Phrases

Preposition	Prepositional Phrase
from	Removing a wild animal *from* its home is not wise.

Underline the preposition twice and the rest of the prepositional phrase once in each sentence.

1. The young turtles stepped slowly into the busy, dangerous road.
2. Ms. Roland spotted the three turtles on her long walk.
3. She treats all animals with respect and kindness.
4. She carried the young turtles to safety.
5. The tiny creatures had wandered from the green, grassy marsh.
6. The marsh beside the forest was a better home than the highway!

Combine each pair of sentences. Write the new sentence on the line. Capitalize and punctuate correctly.

7. Ms. Roland hummed as she walked. She walked to her home.

____

8. She fed her fish and watched them. They swam around their tank.

____

9. You should be happy. You should be happy you live in a safe home.

____

Name ______________________ Date ____________

Word Choice

Using more exact comparative and superlative adjectives and adverbs can make your writing more interesting.

Less Exact	More Exact
Dinner smells better than lunch.	Dinner smells spicier and more delicious than lunch.
The big box is the heaviest.	The big box is the most impossible to fit!

Rewrite each sentence to make it more interesting. Try to use more exact adjectives and adverbs.

1. My favorite star is brighter than a light bulb.

____

2. It is maybe the brightest star.

____

3. Don't you think the sun shines more clearly than your star?

____

4. The sun seems so strong to us because it is the closest to us.

____

5. The sun's role in our lives is bigger than the moon's.

____

6. Sun energy is even better than wind energy.

____

Focus Trait: Evidence

The audience will better understand your ideas if you provide relevant evidence in your writing. All evidence should support the main idea and give details about the topic.

Read the paragraph below. Circle the sentence that would make the best topic sentence to start the paragraph. Underline two details that do not belong in the paragraph.

One of the earliest toothbrushes was called the "chew stick." It was made from a twig about the size of a pencil. One end of the twig was pointed. The other end was chewed until it became soft and brushlike. People brushed with the chewed end. They cleaned between their teeth with the pointed end. New Orleans dentist Levi Spear Parmly (1790–1859) is credited as the inventor of modern dental floss. You might be surprised to learn that people have been using toothbrushes for thousands and thousands of years. The Chinese were the first to make and use toothbrushes with bristles. The handle was carved from bone or bamboo. The bristles were made from animal hair and then attached to one end of the handle. These stiff bristles did a better job cleaning teeth than the chew stick. The first nylon toothbrush was called Doctor West's Miracle Toothbrush.

Name ________________________ Date ____________

I Could Do That!
Esther Morris Gets
Women the Vote

Independent Reading

I Could Do That! Esther Morris Gets Women the Vote

Interview with Mrs. Esther Morris

A reporter has come to interview Mrs. Esther Morris, the first woman to hold public office in America. Help complete the interview by answering the questions below.

Esther, your mother died when you were very young. What effect did your mother's death have on you?

Reread page 657 to give Esther's answer.

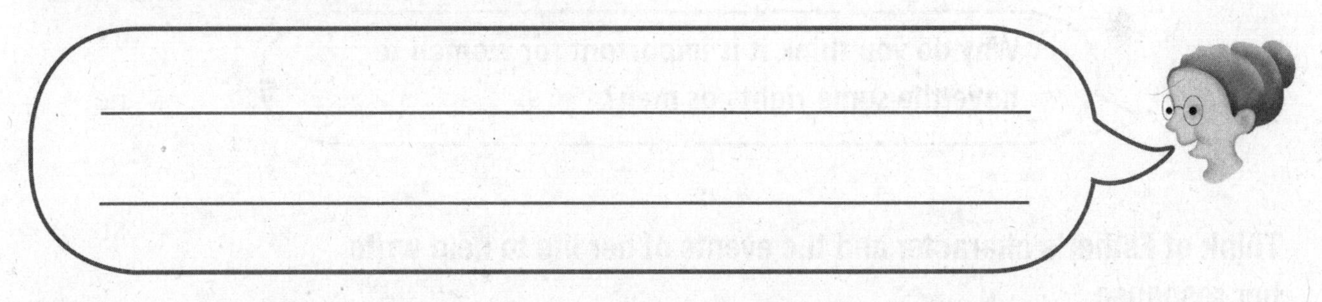

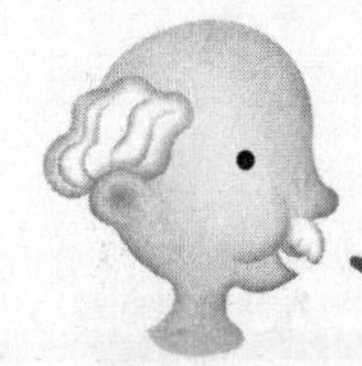

Why did you start your own business at such a young age?

Reread the first paragraph of page 658 to give Esther's answer.

Name ______________________ Date ____________

I Could Do That! Esther Morris Gets Women the Vote

Independent Reading

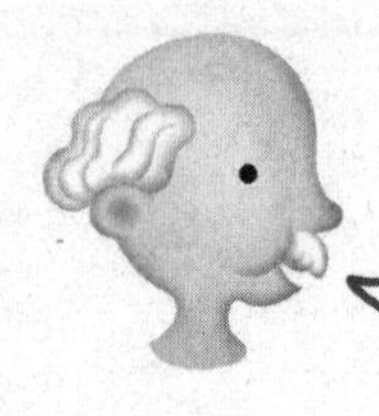

After your husband's death, you moved to Illinois to reclaim his land. The law kept you from owning the land because you were a woman. What effect did this have on you?

Reread page 659. What effect might this have had on Esther? Use these answers to give Esther's response.

Why do you think it is important for women to have the same rights as men?

Think of Esther's character and the events of her life to help write her response.

Name ______________________ Date __________

Adages and Proverbs

I Could Do That!
Vocabulary Strategies:
Adages and Proverbs

Underline the adage or proverb in each sentence. Then explain what it means in your own words.

1. Esther realized it's never too late to right a wrong.

   ____

2. When Esther wanted to get the right to vote, she knew that the longest journey starts with a single step.

   ____

3. In the Wyoming Territory, Esther found that a woman's work is never done.

   ____

4. Esther would not have listened to someone who said, "Don't rock the boat."

   ____

5. For Esther, there was no time like the present for getting the right to vote.

   ____

6. Esther seemed to believe that if at first you don't succeed, you should try again.

   ____

7. Esther proved that where there's a will, there's a way.

   ____

Name ______________________________ Date ____________

VCCV and VCV Patterns

Basic 1–11. Complete the puzzle by writing the Basic Word for each clue.

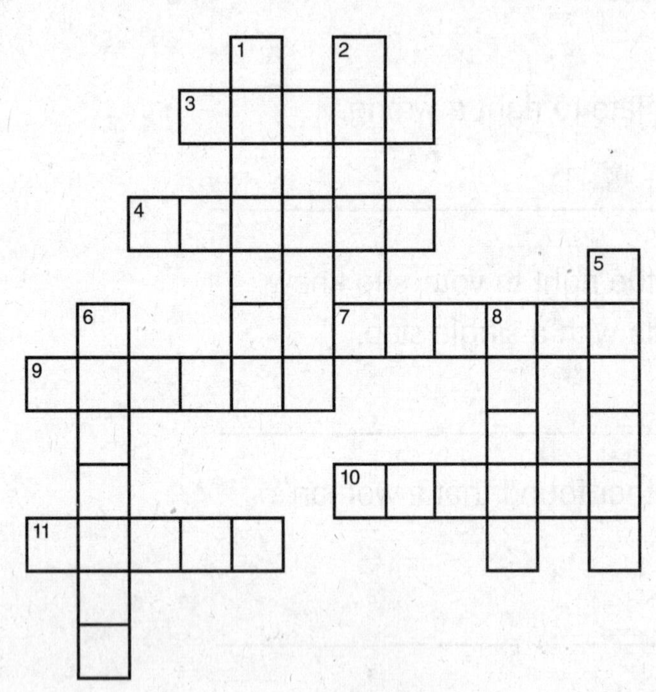

Across

3. in front of
4. having a space or opening inside
7. shiny, white metal
9. something given in return for a worthy act
10. sixty seconds
11. in math, to take away from

Down

1. something that protects or covers
2. very well known
5. not working properly
6. person qualified to treat people's teeth
8. to believe to be of worth

Challenge 12–14. You just watched a movie called "I Could Do That!" Describe a scene from the movie. Use three Challenge Words. Write on a separate sheet of paper.

Spelling Words

1. dentist
2. final
3. finish
4. narrow
5. shelter
6. ahead
7. corner
8. hollow
9. divide
10. famous
11. recent
12. silver
13. capture
14. cabin
15. dinner
16. minus
17. minute
18. value
19. reward
20. broken

Challenge

decent
secure
standard
frontier
stampede

Name ______________________ Date ____________

I Could Do That!
Spelling: VCCV and VCV Patterns

Spelling Word Sort

Write each Basic Word beside the correct heading.

VC/CV Pattern: Divide Between the Consonants	**Basic Words:** **Challenge Words:** **Possible Selection Words:**
V/CV Pattern: Divide Before the Consonant	**Basic Words:** **Challenge Words:** **Possible Selection Words:**
VC/V Pattern: Divide After the Consonant	**Basic Words:** **Possible Selection Words:**

Spelling Words

1. dentist
2. final
3. finish
4. narrow
5. shelter
6. ahead
7. corner
8. hollow
9. divide
10. famous
11. recent
12. silver
13. capture
14. cabin
15. dinner
16. minus
17. minute
18. value
19. reward
20. broken

Challenge

decent
secure
standard
frontier
stampede

Challenge Add the Challenge Words to your Word Sort.

Connect to Reading Look through "I Could Do That!" Find words that have the VCCV or VCV patterns on this page. Add them to your Word Sort.

Name ________________________ Date ____________

Proofreading for Spelling

I Could Do That!
Spelling: VCCV and VCV Patterns

Find the misspelled words and circle them. Write them correctly on the lines below.

Susan B. Anthony was a famus woman at the end of the nineteenth century. In 1872, she broke the law by casting a vote in a presidential election. She knew that the resent Civil War had shown the valew of voting, a reaward that should be given to all people, not just men. She would devide her time between big cities and small towns. Susan wanted to captore the attention of women and convince them of their rights. Women would finich household chores early to host a tea or invite friends to diner just to discuss what Susan had to say. Susan would speak anywhere—a big meeting hall or a small kabin. Everywhere she went, there were crowds. Some women waited in line around the cornur for hours, while others stood along the nerrow hallways to catch Susan's finel words about civil and political rights.

1. ________ 7. ________
2. ________ 8. ________
3. ________ 9. ________
4. ________ 10. ________
5. ________ 11. ________
6. ________ 12. ________

Spelling Words

1. dentist
2. final
3. finish
4. narrow
5. shelter
6. ahead
7. corner
8. hollow
9. divide
10. famous
11. recent
12. silver
13. capture
14. cabin
15. dinner
16. minus
17. minute
18. value
19. reward
20. broken

Challenge

decent
secure
standard
frontier
stampede

Name ______________________ Date ____________

Contractions with *not*

A **negative** is a word that makes a sentence mean *no*. A negative contraction is made with a verb and the negative word *not*. An apostrophe takes the place of the letter *o* in each contraction with *not*.

contraction with *not*

Esther isn't at home, but she may be at the hat shop.

Thinking Question
What word is a contraction made with a verb and the negative word not*?*

1–8. Write the contraction for the underlined word or words in each sentence.

1. There are not any blue hats in the window today.

____

2. This hat does not have a ribbon. __________

3. That small cowboy hat will not fit Mr. Fox's head.

____

4. There were not many customers today. __________

5. The seamstress cannot find her sewing needle.

____

6. Please do not sit on my hat. __________

7. Ms. Kelly did not buy the hat with red stripes.

____

8. Esther had not made a hat this large before. __________

Name ______________________ Date ____________

Using Negatives

I Could Do That!
Grammar: Negatives

The words *no, no one, nobody, none, nothing, nowhere,* and *never* are negatives. A contraction with a verb and the word *not* is also a negative. When making a negative statement, make sure to use just one negative.

positive
I understand the candidates' opinions.
negative
I don't understand the candidates' opinions.
I understand none of the candidates' opinions.

Thinking Questions
What word will change the sentence to have a negative meaning? Does the sentence still make sense?

1–6. Use a negative to change the meaning of the sentence from positive to negative. Write the negative sentence on the line below.

1. Anybody in the fifth grade can run for class president.

____

2. Roger is running for class president.

____

3. Tom has asked Roger if he can be his vice president.

____

4. Myung-Yun always likes to help make campaign posters.

____

5. Everyone is excited about the school elections this year.

____

6. The class president can do something about all of the issues that bother students.

____

____

Name ______________________ Date __________

Avoiding Double Negatives

I Could Do That!
Grammar: Negatives

Words such as *not*, *no*, and *never* are negatives. Using two negatives together is called a **double negative**. Never use two negatives together in a sentence.

double negative

My mother won't tell nobody how she voted.

corrected sentences

My mother won't tell anybody how she voted.
My mother will tell nobody how she voted.

Thinking Question
What two negatives are used together in the sentence?

1–8. Write the correct word shown in parentheses to complete the sentence.

1. There (is, isn't) no presidential candidate that my parents completely support. __________
2. That candidate hasn't said (anything, nothing) about the important issues. __________
3. He doesn't support (any, none) of the laws to help the environment. __________
4. Don't vote for (anyone, no one) without learning his or her political views. __________
5. Doesn't (anybody, nobody) agree with that candidate's views? __________
6. Isn't there (anywhere, nowhere) I can get better information about the candidates? __________
7. The voters (have, haven't) no choice but to support the new law. __________
8. This candidate (has, hasn't) never been honest with the voters. __________

Name ____________________ Date __________

Relative Pronouns and Adverbs

The words *who*, *whose*, *whom*, *which*, and *that* can be used to begin clauses that explain *which one* or *what kind.* Other clauses explain *where*, *when*, and *why* about another clause.

Clause telling what kind of girl Esther was:
Esther was a smart girl **who wanted to do all she could.**

Clause telling why Esther wanted to do things:
When adults said, "Girls don't do that," Esther only wanted to do that thing more.

1–4. Underline the clause that tells which one or what kind. Circle the word that begins the clause.

1. Esther was born into a family that included eleven children.
2. What made Esther different? She was a girl who was eager to learn.
3. As a young woman, Esther ran a millinery business that was very successful.
4. Votes for women was an idea whose time had come.

5–6. Underline the clause that tells where, when, or why. Circle the word that begins the clause.

5. In 1869, when she was fifty-five, Esther and two sons moved to Wyoming Territory.
6. The gold rush town where they settled had many men and few women.

Name ________________________ Date ____________

Conventions

I Could Do That!
Grammar: Connect to Writing

Proofreading can help you make certain that you have used contractions and negatives correctly in your writing.

incorrect, with proofreading marks

Learning to sew ^was ~~wasn't~~ never difficult for Esther.

correct

Learning to sew was never difficult for Esther.

1–6. Correct the use of contractions or double negatives in each sentence. Write the sentence correctly on the line below.

1. Esther doesnt' like that dress pattern.

____

2. Esther never sewed nothing before she was eight.

____

3. She couldn't find no silk for Ms. Kelly's dress.

____

4. Sewing these pants wont take long.

____

5. There isn't no one in town who sews better than Esther.

____

6. The stitching on this shirt isnt neat and even.

____

Name ______________________ Date ____________

I Could Do That!
Writing: Informative Writing

Focus Trait: Elaboration

Using Transition Words

Cause-and-Effect Sentences	Transition Added
When Esther was a girl, only men could vote. Her mother could not vote for president.	When Esther was a girl, only men could vote. **Therefore**, her mother could not vote for president.

Read each pair of sentences. Connect the ideas in the sentences using a cause-and-effect transition word or phrase.

Cause-and-Effect Sentences	Transition Added
1. Esther made nice clothes. Women paid her to make clothes for them.	Esther made nice clothes. __________ women paid her to make clothes for them.
2. Esther heard Susan B. Anthony speaking out about women's rights. She wanted to help women get the vote, too.	Esther heard Susan B. Anthony speaking out about women's rights, __________ she wanted to help women get the vote, too.

Pair/Share **Work with a partner to brainstorm how to add transition words or phrases to make the sentences read smoothly.**

Cause-and-Effect Sentences	Transition Added
3. Esther liked to do things for herself. She painted the sign for her hat shop.	
4. People thought that Esther was too young to run a business. They were shocked to see her open a hat shop.	

The Ever-Living Tree: The Life and Times of a Coast Redwood

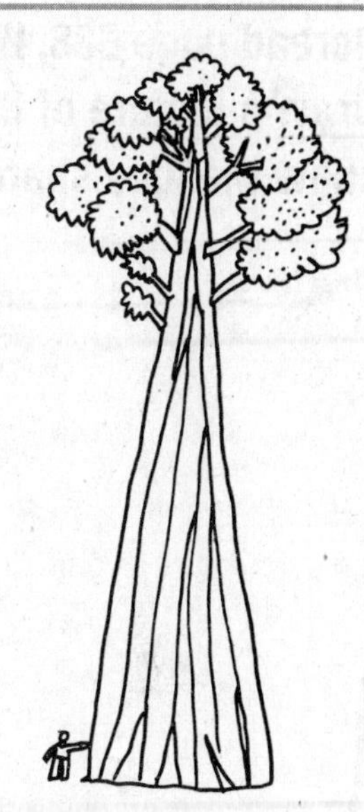

Draw the Idea

Compare the events in the selection "The Ever-Living Tree: The Life and Times of a Coast Redwood."

Turn to page 687. Read the paragraph marked with the icon for Alexander the Great. What is the paragraph mainly about? How does the map help you understand the text?

____

____

Read the next paragraph on page 687 marked with the icon for the sequoia tree. What is the paragraph mainly about? What do the layers of the tree show?

____

____

How are the main ideas of each section similar?

____

____

Why might the author have structured the text this way putting these ideas together?

____

____

Name ______________________ Date ____________

The Ever-Living Tree: The Life and Times of a Coast Redwood

Independent Reading

Reread page 688. How are the ideas of the two sections similar? Draw a picture of the Great Wall of China. Use at least one label to show the idea shared between the sections.

Name ______________________ Date ____________

Prefixes *pre-*, *inter-*, *ex-*

prearrange	interact	intermingle	ex-mayor
precaution	international	exceed	intercontinental

Each sentence shows a word in parentheses with the prefix *pre-*, *inter-*, or *ex-* in parentheses. Use each word in parentheses and your own words to complete each sentence.

1. (prearrange) I will call you to
____
2. (precaution) Buckling your safety belt in the car is
____
3. (interact) When you go to a new school,
____
4. (international) The world-famous film actor was
____
5. (intermingle) Because he's shy, he doesn't like it when
____
6. (exceed) I know that your work will
____
7. (ex-mayor) When the election comes,
____
8. (intercontinental) The family traveled from North America to South America
____

Name ______________________ Date ____________

Words with the VCCV Pattern

Basic 1–10. Write the Basic Word that each sentence describes.

1. No one else knows this.

   ____

2. Cats and dogs have these.

   ____

3. You buy this to see a movie in the theater.

   ____

4. Someone who writes a book is called this.

   ____

5. You can hang this on a wall for decoration.

   ____

6. You can put sand in this at the beach.

   ____

7. People travel into outer space using this.

   ____

8. This is a type of food to eat.

   ____

9. This protects your clothes when you cook.

   ____

10. This is to pick things up and put in one place.

    ____

Challenge 11–14. You have been invited to a friend's party, but you can't attend because you're going to your family reunion that day. Write a letter to your friend explaining why you can't attend the party. Use four Challenge Words. Write on a separate sheet of paper.

Spelling Words

1. poster
2. secret
3. whether
4. author
5. rocket
6. bushel
7. agree
8. bucket
9. ticket
10. declare
11. chicken
12. clothing
13. apron
14. whiskers
15. degree
16. gather
17. achieve
18. rather
19. bracket
20. machine

Challenge

regret
nephew
method
decline
vibrate

Name ______________________ Date __________

Spelling Word Sort

Write each Basic Word beside the correct heading.

V/CCV: Divide before the consonant blend or digraph	**Basic Words:** **Challenge Words:** **Possible Selection Word:**
VCC/V: Divide after the consonant blend or digraph	**Basic Words:** **Challenge Words:** **Possible Selection Words:**

Challenge Add the Challenge Words to your Word Sort.

Connect to Reading Look through "The Ever-Living Tree: The Life and Times of a Coast Redwood." Find words that have the VCCV spelling pattern. Add them to your Word Sort.

Spelling Words

1. poster
2. secret
3. whether
4. author
5. rocket
6. bushel
7. agree
8. bucket
9. ticket
10. declare
11. chicken
12. clothing
13. apron
14. whiskers
15. degree
16. gather
17. achieve
18. rather
19. bracket
20. machine

Challenge

regret
nephew
method
decline
vibrate

Proofreading for Spelling

Find the misspelled words and circle them. Write them correctly on the lines below.

In 1903, Colonel Charles Young was ordered to take his troops to Sequoia National Park. He would rathar have stayed in San Francisco, where the temperature rarely registered a degre under 45 in the winter. But whehter or not he wanted to go, he had to agre to the U.S. Army orders. Traveling on horseback for 16 days, Young and his troopers arrived in Sequoia. They brought clotheng and food. To make sure there was enough to eat, each man had to gathar a bushal of fruit and fill a buket with water. The supplies were so heavy the braket on the shelf broke. The men had no mashine to fix it. Hammer and nails would do. Young and his men were able to acheive their goal of making the wagon road long enough for people to be able to get to the park. Colonel Young, the first African-American superintendent of a national park, could deklare his work a success.

1. ______________ 7. ______________
2. ______________ 8. ______________
3. ______________ 9. ______________
4. ______________ 10. ______________
5. ______________ 11. ______________
6. ______________ 12. ______________

Spelling Words

1. poster
2. secret
3. whether
4. author
5. rocket
6. bushel
7. agree
8. bucket
9. ticket
10. declare
11. chicken
12. clothing
13. apron
14. whiskers
15. degree
16. gather
17. achieve
18. rather
19. bracket
20. machine

Challenge

regret
nephew
method
decline
vibrate

Name ______________________ Date ____________

End of Sentence Punctuation

Different kinds of sentences end with different punctuation marks.

Kind of Sentence	End Punctuation	Example
statement or command	period (.)	Look at this tree. It is more than 500 years old.
question	question mark (?)	Have you ever planted a tree?
exclamation	exclamation mark (!)	What a remarkable life!

1–7. Write the appropriate end mark at the end of each sentence.

1. Many animals live in and on trees _____
2. Do they harm the tree they call home _____
3. For the most part, they do not _____
4. However, some insect pests can kill a tree _____
5. What a spectacular leap that squirrel made _____
6. Look at the top branch of that tree _____
7. Is that a squirrel's nest I see _____

8–11. Rewrite the sentences on the lines. Use capital letters and end marks correctly.

our class is planting trees in the park today can you help us bring a shovel with you we are excited about this project

____

____

____

Name ______________________ Date __________

Capital Letters and Punctuation in Quotations

Use capital letters and punctuation to write direct quotations correctly. Always capitalize the first word of a quotation. Use a comma to separate a quotation from the words that tell who is speaking. Put punctuation inside the last quotation marks.

When a quotation starts a sentence, put a comma at the end of a statement. Use the usual end punctuation for questions and exclamations.

direct quotations
Angela exlaimed, "What a big tree!"
"The redwood is a unique tree," Jee agreed.
"Do you think we can climb it?" asked Angela.

Thinking Questions
What kind of sentence is this quotation? Does the quotation come first or last in the sentence?

1–5. Write the quotations correctly.

1. shall we look for something to eat the woodpecker asked

____

2. the chipmunk asked do you see any acorns

____

3. bugs sound good to me said the woodpecker.

____

4. the chipmunk exclaimed that sounds absolutely awful

____

5. most birds eat worms and bugs said the woodpecker

____

Name ______________________ Date ____________

Punctuation for Effect

Punctuation can show emotion or emphasize an idea.

Ellipses	To show tension, threat	It suddenly grew cold, and a raging wind ripped the branches. . . What would happen?
Exclamation mark (!)	To show surprise	A huge flash lit the forest!
Dash (—)	To emphasize	Lightning struck a pine tree—it was completely shattered in a flash.

1–4. Read each sentence. Rewrite it with appropriate punctuation on the lines. Capitalize the first word in each sentence.

1. we are going to a redwood forest an amazing place and we are really looking forward to it.

____

____

2. whoa look at the size of those creatures

____

____

3. they want to drive through the dark forest that sounds spooky to me

____

____

4. there's a bear coming run

____

____

Name ______________________ Date __________

Ordering Adjectives

Adjectives tell *which one*, *what kind*, or *how many* about a noun or pronoun.

What kind? **Giant** trees may produce tiny seeds.
Which one? **That** huge tree is a redwood.
How many? **Numerous** redwoods were cut down.

When several adjectives describe one noun or pronoun, put them in order by category.

Number or Article	Opinion	Size, shape, age, color	Material	Purpose	Noun
The	beautiful	oval			brooch
One		ancient	gold		coin
Six	talented	young		basketball	players

1–3. Complete each sentence with adjectives that answer the question in parentheses ( ).

1. (what kind?) The little tree spread its ____________ roots far out.
2. (how many?) For ____________ years, the tree remained small.
3. (which one?) ____________ tree is the tallest tree in the forest.

4–5. Choose three adjectives to describe each noun below. Be sure to put the adjectives in the correct order.

4. ________________________ bark

5. ________________________ needles

Conventions

Use quotation marks around the exact words of a speaker. Place punctuation that ends the exact words inside the closing quotation marks. Words that name the speaker are set off by commas if they appear at the beginning or middle of the quotation. They end with a period if they come at the end of the sentence.

"Have you seen my book?" asked Josh.

"I saw it," said Dad, "in the the car."

Josh recalled, "That's right. I took it to our campout last weekend."

Rewrite each sentence to add needed capital letters, quotation marks, and other missing punctuation. Use ellipses (. . .) and exclamation marks (!) for effect, where they are appropriate.

1. you have a lot of big trees in your yard said Jeff

____

2. Marla replied yes and we enjoy the shade they give us

____

3. did you know Marla asked that trees produce oxygen

____

4. wow look at that red-headed woodpecker exclaimed Jeff

____

Focus Trait: Organization

Writing Paragraphs

A paragraph has sentences about one topic, such as how to do something. Writers organize their ideas or instructions to make them clear to the reader. For example, if you write directions, put the steps in the order they should be done. Use process transitions, such as *first* and *next*, to show the sequence of steps.

It is simple to make a tasty French toast breakfast. **First,** beat two eggs and half a cup of milk together until smooth. **Next,** dip each slice of bread into the egg mixture, turning it to coat both sides well. **Finally,** sprinkle cinnamon on the bread. Have an adult fry the slices in hot oil until they are brown.

Read the sentences below. Cross out any sentences that do not belong. Number the steps in order. Then write them in a paragraph on another sheet of paper. Put the directions in the correct order. Add transition words such as *first, next,* and *then*.

How to Plant a Tree

_____ Spread the seedling roots outward and downward while keeping the top of the root even with the top of the hole.

_____ Dig a hole large enough to hold the roots' full length.

_____ Give the planted seedling water and add mulch around its base.

_____ While holding the tree in place, fill the hole with dirt and tamp around the roots with your foot.

_____ Most bare-root seedlings are planted in the winter months.

Name _______________________ Date ___________

Owen & Mzee

Trip to Haller Park

You are a scientist visiting Haller Park to find out more about hippos and tortoises. Take a close look at the following pages: 720 (to find out about where Owen lives), 722 (to find out what the animals eat and how they behave), 724 (for facts about tortoises and hippos).

Based on what you have read, write field notes about your observations. Remember that you are a scientist, so you want to focus on facts. What do you observe?

Name _______________ Date _______________

You focused on the facts—now how about your opinion? Your friends are not sure if they want to make the long trip to Haller Park to see Owen and Mzee. Should they visit? Why or why not? Write a postcard to a friend. Explain why Haller Park is—or is not—a great place to visit!

Name ______________________ Date ____________

Suffixes *-ed, -ly*

wrapped	frequently	displayed	exhausted
normally	naturally	fairly	suffered

1–8 Complete each sentence using a word from the box.

1. It snows ________________ in cold places like Alaska.
2. I would not ________________ be so excited, but today is my birthday.
3. It is important to divide a treat ________________ so that everyone gets the same amount.
4. After running ten miles, she was ________________ .
5. During the spelling bee, he ________________ the embarrassment of being on stage.
6. The books were ________________ in the store window.
7. The actor read his lines very ________________ .
8. ________________ in a warm coat, I went out into the cold December snow.

Name ______________________ Date ____________

Words with VCCCV Pattern

Owen and Mzee
Spelling: Words with VCCCV Pattern

Basic 1–12. Write the Basic Word that belongs in each group.

1. example, model, ____________
2. stock, inventory, ____________
3. describe, clarify, ____________
4. locate, live, ____________
5. traveler, seeker, ____________
6. beast, creature, ____________
7. empire, monarchy, ____________
8. midpoint, halfway, ____________
9. lone, solo, ____________
10. sportsperson, player, ____________
11. finish, conclude, ____________
12. in place of, rather than, ____________

Challenge 13–15. Write an e-mail message to your friend telling about an art exhibit you have seen—perhaps at an art museum, an art fair, or a school art exhibit. Use three Challenge Words. Write on a separate sheet of paper.

Spelling Words

1. hundred
2. supply
3. single
4. middle
5. explain
6. surprise
7. pilgrim
8. sandwich
9. instead
10. complete
11. monster
12. settle
13. address
14. farther
15. sample
16. although
17. turtle
18. athlete
19. orchard
20. kingdom

Challenge

fortress
instant
exclaim
mattress
sculptor

Name ______________________ Date __________

Spelling Word Sort

Owen and Mzee
Spelling: Words with VCCCV Pattern

Write each Basic Word beside the correct heading.

VC/CCV Pattern: Divide before consonant blend or digraph	**Basic Words:** **Challenge Words:** **Possible Selection Words:**
VCC/CV Pattern: Divide after consonant blend or digraph	**Basic Words:** **Challenge Words:** **Possible Selection Words:**

Challenge Add the Challenge Words to your Word Sort.

Connect to Reading Look through "Owen and Mzee: The True Story of a Remarkable Friendship." Find words that have the VCCCV patterns on this page. Add them to your Word Sort.

Spelling Words

1. hundred
2. supply
3. single
4. middle
5. explain
6. surprise
7. pilgrim
8. sandwich
9. instead
10. complete
11. monster
12. settle
13. address
14. farther
15. sample
16. although
17. turtle
18. athlete
19. orchard
20. kingdom

Challenge

fortress
instant
exclaim
mattress
sculptor

Name ________________________ Date ____________

Proofreading for Spelling

Find the misspelled words and circle them. Write them correctly on the lines below.

This is a story about a rare hawksbill tirtle whose adress is Hanauma Bay Nature Preserve in Hawaii. The turtle was seen with a hook caught in its left flipper. Everyone assumed the turtle would die so it was a surprize when a scuba diver spotted it swimming farthur out in the bay. Divers were able to rescue the hawksbill, altheugh the vet's X-ray showed a sengle rusty fishing hook embedded in the animal. The vet decided to cut away as much of the hook as possible insteed of removing it. After the hawksbill was treated with antibiotics, it was released back into Hanauma Bay with "HB" painted on its shell. Several hundrid people visit the bay daily. Some will bring a sandwitch and fruit from a nearby orcherd. They hope to catch a glimpse of "HB" swimming in the midle of the bay.

1. ____________ 7. ____________
2. ____________ 8. ____________
3. ____________ 9. ____________
4. ____________ 10. ____________
5. ____________ 11. ____________
6. ____________

Spelling Words

1. hundred
2. supply
3. single
4. middle
5. explain
6. surprise
7. pilgrim
8. sandwich
9. instead
10. complete
11. monster
12. settle
13. address
14. farther
15. sample
16. although
17. turtle
18. athlete
19. orchard
20. kingdom

Challenge

fortress
instant
exclaim
mattress
sculptor

Name ____________________ Date __________

Commas with Direct Speech and Names

When you write, use a comma to set off the name of a person addressed directly and to set off introductory words such as *yes*, *no*, and *well*.

Yolanda**,** can you tell me about the giant tortoise?
Well**,** the giant tortoise eats both plants and animals.
I wonder**,** Mr. Scorzo**,** if a tortoise is the same as a turtle?

Thinking Questions
Does the sentence include an introductory word or the name of a person being addressed? Does the quotation include words that tell who is speaking?

1–5. Write the sentences correctly. Add commas where they are needed.

1. Yes giant tortoises sleep inside their shells.

____

____

2. Randy have you ever picked up a tortoise?

____

____

3. No I would be afraid it might bite me.

____

____

4. These animals cannot walk fast Brenda though their legs are strong.

____

____

5. Well their legs have to hold up those very heavy shells.

____

____

Name ______________________ Date ____________

Commas in Compound Sentences

A **compound sentence** joins two complete ideas using a coordinating conjunction such as *and*, *but*, *or*, or *so*. Each half of a compound sentence has its own subject and predicate. Use a comma before the conjunction in a compound sentence.

subject **verb** **subject verb**
Hippopotamuses live in lakes and rivers, **but** they graze on land every day.

Thinking Questions
Which word is the coordinating conjunction? Where does the comma go in the sentence?

1–3. Join each pair of sentences using the conjunction in parentheses ( ). Be sure your compound sentence has a comma before the conjunction.

1. Hippos graze for hours each evening. They eat up to 150 pounds of food a day. (and)

____

____

2. Hippos have eyes, ears, and nose on the top of their heads. They can keep most of their body underwater. (so)

____

____

3. Hippos cannot sweat. They keep cool in the mud and water. (but)

____

____

Name ______________________ Date __________

More Uses of Commas

Use a comma to separate the words in a series.

We saw tortoises, hippopotamuses, and birds.

There are sea lions, sea otters, fur seals, and elephant seals at the zoo.

Use a comma between a date and a year.

Today is May 4, 2013.

Use a comma between a city and a state.

I live in Glendale, Arizona.

Thinking Questions
How are commas used to separate items in a series? How are commas used in dates and place names?

1–4. Add commas where they are needed. Write the sentence correctly on the line.

1. My report on the marine sanctuary is due on December 12 2014.

____

____

2. People who drill dump or dig up the sea floor are not allowed in the sanctuary.

____

____

3. The sanctuary is located in Monterey California.

____

4. A layer of fat a thick coat of fur and a dry spot in the sun all help sea mammals to stay warm.

____

____

Name ______________________ Date __________

Interrogative Pronouns and Relative Pronouns and Adverbs

A **dependent clause** has a subject and verb, but it cannot stand alone. A dependent clause is joined to an **independent clause** that expresses a complete thought. The relative pronouns *who*, *whom*, *whose*, *that*, and *which* begin dependent clauses that answer the question *Which one?* or *What kind?* Relative adverbs begin dependent clauses that tell *where*, *when* or *why*. Interrogative pronouns introduce questions.

Dependent clause beginning with relative pronoun

A hippopotamus is a fierce fighter **that** protects its young.

Dependent clause beginning with relative adverb

The mother springs into action **when** her baby is attacked.

Interrogative Pronoun

Which animal do you prefer?

1–8. In each sentence, look for interrogative pronouns, relative pronouns, or relative adverbs. Underline interrogative pronouns. Circle relative adverbs or pronouns, and double underline the dependent clause.

1. Many hippos lost their lives when a tsunami struck the African coast.
2. The only hippo who survived was a six-hundred-pound baby named Owen.
3. Who can help Owen?
4. Rescuers were not sure where Owen should go.
5. Which place became Owen's home?
6. The giant tortoise Mzee at first thought that Owen should leave him alone.
7. The two soon became friends who could not be separated.
8. No one knows for sure why Owen and Mzee became such good friends.

Sentence Fluency

Proofreading can help you make certain that you have used commas correctly in your writing. Using commas makes your writing clear and easy to understand.

Incorrect with proofreading marks

Mark: You know, Dad‸ the population of hippos in Africa has shrunk tremendously.

Dad: That's a serious problem‸ Mark.

Correct

Mark: You know, Dad, the population of hippos in Africa has shrunk tremendously.

Dad: That's a serious problem, Mark.

Activity **This part of a script has 16 missing commas. Add a comma or commas to each part in the script.**

Mark: Yes I agree. Did you know Dad that people are the greatest threat to the hippo population?

Dad: No I wasn't aware of that.

Mark: Well it's true. Hippos are killed for their fat their ivory teeth and because they eat so much grass.

Dad: Is anything being done to save the hippos Mark?

Mark: Yes some of the areas where hippos live are protected.

Dad: Well that makes sense. I think Mark that we should do our part to save the hippos.

Mark: That's a great idea Dad! Let's get a hippo for a pet!

Dad: No let's not. You were kidding weren't you Mark?

Name ______________________ Date __________

Owen and Mzee
Writing: Informative Writing

Focus Trait: Purpose

Finding and Using the Best Information

Source	Information
Encyclopedia	Articles about many different topics
Atlas	Maps of places all over the world
Internet	Web sites of organizations as well as electronic reference materials
Interviewing an expert	Unique information
Newspaper and magazine articles	Up-to-date information on different topics
Nonfiction books	Facts about real people, places, and things

1–3. Answer the following questions about using sources to find the best information.

1. Maggie is researching tortoises. She wants to answer the question, *Where do tortoises live?*

a. Which source could Maggie use? ______________

b. What other question could she answer by using this source?

____

2. Luis is researching how zoos are run. He wants to answer the question, *How many people work at the zoo in my city?*

a. Which source should Luis use? ______________

b. What other question could he answer with this source?

____

3. Nina is researching Kenya. She wants to answer the question, *What ocean is closest to Kenya?*

a. Which source should Nina use? ______________

b. What other question could she answer with this source?

____

The Fun They Had: from *Isaac Asimov: The Complete Stories*

I Want a Live Teacher!

Margie would like to try learning the old-fashioned way, from a live teacher. She is writing an e-mail to the Inspector to try and convince him to give up the mechanical teacher. But Margie understands that she should use language with which the Inspector is comfortable.

Look closely at the way the Inspector talks on page 749. Help Margie finish her e-mail using the formal language that the Inspector uses.

New Message

To: **Inspector**

From: **Margie**

Subject: **Replacing the Mechanical Teacher**

Dear Inspector:

I am writing to you to suggest that you remove the mechanical teacher from my home and let me learn from a human teacher instead.

____

____

____

____

Sincerely,

Margie

Name ______________________ Date ____________

The Fun They Had: from *Isaac Asimov: The Complete Stories*
Independent Reading

Margie would like Tommy to take classes with her from a human teacher. She e-mails him to ask for his help in changing to a human teacher.

Look closely at the way Margie and Tommy talk to each other on page 750. Help Margie finish her e-mail using the informal language that they use.

New Message

To: **Tommy**

From: **Margie**

Subject: **Replacing the Mechanical Teacher**

Hey Tommy!

I have an idea that you can help me with. We could get rid of the stupid mechanical teacher and get a real person to teach us!

____

____

____

____

____

____

____

Your buddy,

Margie

Name ______________________ Date ____________

Greek and Latin Word Parts *meter*, *therm*, *aud*, *fac*

The words in the box each have a part that comes from Greek or Latin. In Greek, *therm* means "heat" and *meter* means "measure." In Latin, *aud* means "to hear" and *fac* means "to make" or "to do."

thermometer	barometer	audible	manufacture
thermal	chronometer	audience	factory

1–8 Write the correct word from the box to complete each sentence.

1. When the concert ended, the orchestra stood and bowed to the ______________.
2. The captain used a ______________ to help determine the ship's time of departure.
3. The automobile plant will ______________ cars.
4. Check the ______________ outside to see if you need a sweater.
5. Mr. Wilson makes chocolate candy at his ______________.
6. The weather forecast predicts rain, because the ______________ reading shows a drop in air pressure.
7. The park ranger wears his ______________ socks in winter to keep warm.
8. With everyone talking at once, Solomon's voice was barely ______________ above the noise.

Words with VV Pattern

Basic 1–10. Write the Basic Words that fit the clues to complete the crossword puzzle.

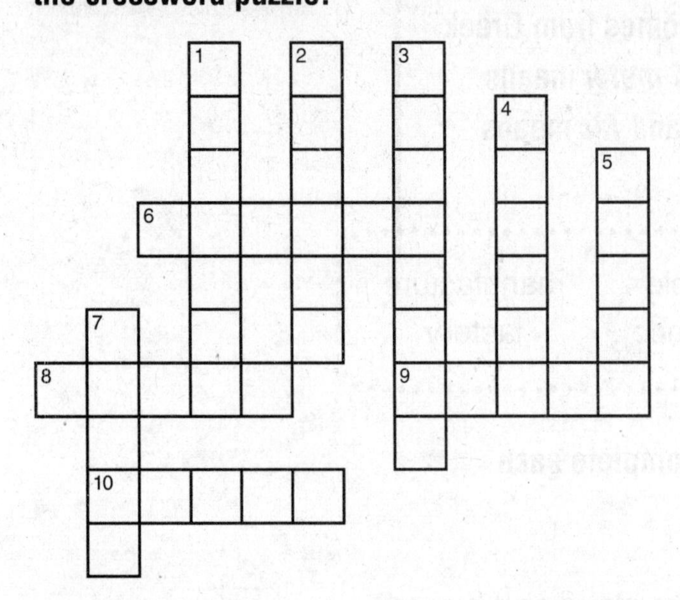

Across

6. piece of rock flying through space
8. tape that records TV programs
9. where cowhands show skills
10. equipment used to receive signals

Down

1. study of natural things
2. food made from grain
3. second month of the year
4. punctuation mark
5. large musical instrument
7. daily written record

Challenge 11–14. You are asked to be student teacher for your geography class today. Give instructions to the class about a writing assignment in which they describe the features of the region in which they live. Use four of the Challenge Words. Write on a separate sheet of paper.

Spelling Words

1. idea
2. lion
3. usual
4. radio
5. liar
6. poem
7. India
8. piano
9. January
10. quiet
11. poet
12. science
13. diary
14. violin
15. period
16. February
17. cereal
18. video
19. meteor
20. rodeo

Challenge

variety
gradual
geography
diagram
punctuate

Name ______________________ Date ____________

Spelling Word Sort

Write each Basic Word beside the correct heading.

VV Pattern with two syllables: Divide between the vowels	**Basic Words:** **Possible Selection Words:**
VV Pattern with three syllables: Divide between the vowels	**Basic Words:** **Challenge Words:**
VV Pattern with four syllables: Divide between the vowels	**Basic Words:** **Challenge Words:** **Possible Selection Words:**

Spelling Words

1. idea
2. lion
3. usual
4. radio
5. liar
6. poem
7. India
8. piano
9. January
10. quiet
11. poet
12. science
13. diary
14. violin
15. period
16. February
17. cereal
18. video
19. meteor
20. rodeo

Challenge

variety
gradual
geography
diagram
punctuate

Challenge Add the Challenge Words to your Word Sort.

Connect to Reading Look through "The Fun They Had." Find words that have the VV patterns on this page. Add them to your Word Sort.

Proofreading for Spelling

Find the misspelled words and circle them. Write them correctly on the lines below.

It was in Janeary that Talia got the idear to enter the Galactic Music Contest. She wrote a composition for her violen using a pome for inspiration. It was early Febuary when she heard.

"Mamma, guess what?" said Talia, smiling. "I placed in the contest. I have to go to Indea for the final competition. I may get to see a lyin there!"

"That's wonderful news," said Mrs. Simms as she handed Talia the sereal.

Talia left the next morning on the shuttle. Everyone was quiat and focused on the captain's vidio. She explained that in the usueal way, after blast-off, they would shut off the engines to conserve fuel and switch to solar power. As Talia looked out the window, she saw a metear streak past her. To her, that was a sign of good luck!

1. ______________ 7. ______________
2. ______________ 8. ______________
3. ______________ 9. ______________
4. ______________ 10. ______________
5. ______________ 11. ______________
6. ______________ 12. ______________

Spelling Words

1. idea
2. lion
3. usual
4. radio
5. liar
6. poem
7. India
8. piano
9. January
10. quiet
11. poet
12. science
13. diary
14. violin
15. period
16. February
17. cereal
18. video
19. meteor
20. rodeo

Challenge

variety
gradual
geography
diagram
punctuate

Capitalization and Writing Titles

Capitalize important words in the titles of movies, books, chapters, and articles in a newspaper or magazine. Short words such as *in*, *if*, *of*, *a*, and *the* are not capitalized unless they are the first word in the title.

When writing the title of a shorter work, such as a story or news article, use quotation marks. When writing the title of a longer work, such as a book, magazine, or movie, underline the title.

book title	**story**
A Pizza for Jin	"The Diary of a Mouse"

Thinking Questions
Which words in this title should be capitalized? Does the title name a long work or a short work?

1–4. Rewrite each sentence. Add capital letters, underlining, and punctuation where they are needed.

1. The headline in Friday's newspaper read "clowns lead parade."

____

____

2. the little mermaid is my little sister's favorite movie.

____

____

3. Jesse's story about his trip to Mexico was called "crossing the border."

____

____

4. benson elementary wins trophy was the front page headline in the school paper.

____

____

Name ______________________ Date __________

End Punctuation

The Fun They Had
Grammar: Proper Mechanics

The punctuation at the end of a sentence helps to show its meaning. Use a period (.) at the end of a statement or a command. Use a question mark (?) at the end of a question and an exclamation mark (!) to show strong feeling.

declarative	I like to play basketball.
imperative	Hand me the ball, please.
interrogative	What is the score?
exclamatory	What a great game!

Thinking Questions
What kind of sentence is it? Does the sentence tell something, ask a question, or show excitement?

1–8. Add the correct end mark for each sentence. Write *declarative*, *interrogative*, *imperative*, or *exclamatory* on the line.

1. A voice command can make the mechanical dog walk and sit ______________
2. Insert a quarter into the machine ______________
3. How many centuries have passed since the Revolutionary War ______________
4. The building inspector will come here to check next week ______________
5. Your picture is amazing ______________
6. What a waste of time this is ______________
7. How much progress have you made with your work ______________
8. Try not to miss your bus ______________

Name ______________________ Date __________

Commas Before Coordinating Conjunctions

A compound sentence joins two independent clauses using the coordinating conjunctions *and*, *but*, *or*, *nor*, *for*, or *so*. Use a comma before the conjunction.

The children were curious about the book**, for** they had never seen one.
Children can learn in a classroom**, or** they can learn through computer lessons.

Thinking Questions
How many independent clauses are in the sentence? What word should connect the clauses?

1–4. Join each pair of sentences to make a compound sentence using the conjunction shown in parentheses. Use commas correctly.

1. Computers are here to stay. They run many systems in our society. (and)

____

____

2. Schools might become unnecessary. Each child may be taught by a machine. (for)

____

____

3. Any book could be put on a computer. Books might also disappear. (so)

____

4. Computer school would be convenient. I would miss books and teachers. (but)

____

____

Name ______________________ Date ___________

Use Quotation Marks and Other Punctuation Marks

When writing someone's exact words, enclose them in quotation marks (""). Capitalize the first word of a quotation. Use a comma to separate a quotation from the words that tell who is speaking. Put end marks inside the last quotation marks. When a quotation starts a sentence, put a comma at the end of a statement instead of a period. If the quotation ends with a question mark or exclamation point, a comma is not used.

Tommy cried, "Look! I found a real book!"
"Where on Earth did you find that?" asked Margie.
"I searched for days," Tommy replied.

1–5. Rewrite each quotation. Add the punctuation marks and capital letters that are needed.

1. My computerized teacher is broken said Margie

____

2. Why don't we read this book instead suggested Tommy.

____

3. But it's so heavy exclaimed Margie.

____

4. Tommy said I like turning the paper pages.

____

5. Margie added they feel cool and crisp.

____

Name ______________________ Date __________

Lesson 25
READER'S NOTEBOOK

The Fun They Had
Grammar: Connect to Writing

Conventions

Incorrect Mechanics	Correct Mechanics
At last! the day of the science fair has finally arrived and everyones excited. mr. joness class will present it's project first? Our class will be last.	At last! The day of the science fair has finally arrived, and everyone's excited. Mr. Jones's class will present its project first. Our class will be last.

1–4. Rewrite the sentences on the lines below. Use the correct capitalization and punctuation.

1. dont forget to bring treats to school on Friday. they are for Miss Smiths birthday party

____

____

2. simons boots were covered with mud they were also filthy and smelly

____

____

3. be careful didnt I tell you the sidewalk was slippery its covered with ice, too

____

____

4. kim wrote a scary story about an imaginary friend named Bindi its called the secret staircase

____

____

Name ______________________ Date ____________

Focus Trait: Elaboration

Using Precise Language

Sentence Using General Language	Sentence Using Precise Language
The computer screen said things, and Margie put her work into a slot.	The computer's monitor flashed commands, and Margie slid her homework on a disk into a gleaming slot.

1–4. The sentences below are vague and overly general. Rewrite each sentence to use precise language about computers. Use some words from the box to help you be more precise. If necessary, look up these words in a dictionary.

browser	microchip	data	memory	hard drive	Internet
memory	monitor	software	CPU	keyboard	browse

1. A computer stores information and lets users find more information.

____

____

2. A computer's brain is on these little pieces that carry electricity and hold information.

____

____

3. A computer contains programs that tell it what to do.

____

____

4. Information appears on a screen.

____

____

Name ______________________ Date ____________

The Girl Who Loved Spiders

Dear Dr. Help

Imagine that Luis is so afraid of spiders he writes to an advice columnist for help just after he moves to Florida. Take a close look at pages 4 and 5. What would Luis say about why he is afraid of spiders?

Dear Dr. Help,

____

____

____

____

____

____

____

____

How can I get over my fear of spiders?

Thanks,

Luis

Name ______________________ Date ____________

Now take a close look at pages 7, 9, and 11. Imagine that you are the advice columnist responding to Luis. Using what you learned from the selection, what would you tell Luis?

Dear Luis,

____

____

____

____

____

____

____

____

Good luck!

Dr. Help

Name ______________________ Date __________

Final Schwa + /r/ Sounds

Basic 1–16. Write the Basic Word that best fits each clue.

1. One of five digits on each hand: __ __ (__) __ __ __
2. A person who acts in a play: __ __ __ (__) __
3. A kind act that helps a friend: __ __ (__) __ __
4. Disturb: __ __ __ __ (__) __
5. Provides power to a car: (__) __ __ __ __
6. A sign with words or a design: (__) __ __ __ __ __
7. A body temperature higher than normal: __ (__) __ __ __
8. Shows your reflection: __ __ __ (__) __ __
9. Treats people who are sick: (__) __ __ __ __ __
10. Come into: (__) __ __ __ __
11. Part of a shirt that fits around your neck: (__) __ __ __ __ __
12. Sprays water to clean: __ __ __ __ (__) __
13. A person's state of mind: __ __ (__) __ __ __
14. Person who begs for a living: (__) __ __ __ __ __
15. Can be worn for warmth: __ __ (__) __ __ __ __
16. Hard work: __ __ __ __ (__)

Now write the circled letters in order to name two months of the year.

Answer: __ __ __ __ __ __ __ __ and __ __ __ __ __ __ __ __

Challenge 17–18. Write a sentence using two of the Challenge Words. Write on a separate sheet of paper.

Spelling Words

Basic

1. enter
2. banner
3. sugar
4. shower
5. motor
6. collar
7. labor
8. finger
9. mirror
10. beggar
11. favor
12. bother
13. fever
14. doctor
15. temper
16. actor
17. polar
18. sweater
19. traitor
20. whenever

Challenge

calendar
error
popular
barrier
director

Name ______________________ Date __________

Word Sort

Write each Basic Word next to the correct heading.

final /ər/ spelled *ar*	**Basic Words:** **Challenge Words:**
final /ər/ spelled *er*	**Basic Words:** **Challenge Word:** **Possible Selection Words:**
final /ər/ spelled *or*	**Basic Words:** **Challenge Words:** **Possible Selection Word:**

Spelling Words

Basic

1. enter
2. banner
3. sugar
4. shower
5. motor
6. collar
7. labor
8. finger
9. mirror
10. beggar
11. favor
12. bother
13. fever
14. doctor
15. temper
16. actor
17. polar
18. sweater
19. traitor
20. whenever

Challenge

calendar
error
popular
barrier
director

Challenge Add the Challenge Words to your Word Sort.

Connect to Reading Look through "The Girl Who Loved Spiders." Find words that have the final schwa + /r/ spelling patterns. Add them to your Word Sort.

Name ____________________ Date __________

Proofreading for Spelling

Find the misspelled words and circle them. Write them correctly on the lines below.

I pulled the coller of my sweeter up around my ears. Even though I had a fevre, I still felt cold. I needed a docter. Instead a polor bear walked up to me and said, "Whennever I look in the miror, I see shugar. Is that normal?" The bear was wearing a red shirt and blue jeans. I reached out my hand to touch him. He felt real. Maybe I was sicker than I thought.

I told him he shouldn't bothar me with silly questions. Then I asked if he was real or an actur. He lost his tempir and called me a trator to the cause. He held up a bannor that said "Bears Should Rule the World," wagged his fingir at me, and left. Then the door opened and my mom came in to check on me. She sighed and said, "You are burning up!" I took my sweater off and went to sleep.

1. ____________ 8. ____________
2. ____________ 9. ____________
3. ____________ 10. ____________
4. ____________ 11. ____________
5. ____________ 12. ____________
6. ____________ 13. ____________
7. ____________ 14. ____________

Spelling Words

Basic

1. enter
2. banner
3. sugar
4. shower
5. motor
6. collar
7. labor
8. finger
9. mirror
10. beggar
11. favor
12. bother
13. fever
14. doctor
15. temper
16. actor
17. polar
18. sweater
19. traitor
20. whenever

Challenge

calendar
error
popular
barrier
director

Name _______________ Date _______________

Making Comparisons

Comparative adjectives are used to compare two things. Superlative adjectives are used to compare more than two things.

Adjective	Comparative	Superlative
slow	slower	slowest
cute	cuter	cutest
fast	faster	fastest
happy	happier	happiest

Thinking Question
How many persons, places, or things are being compared?

A turtle is *slower* than a lizard.

A snail is the *slowest* of the three.

1–6. Circle the correct form of the adjective to complete each sentence. Write C if the adjective is the comparative form. Write S if the adjective is the superlative form.

1. Jana is (tall, taller) than her sister Sasha. ________
2. My little sister is the (cutest, cuter) baby in the whole world. ________
3. Kelli insisted that ghost stories are (scariest, scarier) to read than biographies. ________
4. That is the (funnier, funniest) joke I have ever heard. ________

5–6. Matt is a (fastest, faster) runner than Saleem, but Juan is the (fastest, faster) runner of the three boys. ________

Name ______________________ Date ____________

Making Comparisons with *more* and *most*

With long adjectives, use *more* to compare two persons, places, or things. Use *most* to compare three or more.

The ant is **more** interesting than the grasshopper.
The ant is the **most** interesting of all insects.

Thinking Question
How many persons, places, or things are being compared?

1–5. Rewrite each sentence, adding either *more* or *most* to the adjective in parentheses.

1. The _____ things I learned to do when I moved to Florida were to always wear shoes, to always shake out my shoes, and to watch my step when walking. (important)
____
____
____

2. Spiders are _____ in Florida than in New York. (plentiful)
____
____

3. I think the _____ part about moving is making new friends. (difficult)
____
____

4. I think running road races is ____ than looking for bugs. (satisfying)
____
____

5. What is the _____ insect to be found in the area where you live? (common)
____
____

Name ______________________ Date ____________

Comparing with *good* and *bad*

Some adjectives need to change forms when they are used to compare things.

The adjectives *good* and *bad* are two examples.

Adjective	Comparative	Superlative
good	better	best
bad	worse	worst

Thinking Question
How many persons, places, or things are being compared?

Getting out of school early is good. Weekends are better. Summer break is best of all.

1–5. Complete the sentence by writing the correct form of the adjective shown in parentheses.

1. The __________ news I heard was that 120 amphibian species are now extinct. (bad)
2. David was happy that his second paper was ________ than his first. (good)
3. What is the ________ book you have ever read? (good)
4. I liked the first book ________ than the second. (good)
5. The ________ part of our museum trip was the ride home. (bad)

Correct Adjectives

- The words *a, an,* and *the* are special adjectives called **articles.**

Articles	
Use *a* if the next word begins with a consonant sound.	Ron found **a** giant beetle.
Use *an* if the next word begins with a vowel sound.	**An** ant is a social insect.
Use *the* if the noun names a particular person, place, or thing.	**The** grasshopper landed right on Maria's book.

- Capitalize adjectives formed from proper nouns.

  Wayne studied **Amazon** ants.

1–5. Rewrite the sentences, supplying the correct article.

1. Roberto wrote ___ report on dragonflies.

____

2. _____ class visited a museum last Thursday.

____

3–4. The spider is ____ arachnid and not ___ insect.

____

5. I want to learn everything I can about ____ moth.

____

6–8. Rewrite the sentences, correcting errors in the use of proper adjectives.

6. The canadian guide told us what to look for.

____

7. The arabian horse has great energy and intelligence.

____

8. For a solid week the group investigated the mexican coast.

____

____

Name ______________________ Date ____________

Sentence Fluency

Combine two short, choppy sentences into one sentence to make sentences flow smoothly.

Sentence 1	Sentence 2
The elephant is the biggest animal in the zoo.	The elephant is also the most magnificent animal.

The elephant is the biggest and most magnificent animal in the zoo.

1–3. Combine these short, choppy sentences to make one sentence.

1.

Sentence 1	Sentence 2
The Taipan snake has the most poisonous venom of any snake in Australia.	It also has the longest fangs.

____

____

2.

Sentence 1	Sentence 2
The largest shark on the Australian coast is the great white.	It is also the scariest shark.

____

____

3.

Sentence 1	Sentence 2
My science teacher, Mrs. Welles, is the most interesting teacher I have ever had.	She also is the most knowledgable.

____

____

Name ______________________ Date ____________

Lesson 26
READER'S NOTEBOOK

The Girl Who Loved Spiders
Writing: Opinion Writing

Focus Trait: Evidence

Precise Language

As you describe the characters, setting, and plot in your response, choose clear, exact words to show the reader clearly the features of the story.

Topic	*Exact Details*
Characters	fascinating, realistic, sympathetic, evil

List three or more details that you might use to express your opinion about the following parts of a story you have read recently. Include interesting word choice.

Topic	Exact Details
1. Place	
2. Time	
3. Events	
4. Ending	

Name ______________________ Date ____________

Amphibian Alert!

Amphibian Conservation Group

Suppose you work for a conservation group working to protect amphibians. Help create a pamphlet about your organization.

On this side of the pamphlet, tell why your group exists. Look closely at pages 22–23 (to find details that tell what amphibians are and where they live) and pages 24 and 25 (to find details about threats to amphibian life). Use two synonyms for the noun *threat* in your pamphlet.

What Is an Amphibian?

____

____

____

Threats to Amphibian Life:

____

____

____

____

____

____

____

Name ______________________ Date ____________

Amphibian Alert!
Independent Reading

On this side of the pamphlet, tell what people can do to help protect amphibians. Look closely at pages 26 and 27 to find details to help you write. Use two antonyms for the word *threaten* in this part of the pamphlet. Remember, you work for a conservation group.

What Conservation Groups Do:

____

____

____

____

____

What You Can Do to Help:

____

____

____

____

____

____

____

____

Name ______________________ Date __________

The Final Schwa + /l/ Sound

Basic 1–10. Read the paragraphs. Write the Basic Words that would best replace the numbers in parentheses to complete the sentences.

It was an exciting and **(1)** day. Ana arrived at a bicycle race. She stopped to **(2)** at the colorful balloons and streamers decorating the starting line. A **(3)** of ten other racers were standing by their bicycles.

"Don't be nervous," Ana told herself. "This will be **(4)** compared to all the training that I did."

Ana remembered to tie her shoelaces so they would not **(5)** in her bicycle wheels. The last time that had happened, Ana hurt her **(6)**. Ana used a **(7)** to wipe mud off the shiny **(8)** bicycle frame.

At the starting line, Ana prepared to **(9)** fast. She and the other racers burst forward. It was going to be a **(10)** for the prize!

1. ______________ 6. ______________
2. ______________ 7. ______________
3. ______________ 8. ______________
4. ______________ 9. ______________
5. ______________ 10. ______________

Challenge 11–12. Imagine that your teacher asks you to write about your favorite subject, which is math. Use two of the Challenge Words. Write on a separate sheet of paper.

Spelling Words

Basic

1. title
2. towel
3. battle
4. pedal
5. metal
6. simple
7. eagle
8. special
9. total
10. trouble
11. nickel
12. gentle
13. barrel
14. model
15. tangle
16. ankle
17. marvel
18. juggle
19. squirrel
20. riddle

Challenge

cancel
decimal
material
pretzel
triangle

Name ______________________ Date ____________

Word Sort

Amphibian Alert!
Spelling:
The Final Schwa + /l/ Sound

Write each Basic Word next to the correct heading.

Final /l/ or /əl/ sound spelled *el*	**Basic Words:** **Challenge Words:**
Final /l/ or /əl/ sound spelled *al*	**Basic Words:** **Challenge Words:** **Possible Selection Word:**
Final /l/ or /əl/ sound spelled *le*	**Basic Words:** **Challenge Word:** **Possible Selection Words:**

Challenge: Add the Challenge Words to your Word Sort.

Connect to Reading: Look through "Amphibian Alert!" Find words that have the final schwa + /l/ spelling patterns on this page. Add them to your Word Sort.

Spelling Words

Basic

1. title
2. towel
3. battle
4. pedal
5. metal
6. simple
7. eagle
8. special
9. total
10. trouble
11. nickel
12. gentle
13. barrel
14. model
15. tangle
16. ankle
17. marvel
18. juggle
19. squirrel
20. riddle

Challenge

cancel
decimal
material
pretzel
triangle

Name ____________________ Date ____________

Proofreading for Spelling

Find the misspelled words and circle them. Write them correctly on the lines below.

In 1799, a French army officer named Pierre-Francois Bouchard was working near the city of Rosetta in Egypt. Bouchard and his men saw many ancient things, including a moddel of a house made of a mettal that looked like nikel. For fun, the men would juggil small stones. One day Bouchard found a stone slab that was different from the others. He was very gentil with it as he used water from a nearby barel to wash off the layers of dirt.

Bouchard saw strange symbols. The treuble was that he did not know what they meant. Bouchard took the stone to scholars. They all had to marvell at it, but they were unable to understand it. Was that a reddle or the titil of a play? Was the bird an eagel? Was that little creature a flying squerrel? More than 20 years passed before anyone could translate the Rosetta Stone.

Spelling Words

1. title
2. towel
3. battle
4. pedal
5. metal
6. simple
7. eagle
8. special
9. total
10. trouble
11. nickel
12. gentle
13. barrel
14. model
15. tangle
16. ankle
17. marvel
18. juggle
19. squirrel
20. riddle

Challenge

cancel
decimal
material
pretzel
triangle

1. ____________ 7. ____________
2. ____________ 8. ____________
3. ____________ 9. ____________
4. ____________ 10. ____________
5. ____________ 11. ____________
6. ____________ 12. ____________

Name ______________________________ Date ____________

Comparing with *good* and *bad*

Comparative *Good* and *Bad*: Use *better* or *worse* to compare two things.
Superlative: Use *best* or *worst* to compare three or more things.

Thinking Questions
Is the comparison comparative *or* superlative? *What form of* good *or* bad *should be used to compare?*

Adjective	Comparative	Superlative
good	better	best
bad	worse	worst

Brad earned a **better** score than Jake, but Amelia earned the **best** grade of all.

Circle the correct form of the word in parentheses. Write C if the word is the comparative form. Write S for the superlative form.

1. John's ideas were (best, better) than Dave's to improve the amphibian display. ________
2. Sean had the (worse, worst) job–repairing the frog terrariums. ________
3. Team A's display was (worst, worse) than team B's. ________
4. Of all the guides at the amphibian display, Marta explains tadpoles (better, best). ________

Name ______________________ Date ____________

Comparing with Adverbs

For most adverbs that end in *-ly*:
- use *more* to compare two actions.
- use *most* to compare three or more actions.

Thinking Question
Does the adverb end in -ly? How many things does the adverb compare?

Adverb	Comparative	Superlative
quickly	more quickly	most quickly
skillfully	more skillfully	most skillfully
easily	more easily	most easily

A horse runs **more quickly** than a human. Cheetahs run the **most quickly** of all animals.

1–5. Write the form of the adverb shown in parentheses that correctly completes the sentence.

1. Do you think turtles can swim ______________ than frogs? (quickly)
2. The third doctor cared for the injured newt ______________. (skillfully)
3. Jason handles the salamanders ______________ than Bill. (carefully)
4. Of all the helpers, Aiden works the ______________. (quietly)
5. Alan identified amphibians ______________ than Mitsuo after taking a class. (easily)

Name ______________________ Date __________

Making Comparisons

1–6. Circle the correct word in parentheses to complete each sentence.

1. Dennis smiles (wider, widest) of all his friends.
2. "I think clothing dries (most, more) quickly in warm air than in cold," said Dana.
3. I shop at Bloom's Market (more, most) frequently than I shop at Lynn's Market.
4. Of all the fruits sold at Bloom's market, the bananas will (more, most) likely sell out first.

5–6. When teams choose players, Beth is (most, more) readily chosen than Brianne because she runs (faster, fastest).

Name ______________________ Date ____________

Lesson 27
READER'S NOTEBOOK

Amphibian Alert!
Grammar: Spiral Review

Negatives

- A word that makes a sentence mean "no" is called a *negative*.
- The words *no*, *no one*, *nobody*, *none*, *nothing*, and *never* are negatives.
- The word *not* and contractions made from *not* are also negatives.
- Never use two negatives together in a sentence.

Incorrect	Correct
There **weren't no** fish in the pond.	There **weren't any** fish in the pond. There **were no** fish in the pond.
I **won't never** give away my frog.	I **won't ever** give away my frog. I **will never** give away my frog.

1–4. Write the negative on the line provided.

1. Nobody wanted to leave. ______________________

2. I can't finish this assignment on time. ______________

3. Before this class, I had never studied reptiles. __________

4. I had no interest in learning about newts. ___________

5–8. Rewrite the sentences, correcting errors in the use of negatives.

5. Jason can't go nowhere until he finishes his chores.

____

6. Before taking this class, Pete didn't know nothing about reptiles.

____

____

7. I don't like nothing about insects.

____

8. Jim doesn't never want to miss a class again.

____

Name ____________________ Date __________

Conventions: Proofreading

Amphibian Alert!
Grammar: Connect to Writing

Use proofreading marks to cross out errors and insert corrections.

Sentence with Errors	Corrected Sentence
Elena's performance was worser than Ralph's.	Elena's performance was ~~worser~~ **worse** than Ralph's.

1–5. Use the proofreading marks to fix the convention errors in the sentences below.

1. Of the five books I read on mammals, this was the worse.

2. Among the 50 essays submitted, Jose's essay was judged the better.

3. Of all my grades, my grade in science was the better.

4. Of the three team members, Kara works the faster.

5. Jenna studied more harder than I did.

Focus Trait: Elaboration

Share Feelings with Descriptive Words

Flat Voice	***Interesting Voice***
I found a salamander. I was surprised.	I lifted the log. Wow! I was amazed at the bright yellow salamander underneath!

Read each sentence. Rewrite it, giving it interest and feeling. Write as if you were giving your opinion in a journal entry.

Flat Voice	**Interesting Voice**
1. My dad and I saw a frog in the pond.	
2. I don't like people throwing things in the pond.	
3. The bullfrogs made funny sounds.	
4. I didn't like holding the toad.	

Name ______________________ Date ____________

Museums: Worlds of Wonder

Visit this Museum!

Choose three museums from the selection that you would like to visit. For each museum, reread the section about the museum. Using what you learned about this museum, tell why this museum is important.

Name of Museum	Type of Museum	Why Museum Is Important

Name ______________________ Date ____________

Lesson 28
READER'S NOTEBOOK

Museums: Worlds of Wonder
Independent Reading

Imagine you visited one of the museums during summer vacation. You want to tell a friend about the great things you saw! Send an e-mail telling your friend what it was like to visit the museum. Make sure to tell your friend why this museum is important.

New Message

To: ______________________

From: ______________________

Subject: You should visit this museum!

____

____

____

____

____

____

____

____

____

____

____

____

____

____

____

Name ______________________ Date ____________

Three-Syllable Words

Basic 1–11. Write the Basic Word that best replaces the underlined word or words.

Dear Grandma,

Our family (1) <u>trip</u> to Washington, D.C., was great! Mom, Dad, Rick, and I had a good time (2) <u>jointly</u>. We saw (3) <u>a few</u> places, including the (4) <u>building that holds books</u> of Congress. (5) <u>An additional</u> place we visited was the White House. The (6) <u>leader of the United States</u> wasn't there. (7) <u>But</u>, we saw a lot of other things during the tour. For (8) <u>instance</u>, we saw a painting of Abraham Lincoln in the State Dining Room. I wasn't allowed to use my (9) <u>photographic device</u>, or I would have taken pictures for you. My (10) <u>preferred</u> place was the Smithsonian. Washington, D.C., is full of (11) <u>stories from the past</u>.

Love,
Matt

1. ______________
2. ______________
3. ______________
4. ______________
5. ______________
6. ______________
7. ______________
8. ______________
9. ______________
10. ______________
11. ______________

Challenge 12–13. An astronaut is speaking at your school about her recent shuttle ride through space. You get to talk to the astronaut after her speech. Write a sentence about your talk, using two Challenge Words. Write on a separate sheet of paper.

Spelling Words

Basic

1. library
2. another
3. hospital
4. example
5. deliver
6. history
7. however
8. several
9. vacation
10. important
11. victory
12. imagine
13. camera
14. potato
15. remember
16. together
17. memory
18. favorite
19. continue
20. president

Challenge

internal
ornament
interview
universe
article

Name ______________________ Date ___________

Word Sort

Write each Basic Word beside the correct heading.

First syllable stressed	**Basic Words:** **Challenge Words:** **Possible Selection Words:**
Second syllable stressed	**Basic Words:** **Challenge Words:** **Possible Selection Words:**

Challenge: Add the Challenge Words to your Word Sort.

Connect to Reading: Look through "Museums: Worlds of Wonder." Find words that have three syllables with first and second syllables stressed. Add them to your Word Sort.

Spelling Words

Basic

1. library
2. another
3. hospital
4. example
5. deliver
6. history
7. however
8. several
9. vacation
10. important
11. victory
12. imagine
13. camera
14. potato
15. remember
16. together
17. memory
18. favorite
19. continue
20. president

Challenge

internal
ornament
interview
universe
article

Name ______________________ Date ____________

Museums: Worlds of Wonder
Spelling: Three-Syllable Words

Proofreading for Spelling

Find the misspelled words and circle them. Write them correctly on the lines below.

In 1906, Hiram Bingham had had enough of studying the histery of the Incas in Peru in the libary at Yale. He knew they were importint to the history of South America for severle reasons. He decided to take a working vacashun to South America. Not wanting to rely on his memery, he took many notes and a kamera so he could remembir all the facts when he went to delivir a speech about his travels.

In 1911, Bingham returned to Peru to lead anether expedition and contincw his quest for knowledge about the Incas. One can only imajin his surprise when he discovered Machu Picchu, the "lost city of the Incas." The expedition turned out to be a huge personal victry for Bingham. The ancient stone city, hidden by five hundred years of jungle growth, is considered by some to be the greatest surviving exampel of Incan architecture.

1. ______________ 8. ______________
2. ______________ 9. ______________
3. ______________ 10. ______________
4. ______________ 11. ______________
5. ______________ 12. ______________
6. ______________ 13. ______________
7. ______________ 14. ______________

Spelling Words

1. library
2. another
3. hospital
4. example
5. deliver
6. history
7. however
8. several
9. vacation
10. important
11. victory
12. imagine
13. camera
14. potato
15. remember
16. together
17. memory
18. favorite
19. continue
20. president

Challenge

internal
ornament
interview
universe
article

Name ______________________ Date ____________

Possessive Pronouns

- A **possessive pronoun** is a pronoun that shows ownership.
- Possessive pronouns can replace possessive nouns in a sentence.

Possessive Pronouns	
my	its
your	our
her	their
his	

The teacher gave her students **the students'** tickets to the museum.
The teacher gave her students **their** tickets to the museum.

Thinking Questions
Are there possessive nouns in the sentence? Do any of them need to be replaced to avoid repetition?

1–5. Rewrite each sentence with the correct form of the possessive pronoun in parentheses.

1. Max and I went to see Max's favorite exhibit. (my, his, our)

 ____

2. We observed a dinosaur fossil and read about the fossil's discovery. (our, their, its)

 ____

3. We learned about dinosaurs, including dinosaurs' habits and diets. (its, her, their)

 ____

4. Mary told me that Mary's brother would love the exhibit, too. (my, her, their)

 ____

5. Marcus and I found Marcus's and my class in the museum shop. (its, our, her)

 ____

Name ______________________ Date ___________

More Possessive Pronouns

Some possessive pronouns are placed before nouns. Others are used by themselves and stand alone.

Possessive Pronouns that Stand Alone	
mine	hers
yours	ours
his	theirs

The tickets to the exhibit are **ours.**

Thinking Question
Is the possessive pronoun followed by a noun?

1–4. Write the possessive pronoun that stands alone on the line.

1. Is the ticket to the polar bear exhibit hers? ___________

2. The airplane ticket is mine. ___________

3. Since we have tickets but cannot attend, would you like to use ours? ___________

4. The teacher will give you yours. ___________

5–6. Rewrite each sentence on the line so that the possessive pronoun stands alone.

5. Which report is your report? ______________________

6. The report about trees is my report.

____

Name ______________________ Date ____________

Possessive Pronouns

- Some possessive pronouns are placed before nouns.
  - Jeff left his backpack on the school bus.
  - My books are in Mom's car.
- Other possessive pronouns are used by themselves and stand alone.
  - I think the museum tickets are yours.
  - The red skates in the locker are mine.

1–6. Replace the underlined word or words with the correct possessive pronoun.

1. Jill's inline skates are sitting on Jill's porch. ____________
2. "The backpack with reflector strips is my backpack," I said. ____________
3. Jane can't find Jane's shoe. ____________
4. Which one of the lunches is your lunch? ____________
5. The three boys rode the three boys' bikes to school. ____________
6. If Ned has my jacket, then I have Ned's jacket. ____________

Name ________________ Date ________

Writing Quotations

- **Quotations** show a speaker's exact words.
- **Capitalize** the first word of a quotation.
- Place **quotation marks** before and after the speaker's exact words.
- Use a **comma** to set off words that tell who is speaking.
- When the quotation comes first, place a **comma** inside the last quotation marks.
- If the quotation is a question or an exclamation, place a **question mark** or **exclamation mark** inside the last quotation marks.

Ms. Winger said, "Listen to your guide carefully."

1–8. Rewrite the quotations, correcting the punctuation errors.

1. "Have you ever been to the City Museum" asked Chloe.
____
2. Yes, I have replied Aiden.
____
3. Charlie said "I hope we see dinosaurs".
____
4. Marta exclaimed "the Enchanted Caves are so awesome"!
____
5. "I like Art City better" said Danielle.
____
6. Mr. West suggested "let's go see the World Aquarium now."
____
7. This will be fun! exclaimed Sam.
____
8. I will have so many things to tell my family, said Luis.
____

Name ______________________ Date __________

Sentence Fluency

To avoid repeated possessive nouns, replace them with possessive pronouns.

Sentence with Repeated Possessive Nouns	Sentence with Possessive Pronouns
Jose wanted Jose's mom to chaperone Jose's field trip to the museum.	Jose wanted his mom to chaperone his field trip to the museum.

1–5. Rewrite each sentence, replacing repeated possessive nouns with possessive pronouns to improve sentence flow.

1. Today, the fourth graders will have fun on the fourth grader's first field trip.

 ____

2. Sarah told about Sarah's visit to the museum.

 ____

3. Kayla saved a piece of Kayla's favorite cake for Kayla's mother.

 ____

4. Pam showed Pam's project to the class.

 ____

5. By running in the museum, Tim broke one of the rules that Tim's teacher had given to Tim's class.

 ____

 ____

Name ______________________ Date ____________

Focus Trait: Organization

A well-organized announcement contains:
- a topic or main idea;
- details that support the main idea;
- a sequence of ideas or events that usually happen in order of first, next, and last;
- a conclusion that restates the main idea.

Use a separate sheet of paper. Organize the sentences below in an order that makes sense.

1. Sunday afternoon: Children's concert. Special appearance by Moosy the Cow!
2. Saturday morning, September 27: Family breakfast with the Museum staff
3. Come join the fun. Questions? Call or email the Museum office for more details.
4. Saturday afternoon: Ribbon-cutting ceremony and museum tours
5. Announcing the Gala Opening of the New Children's Museum!
6. Saturday night: Dinner-Dance with raffle. Adults only
7. Save the weekend of September 27–28 so you can enjoy all the activities.
8. Celebrate with your friends and neighbors!

Name ______________________ Date ____________

Save Timber Woods!

Write a Public Service Announcement

Help neighborhood residents who live near Timber Woods understand the pros and cons of cutting down Timber Woods. Reread pages 49–50 and page 52. Think carefully about Gina's, Laura's, Hector's, and Lucas's arguments on these pages. Use their arguments to fill in the chart below.

Cutting Down Timber Woods	
Pros	**Cons**
1. ______________________	1. ______________________
2. ______________________	2. ______________________
	3. ______________________

Name ______________________ Date ____________

Write a public service announcement that could be broadcast on local radio or television stations in the characters' neighborhood. Help residents understand the consequences of cutting down Timber Woods. Include five lines of dialogue for the speaker to say. Include two stage directions that let him or her know how to deliver the lines.

Line 1: ______________________________

____

Line 2: ______________________________

____

Line 3: ______________________________

____

Line 4: ______________________________

____

Line 5: ______________________________

____

Name ______________________ Date ____________

Words with Silent Consonants

Save Timber Woods!
Spelling: Words with Silent Consonants

Basic 1–10. Write Basic Words on the lines provided that will best complete the sentences.

My aunt's job is to keep the water pipes in people's homes running smoothly. She is a (1) ____________. She has to (2) ____________ down and work under sinks. Sometimes she has to (3) ____________ into small spaces to find the (4) ____________ to the plumbing problem. She often has to use tools from her toolbox to (5) ____________ pipes together. Working with tools, my aunt has to take care not to scrape a (6) ____________ or a wrist. She carries a radio in her toolbox because she likes to (7) ____________ to music as she works. The music helps keep her (8) ____________ and relaxed as she does her job. Her customers (9) ____________ her and praise her work. She says being a plumber is a good, (10) ____________ job to have.

Challenge 11–12. You've watched a documentary film about the building of the Egyptian pyramids. Write a review of the film for your class. Use two of the Challenge Words. Write on a separate sheet of paper.

Spelling Words

Basic

1. half
2. comb
3. mortgage
4. honor
5. fasten
6. kneel
7. wreath
8. calm
9. answer
10. handsome
11. wrinkle
12. listen
13. fetch
14. yolk
15. climb
16. honest
17. knuckle
18. plumber
19. limb
20. folktale

Challenge

tomb
glisten
design
hasten
wrestle

Name ______________________ Date ____________

Save Timber Woods!
Spelling: Words with Silent Consonants

Word Sort

Write each Basic Word next to the correct heading.

/m/ spelled *mb*	Basic Words: Challenge Words:
/n/ spelled *kn*	Basic Words:
/ô/ spelled *ho*	Basic Words:
/r/ spelled *wr*	Basic Words: Challenge Word:
silent *l*, *t*, *d*, or *w*	Basic Words: Challenge Words:
Other silent consonants	Challenge Word:

Challenge: Add the Challenge Words to your Word Sort.

Spelling Words

Basic

1. half
2. comb
3. mortgage
4. honor
5. fasten
6. kneel
7. wreath
8. calm
9. answer
10. handsome
11. wrinkle
12. listen
13. fetch
14. yolk
15. climb
16. honest
17. knuckle
18. plumber
19. limb
20. folktale

Challenge

tomb
glisten
design
hasten
wrestle

Name ______________________ Date ____________

Proofreading for Spelling

Save Timber Woods!
Spelling: Words with Silent Consonants

Find the misspelled words and circle them. Write them correctly on the lines below.

After college, Chef Alice Waters went to France, where she was impressed by the honist food she ate, from an omelet made with the freshest egg yoke to fish cooked the day it was caught. She learned that the French were often willing to spend haff of their income for quality food products. Since 1971, Alice has owned Chez Panisse, a California restaurant famous for the quality of its food. People have been known to komb the woods and neel in mud beneath the lim of a tree to fetsh for Alice special foods, such as a mushroom with an ugly wrinkil and incredible flavor. Other people grow herbs and make a wreth of them for Alice. She has worked hard to teach children about growing and eating fresh food. Today there are children in local schools who prefer to lisen to Alice talk about gardening than hear a folktail about a handsum prince.

1. ____________ 7. ____________
2. ____________ 8. ____________
3. ____________ 9. ____________
4. ____________ 10. ____________
5. ____________ 11. ____________
6. ____________ 12. ____________

Spelling Words

1. half
2. comb
3. mortgage
4. honor
5. fasten
6. kneel
7. wreath
8. calm
9. answer
10. handsome
11. wrinkle
12. listen
13. fetch
14. yolk
15. climb
16. honest
17. knuckle
18. plumber
19. limb
20. folktale

Challenge

tomb
glisten
design
hasten
wrestle

Name ______________________ Date ___________

Using *I* and *me*

Save Timber Woods!
Grammar: Correct Pronouns

- Use the pronoun *I* as the subject of a sentence.
  Eileen and I learned so much!
- Use the pronoun *me* after action verbs and after prepositions such as *to, with, for,* or *at.*
  The council gave **David and me** their complete attention.
  Will you come with **me** to the meeting?
- When you talk about yourself and another person, always name yourself last.

Thinking Question
Is the pronoun the subject or the object of the sentence?

1–6. Rewrite each sentence with the correct word(s) in parentheses.

1. (Dominic and I, Dominic and me) wanted to save the forest.

____

2. Eileen told (I, me) what was happening to the forest.

____

3. Carlos and (I, me) realized the deer had nowhere to go.

____

4. Deer often visited (me and my family, my family and me).

____

5. My brother and (I, me) have seen them look for food.

____

6. (He and me, He and I) watched the deer quietly through the window.

____

Using the Right Pronoun

- **Subject pronouns** are used as the subject of a sentence. They tell whom or what the sentence is about.
- **Object pronouns** follow action verbs or prepositions such as *to, for, with, in,* or *at*.

Subject Pronouns	Object Pronouns
I, you, he, she, it, we, they	me, you, him, her, it, us, them

We gave the information to **her**, and **she** told **them** about the forestry class.

Thinking Questions
Does the pronoun tell who or what does the action? Does the pronoun follow an action verb or the words to, for, with, in, *or* at?

1–5. Rewrite each sentence, using the correct pronoun in parentheses.

1. Isabel read (we, us) the article about the housing development.

____

2. Olivia and (he, him) could not believe what they heard.

____

3. (They, Them) want to cut down huge parts of the forest.

____

4. To (we, us), the forest should be used for hiking and camping.

____

5. Since animals cannot speak, we will speak for (them, they).

____

Name ______________________ Date ____________

Reflexive Pronouns

A **reflexive pronoun** is used when the subject and object of a sentence are the same person/thing or people/things. We use reflexive pronouns with the word *by* to mean *alone* or *without help*.

Subject Pronouns		Reflexive Pronouns
I	it	myself
you	we	yourself
he	you (plural)	himself
she	they	herself
		itself
		ourselves
		yourselves
		themselves

I will take care of *myself* someday. *They* like to walk to school *by themselves*.

1–8. Fill in the blanks with the correct reflexive pronoun.

1. When she was hungry, Jane made ____________ a sandwich.
2. Be careful, Lisa. Don't cut ____________ with the knife.
3. "I think I will build a clubhouse by ____________," said Paul.
4. We blamed ____________ for getting lost in the museum.
5. Please boys, make ____________ feel at home.
6. The girls made five dozen cupcakes by ____________.
7. The dog saw ____________ in the mirror and barked.
8. Jack made ____________ a pizza for lunch.

Name ______________________ Date ____________

Commas in Sentences

Use a comma to set off these types of words and phrases:

- the words *yes, no,* and *well* when they begin a sentence
  No, feeding deer human food is not a good idea.
- introductory phrases and clauses
  If you want to see deer, you have to be still.
- the name of a person directly addressed in a sentence.
  Don't blame the deer, Becky, for being hungry.

1–5. Rewrite the sentences, adding commas where they are needed.

1. No I do not want deer in our yard.

____

2. The poor deer lost their homes Alanna.

____

3. Well my family is losing our favorite tree.

____

4. We should get the facts Denzel before we decide.

____

5. Because we left home late we arrived after the park closed.

____

6–8. Rewrite the following script. Add three missing commas where they are needed.

Eliot: Well that went better than I expected.
Maria: Eliot you were great!
Gerald: What can we do now to raise money guys?

Name ______________________ Date ____________

Save Timber Woods!
Grammar: Connect to Writing

Sentence Fluency

Repeating words in writing is uninteresting and awkward. To avoid using a noun over and over again, replace it with a pronoun.

Sentence 1	Sentence 2
Caleb didn't like the deer eating his tree.	Caleb scared it away.

Caleb didn't like the deer eating his tree. **He** scared it away.

1–3. Replace the repeated noun with a pronoun to improve sentence fluency.

1.

Sentence 1	Sentence 2
Nicole told her friends about the problem.	Nicole wanted to help.

____

____

2.

Sentence 1	Sentence 2
Last year the deer were safer.	The deer had more land.

____

____

3.

Sentence 1	Sentence 2
The people of our community have a problem.	The people of our community need to work together.

____

____

Name ______________________ Date ____________

Focus Trait: Organization Focusing on Addressing Objections

Good writers think about how their audience will react to their ideas. In an opinion essay, they try to address any objections ahead of time. Writers often do this after discussing their own opinions and reasons. This writer addressed the objection by the developer about building houses on Timber Woods.

Opinion: *We should save Timber Woods from being destroyed.*
Possible Objection: *We want to build more houses on the Timber Woods land.*
Revised sentence: *Homes could be built where the Smithfield warehouses are instead of Timber Woods.*

1–3. Read the idea and the possible objection. Rewrite the sentence so that it addresses the objection. You can refer to "Save Timber Woods!" to find information to answer it.

1. **Opinion:** Cutting down the forest will cause a lot of problems.

   Possible Objection: It costs too much money for us to buy the land.

   Revised sentence: ______________________________________

   ____

2. **Opinion:** Saving the woods is good for the local environment.

   Possible Objection: The woods don't help the town in any way.

   Revised sentence: ______________________________________

   ____

3. **Opinion:** Wildlife creatures belong in their natural environments.

   Possible Objection: It's nice to see deer in my backyard.

   Revised sentence: ______________________________________

   ____

Name ______________________ Date __________

Mystery at Reed's Pond

Create a Web Page

Help the Pond Patrol complete their science log. Then, help them draw conclusions about invasive species based on what they saw and learned. Reread page 71 for information about Invasive species from Mr. Roberts to help fill in Pond Patrol's log.

Science Log		
Details	**What I Learned**	**Conclusions about Invasive Species**
1. A western turtle used to live in the pond. Now there is a red-eared slider turtle there.		
2. A nest is crushed and is missing eggs.		

Write the text for a web page from an environmental site informing people about the threats of invasive species. Using what you learned, explain the dangers of introducing a new species to an area.

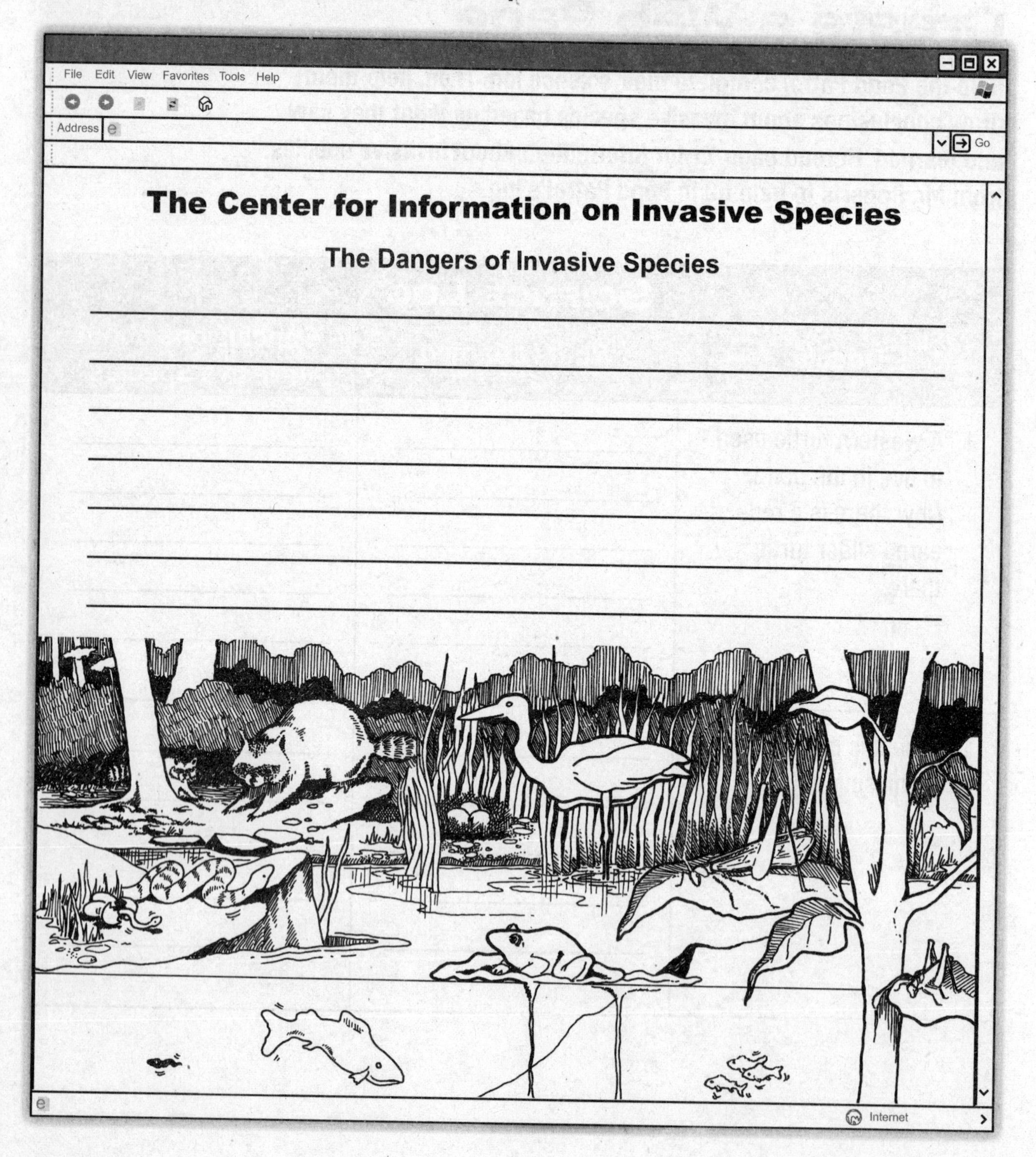

Name _______________ Date _______________

Unusual Spellings

Basic 1–10. Complete the puzzles by writing the Basic Word for each clue.

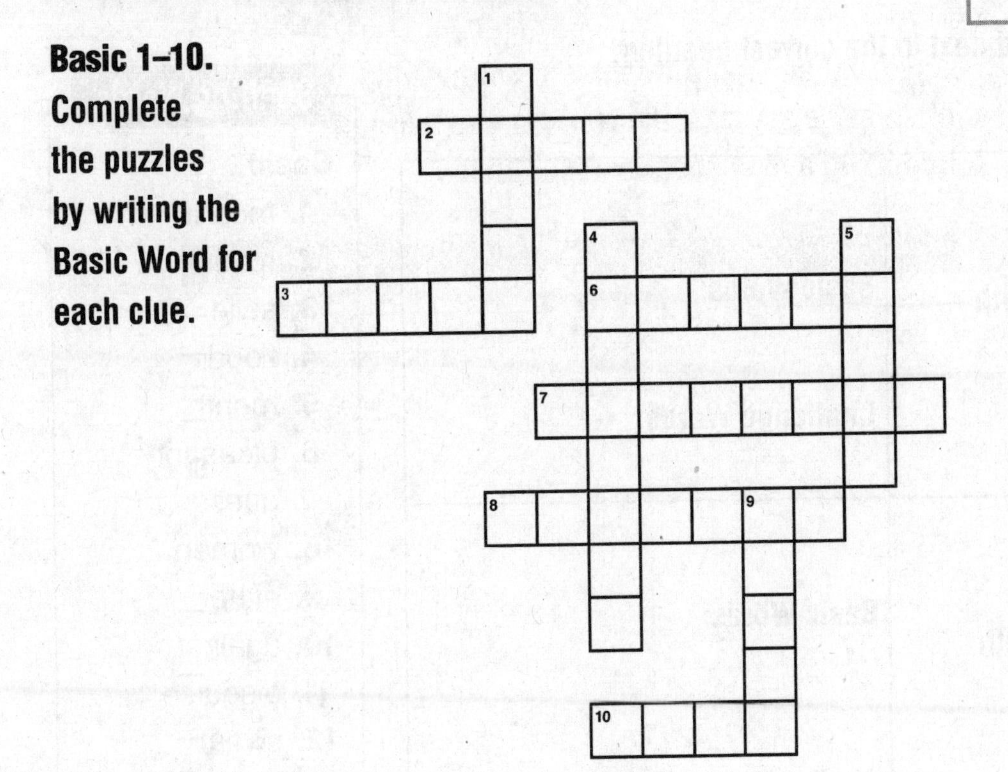

Spelling Words

Basic

1. meant
2. routine
3. style
4. flood
5. month
6. pleasant
7. guess
8. women
9. either
10. against
11. disguise
12. sweat
13. magazine
14. guard
15. receive
16. wonder
17. league
18. type
19. ceiling
20. money

Challenge

plaid
onion
guarantee
rhyme
submarine

Across

2. to form an opinion without being sure
3. to fill or cover with water
6. a group working toward a common goal
7. a weekly or monthly publication
8. in contact with
10. a group sharing common traits

Down

1. someone who watches over or protects
4. enjoyable or attractive
5. past of "to have as its meaning"
9. a way of doing something

Challenge 11–12. Create two book titles: one about a trip to the ocean bottom in a colorful vessel and one about a collection of humorous poetry. Use two of the Challenge Words. Write on a separate sheet of paper.

Name ____________________ Date __________

Word Sort

Write each Basic Word next to the correct heading.

Unusual Spellings with One Syllable	**Basic Words:** **Challenge Words:**
Unusual Spellings with Two Syllables	**Basic Words:** **Challenge Word:**
Unusual Spellings with Three Syllables	**Basic Words:** **Challenge Words:**

Challenge: Add the Challenge Words to your Word Sort.

Spelling Words

Basic

1. meant
2. routine
3. style
4. flood
5. month
6. pleasant
7. guess
8. women
9. either
10. against
11. disguise
12. sweat
13. magazine
14. guard
15. receive
16. wonder
17. league
18. type
19. ceiling
20. money

Challenge

plaid
onion
guarantee
rhyme
submarine

Proofreading for Spelling

Find the misspelled words and circle them. Write them correctly on the lines below.

I was following my rootine for the munth, practicing with the bowling leegue after work. I'm an amateur detective, so I gess I'm always on the lookout for trouble. I arrived at the bowling alley early, and I noticed two strange womin. I couldn't help but wonnder if ether of them was the tipe to bowl. I didn't think so. The tall one wore a disgize. I looked up and began to swet with fear. There was a figure hanging from the seiling. I turned to run.

The tall woman leaned right agenst my face. "You can't go," she said. "I didn't recieve my monie yet." Shaking, I asked her what she ment. She laughed and told me she needed to be paid for the mystery party. Then I realized the figure was just a decoration. It's a good thing I'm just an *amateur* detective.

1. ______________
2. ______________
3. ______________
4. ______________
5. ______________
6. ______________
7. ______________
8. ______________
9. ______________
10. ______________
11. ______________
12. ______________
13. ______________
14. ______________
15. ______________

Spelling Words

Basic

1. meant
2. routine
3. style
4. flood
5. month
6. pleasant
7. guess
8. women
9. either
10. against
11. disguise
12. sweat
13. magazine
14. guard
15. receive
16. wonder
17. league
18. type
19. ceiling
20. money

Challenge

plaid
onion
guarantee
rhyme
submarine

Name ______________________ Date __________

Pronoun Contractions

- Pronouns can be combined with some verbs to form **contractions**.
- An **apostrophe** replaces the letter or letters that are left out.

  I'm going to study that turtle until **it's** engraved in my memory.
- Contractions for the pronouns *he, she,* and *it,* when used with the verbs *is* and *has,* are the same *(he's, she's, it's)*.

Thinking Question
What two words can I combine to make a contraction?

1–5. On the line, write the contraction for the underlined words.

1. We are observing nature with our class. ______________
2. They have taken many notes about the pond. ______________
3. You will have time to observe everything. ______________
4. Adrian said he had never seen a turtle like that. ______________
5. You are responsible for your actions. ______________

6–10. On the line, write the two words that make up each underlined contraction.

6. Lea thinks we've solved the mystery. ______________
7. What do you think they'll do with the red turtles? ______________
8. You've seen the boy put the red turtle in the pond. ______________
9. Mr. Roberts says that it's important to take care of the pond. ______________
10. I've done enough research on turtles to know that this answer is wrong.

    ____

Name ______________________ Date ____________

Pronouns and Homophones

- **Homophones** are words that sound alike but have different spellings and meanings. Some pronoun contractions are homophones.

Homophones	Meaning
it's its	it is belonging to it, of it
they're their there	they are belonging to them in that place
you're your	you are belonging to you

You're very kind to animals and their habitats.
They're enjoying your book on turtles.

Thinking Question
What sentence clues can I use to figure out the meaning and correct spelling of the homophone?

1–6. Read each sentence. Write the correct homophone in parentheses.

1. We found a cracked egg (their, there). ______________

2. The egg should have been in (it's, its) nest. ______________

3. (They're, There) observing the young turtles in the pond. ______________

4. (Your, You're) correct about the effects of pollution. ______________

5. (Your, You're) computer gave us the information we needed. ______________

6. (Its, It's) hard to believe that the boy did not want to keep his pet turtles.

____

Name ______________________ Date ____________

Using Pronouns

Mystery at Reed's Pond
Grammar: Pronoun Contractions

- Pronouns can be combined with some verbs to form contractions.
- An apostrophe replaces the letter or letters that are left out.
  Example: I am = I'm
- Contractions for *he, she,* and *it* when used with verbs *is* and *has* are the same.
  Example: he is = he's he has = he's
- Some pronoun contractions are homophones.
  Example: it's = it is its = belonging to it

1–5. On the line, write the contraction for the underlined words.

1. I am ready to write a report about my field trip.
   ____
2. My teacher says that I will have one week to finish it.
   ____
3. Sylvia said she has decided to do a photo essay as her report.
   ____
4. She said that it is going to be her best report ever.
   ____
5. Les thinks we are going to have fun reading our reports in class.
   ____

6–10. On the line, write the correct homophone for each sentence.

6. (Your, You're) going to visit the science museum next week.
   ____
7. (There, Their) will be students from the whole school district at the museum.
   ____
8. (Their, They're) going on the same guided tour as your class.
   ____
9. (It's, Its) going to be an amazing experience!
   ____
10. Don't forget to bring (you're, your) cameras.
   ____

Name ______________________ Date ____________

Mystery at Reed's Pond
Grammar: Spiral Review

Commas in Sentences

- A **series** is a list of three or more items with the word *and* or *or* before the last item.
- Use *commas* to separate the items in a series. Put a comma after each item except the last one.
- Some choppy sentences can be combined using a series.

  Snakes and lizards are reptiles. So are alligators and crocodiles.

  Snakes, lizards, turtles, alligators, and crocodiles are all reptiles.
- Use a comma to separate the **month and date from the year.**
- Use a comma to separate a **city or town and its state.**

  I will be sixteen on August 4**,** 2010.

  The best park is in Yellowstone**,** Montana.

1–5. Rewrite the sentences, adding commas where they are needed.

1. The scales of a snake are cool dry and hard.

____

2. This park was opened on July 4 1949.

____

3. A turtle in danger can pull its head legs and tail into its shell.

____

4. Most turtles live in ponds lakes rivers or the ocean.

____

5. Next summer I'm going to ecology camp in Orlando Florida.

____

6. Combine the sentences using a series. Write the new sentence on the lines.

Both turtles and tortoises bask in the sun. They both have bony shells. Turtles and tortoises can withdraw inside their shells for protection.

____

____

Name ______________________ Date __________

Conventions: Proofreading

Sentence with Errors	Corrected Sentence
Im sure their excited to have solved the mystery.	I'm sure they're ~~their~~ excited to have solved the mystery.

1–6. Use the proofreading marks to fix the convention errors in the sentences below.

1. Ive never solved a mystery before.

2. Its about time we helped animals by saving their habitats.

3. Youd never guess what my favorite pond animal is.

4. I love frogs because their so interesting.

5. Youll be glad that you did so much to help.

6. The western pond turtle is being squeezed out of it's habitat.

Name ______________________ Date __________

Focus Trait: Conventions Using Different Kinds of Sentences

Writers can give the same information in different kinds of sentences. Be sure to use the correct punctuation for all sentences.

Statement: The western pond turtle needs to have its home protected.

Question: Doesn't the western pond turtle deserve a safe home?

Exclamation: The western pond turtle must have a safe home!

1–3. Rewrite each sentence as the type indicated.

1. If we work together, we can save the animals at Reed's Pond.

Command: ______________________

Question: ______________________

2. The red-eared slider should not be released in Reed's Pond.

Exclamation: ______________________

Command: ______________________

3. Saving the pond's native species is very important.

Question: ______________________

Exclamation: ______________________

Reading and Writing Glossary

Use this glossary to help you remember and use words that you are learning about reading and writing.

A

abbreviation A shortened form of a word.

action verb A word that tells what a person or thing does.

adage A short saying that expresses life lessons that many people believe are true; a proverb.

adjective A word that describes a noun or pronoun.

adverb A word that describes a verb.

adverb of frequency Tells how often an action happens.

adverb of intensity Tells how much or to what degree an action happens.

advertisement An announcement designed to grab people's attention and persuade them to do or buy something.

affix A suffix or prefix attached to a base word, root word, or root that changes the meaning of the word.

allusion A reference to a famous person, place, event, or story.

analogy A comparison of two pairs of words.

analyze To look at or study something carefully.

antecedent The noun that the pronoun replaces.

antonym A word that has the opposite or very different meaning as another word.

apostrophe Punctuation mark used to show possession.

author's purpose The author's main goal in writing a selection, such as to explain, persuade, or entertain.

B

bar graph A diagram that uses bars to compare measurements or amounts.

base word A word to which affixes are added and is a complete word on its own.

behavior The way a character acts.

biography Text that tells about a person's life and is written by another person.

C

capital letter A letter that comes at the beginning of a proper noun and is uppercase.

caption A short description or explanation of a picture.

category A group of similar items.

cause An event that makes another event happen.

character A person or animal in a story.

chart A graphic organizer with columns and rows.

chronological In the order that events happened.

clause A group of words that has a subject and a predicate.

column A vertical (up and down) section of a chart.

comma A punctuation mark that separates elements or ideas.

command A sentence that gives a command; an imperative.

comparative An adjective or adverb that compares two persons, places, things, or actions.

compare To show how things are alike.

complete predicate All the words that tell what the subject of a sentence is or does.

complete subject All the words that tell who or what is doing the action in the sentence.

complex sentence A sentence made up of a simple sentence and a clause joined with a subordinating conjunction such as *because*.

compound sentence A sentence made up of two simple sentences joined by a comma and a connecting word such as *and, or, but,* or *so*.

conclusion A reasonable judgment you make after looking at facts.

conflict The story problem or struggle, which affects events in the plot.

context clues The words that surround an unfamiliar word or phrase that readers can use to figure out the meaning of an unknown word or phrase.

contraction A short way of writing two words, using an apostrophe to replace one or more letters.

contrast To show how things are different.

coordinating conjunction A word that connects other words or groups of words in a sentence.

D

declarative sentence A sentence that tells something; a statement.

demonstrative pronoun A pronoun, such as *this* or *that*, that talks about something nearby or far away.

dependent clause A group of words with both a subject and predicate that is not a complete sentence.

diagram A picture or group of pictures that explains how something works or how parts relate to one another.

diagram A visual that shows ideas.

dialogue What people say to each other in a story or play.

dictionary entry A word listed in the dictionary along with its meaning, pronunciation, and other information.

digital media Print, video, and audio content usually accessed by computer or electronic device.

direct speech The exact words someone says.

directions A set of instructions telling the reader how to do something. Directions may instruct the reader to follow a series of steps.

distinguish To tell one thing apart from another.

domain An area of knowledge that has its own special vocabulary.

domain-specific vocabulary A set of words that belong to an area of knowledge, such as math or medicine.

double negative Using two negatives in a single sentence.

drama A story written to be acted out.

E

effect What happens as a result of a cause.

email Message sent via the Internet from one computer or other electronic device to another.

exclamation A sentence that shows strong feelings; an exclamatory sentence.

exclamatory sentence A sentence that shows strong feelings; an exclamation.

F

fable A short story in which a character, usually an animal, learns a lesson.

fact A statement that can be proved true.

fantasy A fictional story that has characters or events that could not exist in real life.

figurative language A way to use language in which the meaning is different from its literal meaning.

first-person point of view The point of view if one of the characters is telling the story.

firsthand account An account that is written by a person who experienced or witnessed an event.

folktale A story that the people of a country tell to explain or entertain.

formal language Includes precise language and complete sentences; does not include slang expressions.

free verse Poetry without a regular rhyme or regular rhythm.

future tense Verb form that shows action that will happen.

G

generalization A conclusion that is based on a small amount of information that may or may not be true.

graph Shows numerical information in a visual format that allows comparisons to be made.

graphic features Visual organizers, such as charts or diagrams.

H

heading Boldface print that identifies the main idea of a section of text.

helping verb A verb that comes before a main verb and tells more about the action.

historical event Something that happened during a particular time.

historical fiction A story that is set in the past and tells about people, places, and events that did happen or could have happened.

historical text A kind of informational text that gives facts about a topic in history.

homophone A word that sounds the same as another word but has a different spelling and meaning.

humor Funny parts of a story.

hyperbole Exaggerated language that makes something seem better or worse than it actually is.

I

idiom A phrase that means something different from what the individual words say.

imperative sentence A sentence that gives a command; a command.

independent clause A clause that can stand alone because it is a complete sentence.

infer To figure out something that is not stated directly.

informal language A more relaxed form of speaking and writing that includes slang expressions and incomplete sentences.

informational text Text that gives facts and examples about a topic. Informational text may include visuals, such as photographs and diagrams.

informative writing Writing that gives facts about a topic.

interrogative sentence A sentence that asks a question; a question.

irregular verb A verb that does not add *-ed* to the present form to show past action.

J

jargon Special words or phrases used in a particular field.

K

key A graphic feature that tells what different colors, symbols, and patterns stand for.

L

label Text used in a diagram to identify parts of an object or steps in a process.

linking verb A verb that tells what someone or something is or is like.

M

main idea The big idea an author wants to state.

main verb The verb that tells the action when a verb is more than one word.

map An illustration of an area.

metaphor A phrase that compares two things without using the word *like.*

meter Rhythmic patterns in poetry.

modal auxiliary A helping verb that shows how things could be or should be.

moral A lesson that a fable or other tale teaches about good and bad behavior.

multiple-meaning word A word that has different meanings depending on how it is used.

mystery A type of fiction story in which the main characters solve a crime.

myth An imaginative story that shows what a group of people in the past believed.

N

narrative nonfiction Text that tells about people, things, events, or places that are real.

narrative poem A poem that tells a story.

narrative writing Writing that tells a story. A narrative tells about something that happened to a person or a character.

narrator The person who says the words that are heard as part of a drama and that describe what is being seen.

negative A word that makes a sentence mean "no."

noun A word that names a person, place, or thing.

O

object pronoun A type of pronoun that tells who or what receives the action of the verb.

onomatopoeia A way authors help readers imagine what something sounds like.

opinion A statement that tells someone's thoughts, feelings, or beliefs.

opinion writing Writing that tells what the writer believes and gives reasons.

order words Words such as *first, now, next,* and *finally* that show sequence.

P

participial phrase Phrase that describes a noun.

participle A verb form that can be used as an adjective.

past participle The past-tense form of a verb.

past tense Verb form that shows action that has already happened.

personification A metaphor that describes a nonliving thing as if it were human.

persuasive technique A method or way of doing things to convince people to do or believe things.

pie chart A type of chart that uses portions of a circle to show how amounts of something relate to one another.

play A story that can be performed by an audience.

plot The sequence of story events, including a problem and a solution.

poetry Uses the sound and rhythm of words to suggest images and express feelings.

point of view The perspective from which an author tells a story.

possessive noun A noun that shows ownership.

possessive pronoun A pronoun that shows ownership, such as mine, yours, his, and *theirs*.

predicate The part of a sentence that tells what action is being done.

predict To figure out what might happen later in the story.

prefix An affix attached to the beginning of a base word, root word, or root that changes the meaning of the word.

preposition A word that shows a connection between other words in a sentence.

prepositional phrase A group of words that begins with a preposition and ends with a noun or pronoun.

present participle A verb form that expresses present tense by adding *-ing*.

present tense Verb form that shows action that is happening now or that happens over and over.

problem A person, situation, or difficult question that a character must deal with.

pronoun A word, such as *he, she,* or *they*, that takes the place of one or more nouns.

pronunciation key An explanation of the symbols used to show how a word is divided into syllables and pronounced.

proper noun A word that names a particular person, place, or thing and is capitalized.

proverb A short saying that expresses life lessons that many people believe are true; an adage.

punctuation Marks or signs in writing that help make meaning clear and separate parts of sentences.

Q

question To ask oneself questions about a selection before, during, and after reading.

question sentence A sentence that asks a question; an interrogative sentence.

quotation The exact words taken from a text.

quotation marks Punctuation used to show the exact words someone says or the exact words taken from a text.

R

realistic fiction Story that has characters and events that are like those in real life.

reference materials Printed books and online resources, such as dictionaries, that contain information about words and word meanings.

reflexive pronoun A pronoun whose antecedent is the subject of the sentence.

regular verb A verb that uses *-ed* to form its past tense.

relative adverb A type of adverb used to introduce a dependent clause that gives information about time, place, or reason.

relative pronoun A type of pronoun used to introduce a dependent clause that gives more information about a noun.

research report Writing that tells what a writer learned from doing research about a topic.

resolution The way the main characters solve a problem; a solution.

rhyme Repeated sounds at the ends of words.

rhythm A regular pattern of sound in poetry or music.

root A word part to which affixes are added to make a complete word.

root word A word to which prefixes and suffixes are added.

row A horizontal (left to right) section of a chart.

run-on sentence A sentence that has two complete thoughts, or sentences, that run into each other.

S

scene A section of a play that presents a single event.

science fiction Stories with futuristic settings and plots driven by technological advancements.

scientific concepts Terms or ideas about topics in science.

secondhand account An account that is based on reading and research.

sentence A group of words that tells a complete thought.

sentence fragment A group of words that does not tell a complete thought.

sequence The order in which steps are completed in directions.

sequence of events The order in which events happen in a story.

setting The time and place where story events happen.

shades of meaning Small differences in the meanings of words that have similar meanings.

signal word A word such as *because* or *so* that alerts a reader to key ideas.

simile A phrase that compares two things using the word *like* or *as*.

simple predicate The main word in a sentence that tells what the subject does or is.

simple subject The main word in a sentence that tells who or what the sentence is about.

split quotation Direct speech that is interrupted in the middle by words that tell who is speaking.

stage directions Instructions to actors on how to move and speak.

stanza A group of lines in a poem; a verse.

statement A sentence that tells something; a declarative sentence.

steps The stages or actions involved in completing a project or process.

story elements The important parts of the story, including characters, setting, and plot.

structure The way something is shaped or organized.

subject The part of a sentence that tells who or what is doing the action.

subject pronoun A type of pronoun that tells who or what performs the action in a sentence.

subordinating conjunction A word, such as *because, although, until, if,* or *since,* that links two sentences.

suffix An affix added to the end of a word that changes the meaning of the word.

summarize To briefly tell the important parts of a text in one's own words.

superlative An adjective or adverb that expresses the extreme degree of comparison.

supporting detail A fact or example that backs up the main idea.

symbol A shape or design that stands for things in real life.

synonym A word with almost the same meaning as another word.

T

tall tale A humorous story about impossible or exaggerated happenings.

text evidence Details such as facts, the author's words, and quotations in the selection that support an inference or opinion.

text features Parts of the text, such as titles, headings, and captions.

theme The message or lesson in a work of literature.

thesaurus A reference book that contains words and their synonyms.

third-person point of view The point of view if a narrator is telling the story.

traits Ways of speaking and acting that show what a character is like.

V

verb A word that shows action.

verse A group of lines in a poem; a stanza.

visualize To use text details to form pictures in your mind.

visuals Maps, charts, graphs, photographs, and other images.

W

word choice An author's use of exact words in writing.